# COMPUTING
# AS WRITING

# COMPUTING AS WRITING

DANIEL PUNDAY

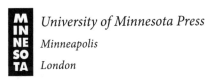

University of Minnesota Press
*Minneapolis*
*London*

An earlier version of chapter 4 was published as "Ebooks, Libraries, and Feelies," *Electronic Book Review,* February 2, 2010.

Published by the University of Minnesota Press
111 Third Avenue South, Suite 290
Minneapolis, MN 55401-2520
http://www.upress.umn.edu

Library of Congress Cataloging-in-Publication Data

Punday, Daniel.
Computing as writing / Daniel Punday.
Includes bibliographical references and index.
ISBN 978-0-8166-9699-4 (hc)
ISBN 978-0-8166-9702-1 (pb)
1. Literature and technology. 2. Digital media—Social aspects.
3. Authorship—Data processing. 4. Communication and technology.
5. Literature and society. 6. Narration (Rhetoric). I. Title.
PN56.T37P86 2015
802.85—dc23          2014043042

Printed in the United States of America on acid-free paper

The University of Minnesota is an equal-opportunity educator and employer.

21 20 19 18 17 16 15          10 9 8 7 6 5 4 3 2 1

Writing, in the sense of placing letters and other marks one after another, appears to have little or no future. Information is now more effectively transmitted by codes other than those of written signs. What was once written can now be conveyed more effectively on tapes, records, films, videotapes, videodisks, or computer disks, and a great deal that could not be written until now can be noted down in these new codes.

—Vilém Flusser, *Does Writing Have a Future?*

And in all its various uses, the computer is best understood as a new technology for writing. Even computer programming is a kind of writing.

—Jay David Bolter, *Writing Space*

Writing that began in the service of the oral arts has been transformed over the ages to become writing in the service of technological connectivity.

—James Strickland, "Writer's World 2.0"

# Contents

# Preface

This book argues for the value of the metaphorical link between writing and computing—even though that link is fraught with contradiction, vagueness, and instability.

From the moment it emerged into popular consciousness in the middle of the twentieth century, the operation and use of the modern computer has been understood as a form of writing. The essays and books that provided the first popular explanations of the future of computing to a general audience depended heavily on the framework provided by the familiar activities of writing, reading, and storing documents. These include Vannevar Bush's 1945 "As We May Think," J. C. R. Licklider's 1965 report *Libraries of the Future*, Alan Kay's 1968 plan for the "DynaBook," and Theodor Nelson's 1974 manifesto *Computer Lib/Dream Machines*.[1]

This link between writing and computing was reinforced during the 1980s and 1990s, as personal computers became affordable and most day-to-day writing moved from the typewriter to the word processor. The result was a spate of books about the literary uses of electronic media in the near (and not so near) future. These include Jay David Bolter's 1991 *Writing Space*, which explores the new forms of textuality and reading made possible by the electronic medium; Michael Joyce's 1995 *Of Two Minds*, which describes the nature of composition on the computer screen; and Janet Murray's 1997 *Hamlet on the Holodeck*, which imagines "interactive" electronic media as transforming the nature of literary experience.[2] Along with a huge number of works celebrating the emergence of the Internet, like Sherry Turkle's 1995 *Life on the Screen*, these books of the early and mid-1990s framed computing as a broadly literary matter in which interactivity and hypertext linking would transform text, reader, and author.[3]

Since the high-water mark of Murray's book, there has been increasing suspicion about the link between computing and writing—especially writing understood through literature and narrative. Espen Aarseth's 1997 *Cybertext* offered an energetic critique of the way in which "the academic masses . . . since 1984 have increasingly attempted to capture and construct computer-mediated texts as objects of literary criticism."[4] Within a few years, claims of "colonialism" by literary critics became commonplace; Markku Eskelinen summarizes in 2004, "If there already is or soon will be a legitimate field for computer game studies, this field is also very open to intrusions and colonisations from the already organized scholarly tribes."[5] A supporting critique of the computing–writing construction emerged out of the sloppiness of many of the apparent qualities celebrated in electronic texts, such as "interactivity." Lev Manovich's 2001 *The Language of New Media* attacked not only the myths that make up what he calls "new media" but also the tendency to see narrative as an inherent part of our experiences with computing.[6]

As a result, the work over the last decade has tended to view any broad equation of writing and computing with suspicion, and instead has pursued terms and concepts native to this emerging digital medium. Probably the best example of this is the call for "platform studies." As Nick Montfort and Ian Bogost wrote when they launched the series in 2009, "The best artists, writers, programmers, and designers are well aware of how certain platforms facilitate certain types of computational expression and innovation. . . . We believe it is time for those of us in the humanities to seriously consider the lowest level of computing systems and to understand how these systems relate to culture and creativity."[7] Attention to a particular platform—the first book in this series focused on the Atari Video Computer System—would allow for "technical rigor." Manovich's 2013 *Software Takes Command* pursues a similar technical specificity in software, particularly Photoshop and After Effects.[8] Other critics have embraced such technical specificity through an emphasis on the archive and archaeology. Matthew Kirschenbaum describes his 2008 *Mechanisms* in this way: it "eschews top-heavy formalist or theoretical approaches to the medium and instead seeks to examine a number of specific digital writing technologies—and individual electronic objects—in their unique textual, technical, and imaginative milieu."[9] As a whole, the field has moved to value terminological and technical specificity over the kinds of broad metaphorical associations that dominated discussion in the 1980s and 1990s.

Although this turn to materialism and media specificity among critics is compelling, the metaphorical link between writing and computing is not going away. This metaphor remains a fundamental part of our experience of computing, from the way that the computer is said to "write" data to the hard drive, search through a "library" of music and code, organize files into "folders," and treat them all as "documents." Apple's decision to name its touchscreen computer the iPad in 2010 only confirms the continuing centrality of writing for envisioning computing. Likewise, the professions of writing and computing seem to be evolving closer together rather than apart. Authors composing for the Web may find themselves including HTML and CSS code for formatting, while programmers often employ simple text editing programs for their day-to-day work. In turn, a number of word-processing applications have appeared in the last few years that subject prose to code-like analysis for structure and pattern.[10] Overall, writing an article for the Web and writing the code that powers its backend server have evolved to feel more alike to many practitioners.

This book, then, is an attempt to carve out a space within our current critical moment for the metaphorical muddiness that characterized early accounts of computing. Bush's 1945 essay has a central role in this book, but early writers like Kay, Licklider, and Nelson will figure prominently. I'll show that the metaphor of writing provides a useful way to hold together tensions within our experience of computing. In particular, writing captures the unstable relationship between work and leisure, between individual and corporate agency, and between creativity and invention. These unstable links between writing and computing provide a space in which to explore the nature of creative work today.

Embracing the writing metaphor in the nuanced way that I advocate here will work to build connections between the many different disciplines affected by the ubiquity of computing. Already I noted the tendency for critics interested in electronic media to resist what they see as the colonializing intent of literary scholars. Likewise, digital humanities scholars have vigorously debated the scope of research that should "count" as part of this field—and have sometimes advocated a narrow definition that insists, for example, on training in programming.[11] In both cases, there has been a justifiable worry that established fields and institutions will absorb digital methods and activities rather than allowing them to develop their own identities. But insisting on narrow (if rigorous) methodological principles runs the risk of siloing the digital from the wider cultural context in which it operates. Because computing is not simply a discipline or set of technologies but also an *idea* that plays a role in contemporary culture, these kinds of cross-disciplinary investigations are so important. For example, in chapter 5 I link debates about the scope of patent law in the United States to design trends within computer user interfaces (UI) because both are wrestling with the nature of invention in an age of networked computing. In chapter 6 I show how representations of archaic writing technologies in the video game *Myst* and the Harry Potter novels help to explore the changing nature of authorship in an age when writing computer code can *do* things. These kinds of cross-disciplinary comparisons are only possible if we are willing to tolerate a broad understanding of the digital and the ways that it can invoke writing.

Finally, the writing metaphor can be helpful for anyone seeking to define their professional identity today—whether inside or outside a formal programming workplace. Calling programming a matter of "writing code" has been frequently criticized as depending on an outdated model of work that does not capture the nature of modern software development. But this link between writing and computing remains common precisely because it gives individuals a way to visualize their own agency and creativity in relation to abstract corporate, legal, and academic institutions. I do not claim that writing is an unproblematic metaphor for these activities but instead advocate for writing as a framework through which to investigate the nature of work today. I conclude this book by arguing that university writing courses can become places where students have the opportunity to think about their professional identities and their relationships to disciplinary and institutional resources more broadly.

## Plan of the Book

This book is organized around six points of intersection between literary and computing culture: the nature of research (chapter 1), the tensions within professions (chapter 2), the job of the programmer (chapter 3), the idea of the library (chapter 4), invention and the technology patent (chapter 5), and the idea of audience (chapter 6). In each chapter a link between writing and computing is established and grows more complex and often contradictory as it is analyzed. Each chapter is organized by one or more tutor texts that provide insight into the relationship between writing and computing. Some of these are obviously engaged in the process of articulating the nature of computing, like early books about the future of computing from the 1960s and 1970s, or the recent movie *The Social Network*. Others reveal their relevance to the nature of computing more slowly, such as Andy Rubin's first tweet or cases about patent law. I have sought out this heterogeneous mixture of texts in order to show how extensively these debates about computing, invention, and individual agency are woven into contemporary culture.

My opening chapter takes Vannevar Bush's 1945 essay "As We May Think" as a tutor text that helps us to understand the transformation of writing as it moves into the age of computing. Bush's essay today is usually understood as a prediction of contemporary forms of document storage and linking; for many Bush is the father of hypertext avant la lettre. Instead of celebrating Bush's foresight as so many critics have done before me, I want to treat this essay as providing a diagnosis of the difficulties that arise when we try to use writing as a model for knowledge production and dissemination in a digital age. Bush's essay, I argue, is profoundly ambivalent about the relationship between the consumption of prior knowledge through reading documents and the production of new knowledge. Bush clearly explains how we move through an archive of prior research by creating a "trail" that is uniquely our own, but he is not at all clear about how this trail produces new research. Is the trail itself the new knowledge or is it merely preliminary to an inquiry? Calling this work *writing,* I suggest, helps to capture these ambivalences.

Chapter 1 reveals that writing means two different things both in Bush's essay and in contemporary culture in general: it can mean work produced in a professional, academic, or corporate context that engages with shared resources, or it can mean an activity broadly literary in nature that allows an individual to produce a work creatively using accessible, mundane tools. These two ways of understanding writing provide the basis for chapters 2 and 3. In chapter 2 I return briefly to Bush's essay to consider the changing role of professions and work that frames his 1945 essay. Starting with the context provided by contemporaries like Norbert Weiner and Herbert Marcuse, I interpret Bush's essay as responding to the emergence of what Alan Liu calls "knowledge work." From here I look at changing ideas about professions in general, and observe the complex role that writing has always played within them. Drawing on Clifford Siskin, I note that the novel has been a liminal space in which writing has been able to comment on the nature of professions. Having shown the complex relationship between the individual writer and this larger corporate, professional context, I close this chapter by turning to the teaching of writing. I note the problems with plagiarism that students often have in working with online resources, which, like Bush's trail, often result from confusing the consumption of prior work with the production of new.

Chapter 3 turns from this corporate model for writing to those that embrace a more literary understanding. I begin by looking at two films that represent programming—the 1957 romantic comedy *Desk Set* and the 2010 film *The Social Network.* Where films in the past treated computers as monoliths dropped into social spaces, forcing people to adapt or resist, this later film represents programming as a form of writing—blurring together, for example, the writing of programming code and the diary-like entries on a personal blog. This shift toward seeing programming as a form of writing brings with it profound changes in our understanding of the profession. Today the lines between programming and writing are blurry, since most writing for the Web depends on markup language that contains coding. Some have advocated a more explicitly "literary" approach to programming, arguing that we would be better to treat the act of writing code as a literary activity. All in all, the professions of writing and programming have evolved to be closer together, and form an essential part of what has been called the "creative economy" by Richard Florida.

These ideas about writing and computing are given an especially clear and suggestive articulation in Neal Stephenson's open-source manifesto *In the Beginning . . . Was the Command Line.* In this book, Stephenson contrasts the graphical user interface (GUI) to the textual command line. For Stephenson, the command line is fundamentally more accurate. He describes the GUI as a rough and lazy approximation. For him the command line is the equivalent of the literary writer working hard to represent the world accurately and fairly—even if that representation is difficult for some people to understand. I employ Stephenson's essay to round out my analysis of the literary writing metaphor used for thinking about the operation of the computer, since he reveals the common belief that the writing embodied in the command line or in coding represents a more fundamental layer of the computer. Programmers and writers are the same, according to Stephenson, because they struggle with the basic challenge of representing the world clearly.

Chapter 4 turns to another point of connection between writing and computing: the library. Although we often think of the library first as a collection of books, in fact it is common to refer to a *library* of shared code. The library's liminal position between writing and computing comes especially to the fore with the recent interest in electronic book publication, especially using devices like the Kindle or iPad. In fact, the idea that the computer organizes a complete library of digital media has been one of the most powerful appeals of the computer: most of us use some program to organize and access our music, photos, and perhaps movies. In this chapter I suggest that we can describe two types of libraries: the *accumulative,* in which each of the items is an individual, and the *modular,* in which each item is meaningless outside of its library. Traditionally we think of book-based libraries as accumulative and computing libraries as modular, but the digital environment increasingly moves even the items of the accumulative library—like songs and pictures—toward the modular library, because doing so provides significant gains in efficiency and storage. The future of electronic books is uncertain, although the popularity of the Kindle certainly suggests a movement toward the modular library, as well.

Chapter 5 turns to contemporary disputes over software patents as another point of connection between writing and computing. In this chapter I argue that debates about software patents actually reflect a broader uncertainty about the nature of creativity in a computing age that was already implicit in Bush's 1945 essay. This chapter begins by investigating the degree to which software can be seen as a tool. In *Being and Time* Heidegger offers a well-known account of tools as "ready to hand," but I am particularly interested in the way that he uses the term *equipment* in this book, since equipment for him represents a set of interrelated technologies such as the pen, paper, and desk for writing. Equipment is a powerful concept today because it captures the way that technological systems interrelate. I argue that these systems pose challenges to our traditional ideas of creativity. I turn to recent U.S. Supreme Court cases—especially the 2010 *Bilski v. Kappos*—to see how computing technologies have challenged our ways of evaluating inventions. Today, I argue, new technologies are increasingly integrated into these systems, and as a result our older models defining what can be patented are very much in flux. Writing's ability to represent the abstract possibilities of invention has frequently been criticized as the basis for "speculative patents" disconnected from concrete objects, but this is another instance where writing embodies the tensions of contemporary culture.

Chapter 6 turns from these technical subjects back to literary writing. In this chapter I am interested in whether the model of computing changes our ideas about the relationship between the literary writer and his or her audience. We conventionally think of programming as *doing* something instead of describing something—giving instructions to be executed. A number of critics have suggested a similar shift toward the performative in contemporary culture as a whole. I link this interest in performativity to a change in audience, as general readerships have given way to increasingly niche subgroups. Today's writers, I suggest, increasingly have ad hoc relationships with their audiences, making the ability to provoke responses especially important to establishing oneself as a writer. In this chapter I am, however, eager to counter the common assumption that readers have somehow gained control over the reader–writer relationship. I turn to Henry Jenkins's analysis of participatory culture, especially online discussion concerning shows like *Survivor* as well as hoaxes like the YouTube Lonelygirl15 series, to show that the image of a controlling author continues in today's computing culture. I unpack these tensions by exploring two examples of literary authors caught between older and performative models of the writer: Jonathan Franzen and J. K. Rowling. Both have provoked controversy through conflicts with their fans, and in their essays, interviews, and court filings they demonstrate a fundamental unease with how the literary writer should be understood today.

In my conclusion, I return to the issue of the teaching of writing raised in chapter 2, and advocate for an expanded understanding of what it means to help students think about themselves as writers. Too often, I argue, we talk about the teaching of writing as a matter of encouraging students to embrace their ability to respond to a variety of rhetorical situations in personal, civic, and professional life. Since writing is the emblematic activity of contemporary knowledge work, the composition classroom is an ideal place to address changing attitudes towards work, creativity, and invention. More broadly, as writing becomes a model for a host of professional activities like programming, we should use these classes to help students to find a balance between the individual and the corporate, between the shared and the new, and between the professional and the personal.

# ONE

# My Documents

*Remembering the Memex*

Vannevar Bush's 1945 *Atlantic Monthly* article "As We May Think" is usually understood to be a prescient description of future "hypertext" forms of information. Bush famously describes the *memex* as "a sort of mechanized private file and library" built into a desk, with "a keyboard, and sets of buttons and levers."[1] As Bush imagines it, the memex allows the reading of documents stored on microfilm, which can be accessed using a "transparent platen" built into the surface, and to which can be added handwritten notes, clippings, and pictures using a kind of photocopying technology. Bush describes the memex as a device that will fundamentally transform the nature of doing research and taking notes.

Bush's essay is striking for how well it anticipates now-ubiquitous electronic document search and retrieval, and it is justifiably famous. Michael Joyce says that "hypertext . . . has its roots in [this] single article."[2] But over the years, this essay has been mythologized and many of its most striking details lost. In particular, I would like to suggest that there are deep ambiguities in "As We May Think" about the relationship between an archive and the creation of new knowledge. This is an especially fraught relationship today, as any undergraduate caught plagiarizing from *Wikipedia* can tell you. I argue that Bush reveals ambiguity in what it means to do research today in a networked environment, and that *writing* in particular often emerges as a figure to represent this ambiguity. Bush's essay functions as a tutor text throughout this book. In this opening chapter, I use it to unpack some of the underappreciated tensions in our understanding of writing in relation to computing, and I return to the essay often in later chapters.

1

The element of Bush's essay that I want to emphasize is the relationship between the memex and the professional scholarly community. This is one of the elements that has been most overlooked in celebrations of Bush's essay, and I argue that it raises uncomfortable but important issues about the nature of research and writing today. Surveying the scientific world in the immediate aftermath of the Second World War, Bush sees a crisis in the disciplines:

> There is a growing mountain of research. But there is increased evidence that we are being bogged down today as specialization extends. The investigator is staggered by the findings and conclusions of thousands of other workers— conclusions which he cannot find time to grasp, much less to remember, as they appear. Yet specialization becomes increasingly necessary for progress, and the effort to bridge between disciplines is correspondingly superficial.[3]

The problem that Bush is describing is familiar, and has even grown more severe in the intervening years. But what is striking about this passage is how far it departs from our common ways of thinking about hypertext and networked computing. Today we are much more likely to see the Internet as a force that transforms all those elements of our lives beyond the job: commerce, leisure, and education. Such concerns are miles away from Bush's emphasis in this 1945 essay. His examples are drawn exclusively from scholarly activity. His most sustained example is a research project on the Turkish bow:

> The owner of the memex, let us say, is interested in the origin and properties of the bow and arrow. Specifically he is studying why the short Turkish bow was apparently superior to the English long bow in the skirmishes of the Crusades. He has dozens of possibly pertinent books and articles in his memex. First he runs through an encyclopedia, finds an interesting but sketchy article, leaves it projected. Next, in a history, he finds another pertinent item, and ties the two together. Thus he goes, building a trail of many items. (104)

I return to this idea of the "trail" shortly, but what we should notice at the outset is that Bush's motivation for consulting the memex is essentially scholarly and connected to professional academic work. He makes no reference to the kinds of uses to which current Internet searches would be put: getting medical advice, researching purchasing decisions, making travel plans, and so on. This emphasis on professional activity is not incidental, but rather an important part of Bush's approach to science funding and administration. Bush himself was heavily involved in advocating for government funding for research important to the military during World War II. Bush was Roosevelt's adviser, and helped to organize the Manhattan Project. In a biography of Bush, G. Pascal Zachary describes his emphasis on professional expertise, especially in the postwar environment: "While not espousing a scientocracy, Bush envisioned a technologically advanced America governed by the masters of science and technology. If this scientific elite could not actually fill the seats of power, it could at least advise those who did. As the war had shown, 'with scientists reaching beyond mere invention to guide military and even diplomatic policy,' in practice 'once-clear distinctions between corporate executives, military officials and research administrators 'were fading,' historian Michael Sherry has noted."[4] Bush, as Zachary describes him, was an "organizer of expertise."

The memex, then, was born out of a vision of research and the archive in which disciplines, bureaucracy, and professional organization are central to the nature of human knowledge. It is this focus on the organization of knowledge that makes Bush's essay such a striking break from the realities of computing at the time: here is a description of what we might think of today as a "computer" that does not calculate but instead merely stores and organizes information. The early ENIAC computer, completed in 1946, stored only a few digits in its vacuum-tube memory as it performed one operation after another, before outputting the results to a punch card. As Paul Ceruzzi explains, "Its purpose was to calculate firing tables for the U.S. Army, a task that involved the repetitive solution of complex mathematical expressions."[5] It wasn't until 1951 and the completion of the UNIVAC that computers could store and access information on magnetic tape, and even then most saw the research application of the computer to be performing large, complex scientific calculations. In this regard, Bush's description of a device for automatic storage and retrieval of information is quite a break from contemporary technology. Even more important, his emphasis throughout the device's operation is not on the mathematical calculations that kept the ENIAC busy but on *reading* and *writing*. Although today a commonplace in our interaction with computers, the centrality of writing and reading to Bush's vision of the memex is ultimately what makes it such a prescient idea.

This link between computing and writing is my subject in this book. Writing provides a model and set of metaphors that help us make sense of computing—how we should use it, what kinds of professions should be responsible for it, what cultural value using it should have. In turn, seeing computing as a form of writing influences what it means to be a writer (and reader) in a literary sense. Computing emphasizes a whole set of capabilities and restraints in writing as a medium, profession, and object. Because Bush's image of computing offered in the memex has little to do with calculation, when I talk about *computing* in this book, I am not following the line of inquiry taken by David Golumbia in *The Cultural Logic of Computation,* which looks at the way contemporary culture subjects more and more of the world to computation as a means of understanding it.[6] Instead, I am interested in the computer in the way that the memex models it, as an object that transforms our relationship to a body of information and to the others who use and produce the information. It is crucial, I show, that Bush imagines this transformation as occurring on the model of writing rather than calculation or any other way of producing information.

In equating Bush's memex with writing, I understand the latter term to be a particular kind of individual activity given meaning by its social (especially professional and institutional) context. In adopting this definition, I am following the work of scholars who focus on workplace writing—what a recent collection called "writing in knowledge societies."[7] As Patrick Dias, Aviva Freedman, Peter Medway, and Anthony Paré write elsewhere, "Writing is a means, a tool in accomplishing larger goals, which may involve actions other than writing and other participants who function in a variety of roles."[8] This focus on workplace writing is especially appropriate when analyzing Bush's scholarly memex, of course. Much of the research on workplace writing is interested in the nature of academic training and the sometimes-informal ways in which new workplace genres are developed and learned. I am less interested in these particular genre considerations and more in the way that writing is understood to be a part of work more generally. As we will see, writing emerges in what is called the "culture of information" as an embodiment of contemporary work. Bruno Latour's analysis of the rhetoric of science, which I return to in chapter 2, provides a model for this. Latour advocates studying the way that science operates not by looking at the truth of individual statements but by studying how earlier scientific assertions are made true by subsequent writing. Latour "asks us not to look for the intrinsic qualities of any given statement but to look instead for all the transformations it undergoes later in other hands. This rule is the consequence of what I called our first principle: the fate of facts and machines is in the hands of later users."[9] These kinds of social actions that create facts are overwhelmingly defined by writing. More broadly, I argue that writing provides a unique but frequently conflicted understanding of how individual actors operate within their professional networks.

Much of the thinking about computers inspired by Bush turns sharply from this focus on professions, and thus loses this essential focus on individual action within a social network. For example, in his influential essay imagining a future laptop computer called the DynaBook, "A Personal Computer for Children of All Ages," Alan Kay shifts his attention from professional life to the education of children. Kay describes not Bush's inquiry into the influence of the Turkish bow but children trying to build a better version of the video game *Spacewar.* He offers a considerably broader definition of the computer as a tool: "What then is a personal computer? One would hope that it would be both a medium for containing and expressing arbitrary symbolic notions, and also a collection of useful tools for manipulating these structures, with ways to add new tools to the repertoire."[10] Here the computer is essentially modeled on the human mind, which develops through just this process of acquiring and extending tools. For Kay, "man is clich[é]d as the 'tool building animal.'"[11] This belief that computer information storage fundamentally mimics the process of human education is deeply embedded in much of our more recent discussion of computers. Theodor Nelson takes a similar approach in *Computer Lib/Dream Machines,* where he describes the computer as a Thinkertoy: "a system to help people think."[12] We might also recall Steve Jobs's description of computers as "bicycles for the mind."[13] In all of these cases, the computer is treated as a tool for thought in general, and its roots in scholarly research are forgotten.

A similar shift toward seeing the computer as mimicking thought in general occurs in J. C. R. Licklider's 1965 *Libraries of the Future,* which itself cites Bush's "As We May Think" essay as "the main external influence that shaped the ideas of this book."[14] Although Licklider sees himself as working in the light of issues raised by Bush, he subtly but fundamentally changes the nature of the inquiry. Much of this book focuses on the same process of imagining what it means to work with a future computing device that would give access to information. Licklider even repeats the description "in which a man sits at a desk, writes or draws on a surface with a stylus, and thereby communicates to a programmed information processor with a large memory" (9). But even in this passage, it is clear Licklider has changed some of the terms of the problem. For him, users interact not just with documents (as in Bush) but with information and facts more abstractly. When he lists the twenty-five criteria for his information system, item number two (after the first rule that it "be available when and where needed") expands Bush's definition of the research archive: this device must "handle both documents and facts" (36). A footnote explains: "'Facts,' used here in a broad sense, refers to items of information or knowledge derived from one or more documents and not constrained to the form or forms of the source passages" (36). Although Licklider pushes this issue into a footnote, this shift from document to data transforms the nature of the research that Bush describes. Gone are the specific materials reviewed and, thus, the trails that connect them. Now we are in the realm of information in general.[15] There should be little surprise that, as a result, when Licklider goes on to imagine his ideal system, he emphasizes not the retrieval of specific documents but a dialogue-like interaction with the computer as an artificial intelligence, which answers questions like the following: "Has any digital-computer system responded to questions phrased in ordinary English, or other natural language, by giving correct answers in natural language?" (51). Here we are far away from the image of research that Bush described, and we are involved in a much more general, document-free inquiry into knowledge. It should be little surprise, then, that when Licklider enumerates the "Steps toward Realization" of this knowledge system, his first item is "overcome interdisciplinary barriers" (59).

## 2

It is clear, then, that Bush's memex reflects a complex understanding of the relationship between an individual researcher and the collective body of information with which he or she is involved, and that this complexity depends in part on placing the metaphor of writing at the heart of computing. This complex relationship produces, in turn, a conflicted understanding of individual creativity. One of the most striking things about Bush's account is that at no point does he provide a clear explanation of how a scholar using a memex produces something new. Let us pick up the example of research into the Turkish bow from where I dropped it:

> Occasionally he inserts a comment of his own, either linking it into the main trail or joining it by a side trail to a particular item. When it becomes evident that the elastic properties of available materials had a great deal to do with the bow, he branches off on a side trail which takes him through textbooks on elasticity and tables of physical constants. He inserts a page of longhand analysis of his own. Thus he builds a trail of his interest through the maze of materials available to him.[16]

Although this passage should be showing how new information is produced through research, Bush's emphasis is strangely on the *consumption* of information: Bush's memex owner is much more a reader than someone producing new information, and most of the materials that he adds to this archive are simply notes and links. Even the "longhand analysis" with which this passage ends implies largely an application of one piece of knowledge (tables of physical constants) to another (the available materials of the bow). Indeed, this passage blurs together the new information produced and the trail that was followed to find it. The analysis is in some sense an inevitable result of the sources consulted.

Bush's description of this *trail* deserves careful attention, since it is his central method for explaining how researchers engage with the memex and thus with the archive as a whole. Paul Kahn and James Nyce note, "For Bush, the body of knowledge in a library is always a evolving, coherent space through which one travels intellectually."[17] What is especially striking about these travels is their personal quality. In the passage above, Bush refers to a "trail of his interest," and elaborates shortly after: "Several years later, his talk with a friend turns to the queer ways in which people resist innovations, even of vital interest. He has an example, in the fact that the outranged Europeans still failed to adopt the Turkish bow. In fact he has a trail on it" (104). Tim Oren has suggested that Bush's emphasis on the trail arises from his desire to mimic the associations that make up human memory,[18] but I think his handling of the trails reveals a more fundamental ambiguity about the nature of productivity in relationship to the archive. In some ways, a trail might seem ephemeral—simply a passing experience that fundamentally leaves the archive unchanged. This passage quoted above shows that Bush sees the trail as adding to and thus transforming the archive, but it also seems clear that the archive itself is *not* simply the sum total of trails, in the same way that the trails through a forest may be part of the identity of that forest without fully defining it. In this regard, a trail seems to be preliminary to producing new work—it is the equivalent of notes and an outline that would then be used to write an article or book. Later in the essay, Bush seems to make this distinction quite clearly: "There is a new profession of trail blazers, those who find delight in the task of establishing useful trails through the enormous mass of the common record" (105). Here "trail blazers" are different from the researchers who produce the content of the archive.

In other places, Bush implies that the memex grows over time as these trails accumulate. In his 1959 revisiting of the topic, "Memex II," Bush describes how the memex evolves over a lifetime:

Memex II will have an enormous memory. Into it may be inserted voluminous material, through a lifetime, and this will remain until called for. It does not need to get in the way, for it will remain quiescent unless and until a trail is purposely followed which leads into its interrelated mass. It will be useful to be able to distinguish recent from ancient trails, and color may be used for this purpose. An item is projected before a man's personal memex, say a letter from a friend received some years before, and inserted and coded by his secretary. On the margins of the item are a dozen code areas, a few of them active.[19]

Here a memex has become personal and an object to be developed over time. In fact, later in the essay, Bush asks, "The race progresses as the experience and reasoning of one generation is handed on to the next. Can a son inherit the memex of his father, or the disciple that of his master, refined and polished over the years, and go on from there?"[20] Here the trail *is* the accumulation of knowledge and not merely a preliminary state of research. This is the way that Theodor Nelson—one of the strongest advocates for the memex and the person who coined the term *hypertext*—understood these paths: "Bush regarded his new text structures as transmissible between individuals, and publishable."[21] Although this is merely Nelson's extrapolation of Bush's essay, the distinction between a personal and shared memex is one that emerges strongly in Bush's later work. In "Memex II," he suggests, "In each [professional] society will be maintained a master memex on the professional field of interest. This will contain all papers, references, tables, and the like, intimately interconnected by trails, so that one may follow a detailed matter from paper to paper, going back into the classics, recording criticism in the margins."[22] The professional memex seems to define the field, but it is hard to imagine how a personal memex is different. Are some trails more officially sanctioned than others? And if so, on what grounds?

That Bush does not answer these questions is less a matter of lack of care and more a feature of the task that he has set himself. Throughout all of these writings is a crucial ambiguity about the relationship between trails and the material of the archive embodied in the memex. In some cases, Bush seems to want to distinguish trail and material; in other places, he seems to blur the distinction. Sometimes he treats the trail as preliminary to research, and at other times he suggests that the movement through the archive is itself work. And throughout these essays he is profoundly ambiguous about what it would mean to "publish" these trails and make a private trail public. Or is it that all trails are inherently public, since they exist within the archive itself?

In *Grammars of Creation*, George Steiner articulates an opposition between *creation* and *invention* that provides language we can use to describe Bush's memex, and on which I depend throughout this book. Steiner describes the concept of creation as having "magnetic fields" of myth and depending on an idea of action that is essential and without precursor: "To found, to begin, is to act essentially."[23] Steiner explains: "No religion lacks a creation-myth. Religion could be defined as a narrative reply to the question of 'why is there not nothing,' as a structured endeavour to demonstrate that this question cannot elude the contradictory presence within itself of the verb 'to be.' We have no stories of continuous creation, of undifferentiated eternity. There would, in a strict sense, be no story to be told. It is the postulate of a singularity, of a beginning in and of time which necessitates the concept of creation" (17–18). In contrast, invention begins in predefined materials and responds to particular needs. "All human constructs are combinatorial," Steiner writes, "Which is simply to say that they are *arte-facts* made up of a selection and combination of pre-existent elements" (141). Such constructs are ultimately *inventions:* "Invention is answerable, as Edison emphasized, to specific needs, to pragmatic possibilities as these are offered by the availability or manufacture of new materials" (183). It is clear that, while invention is immediately rooted in our everyday experiences, creation is much more an idealization; as Steiner remarks, "'creation' is under incessant pressure of its neighbouring religious and philosophical values" (21). But even in the sciences, we are uneasy with wholly embracing invention as the only model by which new things come into the world: "It is where the sciences translate into application, into technologies of every kind, that the notion of 'invention' becomes at once manifest and elusive. It seems difficult to deny that Thomas Edison 'invented' the lightbulb, that he did not simply stumble upon that which was already 'there.' On the other hand, a deep-reaching uneasiness or sense of magnification does attach to the statement that Edison 'created' this useful object. Definitions blur." (110) Throughout *Grammars of Creation,* Steiner notes points at which our cultural attachment to one or another of these models for making new things blurs and shifts.

An important part of the power of the computing-as-writing metaphor arises from writing's basis in invention rather than creation. In fact, Steiner notes that language appears to be fundamentally a medium of invention: "Reflection tells us that even the greatest of poets works in and with the pre-existent means of languages" (112). He asks later, "How, then, is it possible to think new? How can new thoughts be crafted or cobbled out of material—words, sentences—itself 'pre-stressed' and irreparably second-hand (we think in words)" (147). Vilém Flusser makes a similar point when he contrasts the linearity of writing to the circularity of myth: "Writing is about setting ideas in lines, for unwritten ideas, left to their own devices, run in circles. . . . Written signs are quotation marks signaling the onset of linear, directional thinking within mythical thinking."[24] To say that computing is a form of writing—rather than, perhaps, a form of painting or design—is to emphasize the pregiven elements out of which the program is made. Of course, the idea that contemporary culture depends on borrowed source material has been a common observation. Marjorie Perloff coined the phrase *unoriginal genius* to describe the nature of poetic creativity today, an age of citation or *récriture* in which texts "can be appropriated, transformed, or hidden by all sorts of means and for all sorts of purposes."[25] Steiner suggests that language's shared origins have always posed a challenge for aesthetic theories that are based on originality, and that today's equation of writing and the computer might take much of its power from this problematically shared source material of language. This is an essential feature of the memex, as well: it is a personal device, a link to a scholarly archive, and a method of disseminating information to others. Just as it complicates the relationship between the individual researcher and the collective body of information, so too does the memex reflect a conflicted understanding of whether these individual paths of research are mere inventions or new creations.

Bush's memex essay captures, then, an ambiguity about the relationship between writing and a prior archive of research that haunts contemporary thinking. In fact, I would suggest that this particular problem defines in part the cultural meaning of *writing* as it is applied to computing today. To associate the computer with writing—which we will see occurs throughout contemporary culture—is to intervene into our ways of thinking about scholarship, community, and creativity. We see again and again that that intervention is profoundly ambiguous, since the writing metaphor involves not just a way to think about scholarly contributions but also a recognition of the ways that individuals are dependent on larger corporate and institutional structures.

It might seem that linking Bush and writing, specifically, is problematic. Bush himself did not type and instead, like many professional men of his generation, relied on a secretary to prepare his typescripts.[26] He spends a significant amount of time in his original memex essay describing a form of speech recognition:

> To make the record, we now push a pencil or tap a typewriter. Then comes the process of digestion and correction, followed by an intricate process of typesetting, printing, and distribution. To consider the first stage of the procedure, will the author of the future cease writing by hand or typewriter and talk directly to the record? He does so indirectly, by talking to a stenographer or a

wax cylinder; but the elements are all present if he wishes to have his talk directly produce a typed record. All he needs to do is to take advantage of existing mechanisms and to alter his language.[27]

Of course, speech recognition has become an increasingly mundane part of our interaction with computers. Michael Heim notes that for some people, even the shift to typing on a word processor escapes the physical drudgery of writing with pencil and paper; he cites a software developer who claims that "my own experience, particularly with letters composed on a word processor, is that electronic copy more closely resembles speech."[28] However, Bush does not emphasize this oral model for interacting with his memex. It is clear that Bush looks forward to the day when technology will allow him to speak his notes and comments directly into the machine, but his concern in this passage is fundamentally about the tedious nature of "push[ing] a pencil or tap[ping] a typewriter" and not about a different model for creativity. In fact, Bush seems most troubled by his need for having another person involved in the activity of creating these records. He describes the stenographer in these terms: "A girl strokes its keys languidly and looks about the room and sometimes at the speaker with a disquieting gaze."[29] Instead of moving toward some other (perhaps oral) model of communication, Bush wants to get back to the solitary activity of an individual responding and adding to a text; he wants, in other words, to be a writer. Throughout this book, I explore the tension between this literary image of the individual writer and the networked context of contemporary scholarly exchange. In chapter 6, for example, I look at Jonathan Franzen's definition of the writer in his collection of essays on the contemporary novel, *How to be Alone:* "The essence of fiction is solitary work: the work of writing, the work of reading."[30] It seems clear that the memex is likewise a way for Bush to be alone with his notes.

## 3

Bush's memex is not merely a personal vision for the future of computing and our relationship to information; instead, I argue, Bush captures a cultural understanding of the relationship between writing and computing that manifests itself over and over again in late twentieth-century culture. Having shown the crucial role of writing in Bush's vision of the memex, I would like now to look at writing metaphors as they are embodied in actual computing products. Specifically, I would like to look at the role of writing metaphors in modern computer operating systems, and then to turn, in the next section, to the role of writing in the representation of computers themselves—both fictional and real.

The UI built into the computer operating system obviously provides a particularly explicit representation of what the computer can do and how we should interact with it. When we look more closely at the history of computer operating systems, we see a gradual expansion of writing metaphors used to describe aspects of the computer. One of the most basic and extensive uses of writing metaphors is for discussing the storage of information. It seems almost inevitable to describe *reading* from and *writing* to the hard drive, but we should note that internal storage was a later and in some ways secondary feature of the computer. Early computers like the analog "differential analyzer" (1931) were simply that: devices for calculating values. For example, Norbert Wiener's work during World War II, which led to the development of cybernetics, had its roots in the problem of calculating firing trajectories for antiaircraft guns.[31] As I already noted, when contemporaries imagined the future of the computer, it was frequently by extending the power of these calculations to a range of decisions. Thus, for example, in *Dr. Strangelove* (1964) the task of deciding which humans to save from nuclear war is assigned to a computer: "It could easily be accomplished with a computer. And a computer could be set and programmed to accept factors from youth, health, sexual fertility, intelligence, and a cross section of necessary skills."[32] Likewise, the fascination through the 1950s and 1960s with robots and artificial intelligence—for example, in Isaac Asimov's *I, Robot* stories (1950)—essentially treats computing as a matter of decision making and behavior, rather than information storage. As Matthew Kirschenbaum remarks, "Computers themselves were initially engines of prediction and prognostication . . . not recollection and storage."[33]

Of course, the corporate implementations of computers immediately made the value of storing information obvious. In fact, mechanical methods for storing information on punched paper tape or cards was introduced into the United States in service of the 1890 census;[34] "in the late nineteenth century, many businesses adopted a practice that organized work using a punched card machine."[35] The UNIVAC's tape storage system was an important part of its first installation for the U.S. Census Bureau in 1951. In fact, Paul Ceruzzi argues that automatic storage was the primary appeal of UNIVAC for many of its first customers: "For most customers, what was revolutionary about the UNIVAC was not so much its stored-program design or even its electronic processor. It was the use of tape in place of punched cards. To them, the 'Automatic' nature of the machine lay in its ability to scan through a reel of tape, find the correct record or set of records, perform some process in it, and return the results again to tape."[36] Although the popular conception of the computer imagined it as an "electronic brain"—Edmund Collis Berkeley published a book in 1949 called *Giant Brains or Machines that Think*—in practice the businesses that routinely used the computer immediately understood that the storage of information was the real innovation taking place in computing.[37] It took a long time for these popular images to catch up with the reality of computing.

The use of these writing metaphors in early computers was uneven, however. Let us take the example of the pamphlet "Introduction to Computers," prepared by Remington Rand as part of the training materials for the UNIVAC. Here the storage of information onto magnetic tapes is described using a mix of metaphors. At times the language anticipates the current popularity of writing metaphors, describing the tape as "readable" and noting that "a reel of tape can be read or written upon nearly 1,000 times before showing appreciable wear."[38] But more common is referring to storage simply as "recording." The more that the document refers to the tape as a physical thing (rather than an abstract process of storing information), the more likely it is that writing metaphors will emerge. For example, in the 1956 "Preliminary Description of the UNIVAC," the terms *read interlock* and *write interlock* are integrated right into the diagram describing the storage of instructions on the tape.[39] When explaining the computer's operation more generally, however, language about *recording* is much more common.

We see this inconsistency of writing metaphors throughout the history of computers, in the design of both operating systems and programming languages. If we look at the primary disk commands in M-DOS in 1979, we notice that many seemingly natural writing metaphors are missing or de-emphasized: we do not read a file but instead *load* it; we do not erase a file but instead *delete* it; we *save* a file and *deposit* a value into a memory location rather than writing. Likewise, UNIX deletes a file by using the *rm* (remove) rather than a writing-based *erase* command. CP/M uses *load* to place a file into memory rather than *read*. In their book on metaphor and conceptual "blending" in human–computer interaction, Manuel Imaz and David Benyon describe the heterogeneity of our language for discussing the computer.[40] They note metaphors drawn from construction (architecture, foundation, platform); manufacturing (pipeline, tool kit, package); business (client, agent, export); office (files, folders, attachments); biology (taxonomy, tree, virus); geography (domain, site, pathway); and so on.[41] It seems clear that our ways of thinking about computers have no coherent dependence on writing, except in some specific instances.

One such instance is the storage of information on a hard drive. The hard drive itself was first produced commercially for the IBM 305 RAMAC computer in 1956. It replaced the cheaper but slower magnetic tape storage that, as we have already seen, was used by the UNIVAC and gave rise to the language of "recording." The shift from tape to disk drive not only had practical advantages; it also fundamentally transformed the way that users could think about the storage of information. If we look at the patent for the device, filed by Jacob Rabinow in 1951, we find the same mixture of metaphorical language that we see in computer operating systems through the 1960s and 1970s; the device is referred to as "a novel recording and reproducing machine," and information retrieval is described as "playing" the disk. Immediately after this audio metaphor, the patent shifts its terms: "An ordinary printed book is of the same type of recording machine except that the pages must be opened in order to be read. My invention results in a 'book' in which the pages can be read without the book being opened."[42] It is clear from this passage that Rabinow grasps the link between this storage and writing, and yet at the same time recognizes the foreignness of a book whose pages are read without being opened. The metaphor does not appear again in the patent application. Kirschenbaum draws on Rabinow's use of this description of the hard drive for the journal *Electrical Engineering* and notes the complex intellectual work going on in this passage:

> The comparison of disks to pages and of the concentric recording tracks (still a basic feature of magnetic disks today) to the lines on the page is also striking, and acknowledgement of the extent to which efficient inscription demands the rationalization of the writing space, regardless of medium. Perhaps most noteworthy, however, is the final line, the "book [that] can be read without being opened." This image, a throwaway, seems to anticipate much in our own contemporary response to electronic storage media: the book has become a black box, and whatever is inscribed within its pages is destined for other than human eyes.[43]

Kirschenbaum brilliantly unpacks the drive-as-book metaphor, and goes on to note that our language for referring to information storage on the hard drive is not fully committed to this writing metaphor. He notes, "The commonplace is to speak about writing a file *to* a disk; to say writing 'on' a disk sounds vaguely wrong, the speech of someone who has not yet assimilated the relevant vocabulary or concepts" (87).

This use of writing to describe computer storage repeats a pattern that we see throughout this book: writing seems to provide us with a more concrete and familiar way of thinking about computing, but in the process it actually embodies the abstraction of the device and its links to corporate and institutional contexts. This is especially the case with the shift from tape to the hard drive. While the hard drive introduces a more concrete metaphor (*writing* instead of the more general and audio-based *recording*), it also makes the process and information stored more abstract. Kirschenbaum notes that the storage of information on the five-and-a-quarter-inch floppy disks he remembers from his teenage years made the "writing" of data concrete because the only way to keep track of which disk held which document was to write on an adhesive label: "Written labels were therefore indispensable, their legible text standing in implicit counterpoint to the machine-readable markings on the magnetic surface sheathed within the plastic envelope to which the label was affixed" (33). This shift has become even more striking in subsequent years: "Since even routine chores like disk defragmentation are performed far less frequently on the current generation of hard drives, storage has become ever more of an abstraction, defined only by a volume letter (on most Windows machines, 'C'), a graphic hard drive icon, or a pie chart visualization of space remaining" (34). Information on this disk becomes increasingly abstract and intangible even as the concrete writing metaphor becomes more widely accepted.

These examples should make clear that, while writing metaphors have their most direct and consistent usage in talking about the physical act of recording information onto a disk, such recording also suggests an uncertainty about who is writing on the hard disk—the user or the computer itself. This slippage is nicely embodied by the increasingly broad use of the term *document* to refer to all kinds of electronic files. Today we tend to think of a *file* as part of a set of writing metaphors. When Xerox PARC introduced the GUI for its Star computer (1981), one of its central innovations was to represent directories visually as file folders; this is a metaphor that Apple's Lisa and Macintosh computers popularized a few years later in 1983 and 1984. The original meaning of *file* was not related to written documents but instead to the file box that would hold the series of punch cards on which data were stored.[44] *File* in this regard meant a method of holding together a plurality of data-storage cards. Today, however, we contrast the individual computer files to the folder that organizes and holds them. Understood in this way, the computer *file* has come to be a metaphorically written document.

The expanded use of the word *document* in the last fifteen years is another testament to the ubiquity of writing metaphors in computing—one that particularly emphasizes the actions of the "writers" who create them.[45] In a 1982 article summarizing the Star interface, the authors start their inventory of the desktop icons with the document: "A document is the fundamental object in Star. It corresponds to the standard notion of what a document should be. It most often contains text, but it may also include illustrations, mathematical formulas, tables, fields, footnotes, and formatting information."[46] The circularity of these first two sentences suggests a struggle with the metaphorical transfer of this term: a Star document is, more or less, just a document. The authors themselves seem uncertain about whether their language is metaphorical. In the Star interface, document icons sit side by side with other familiar items like folders. But there are other icon types that today we would call simply another variety of document, such as a *record*, which is described as "information [that] will be the variable data from forms."[47] It is clear that in the original conception of the Star interface, documents are those items that have been produced for printing or distribution, and they contrast to the raw data that might occupy another kind of file. Today, documents have moved much more to the center of our understanding of the computer, as any saved data are understood to be a kind of document. Although we recognize that nondocument data exist on our computer (for example, in the playlists in iTunes or the mailboxes in Outlook), we have very little language for discussing these data, and they remain invisible to the user when at all possible.

A convenient reference point for this transition is the introduction of the "My Documents" folder in Windows 95. Of course, traditionally a document is a written object. Although sometimes used to refer to evidence in general, the *Oxford English Dictionary* shows that a document is "something written, inscribed" by 1728. But, as we are all familiar with, the documents housed in the "My Documents" folder are not simply written texts; instead, "My Documents" has standard subfolders for pictures and music. Writing in 1997 in the *Journal of the American Society for Information Science,* Michael Buckland focused exactly on this shift of meaning: "Ordinarily information storage and retrieval systems have been concerned with text and text-like records (e.g., names, numbers, and alphanumeric codes). The present interest in 'multimedia' reminds us that not all phenomena of interest in information science are textual or text-like. We may need to deal with any phenomena that someone may wish to observe: Events, processes, images, and objects as well as texts."[48] Buckland instead broadens the definition of *document* to refer to all objects that have a documentary function: "if the term 'document' were used in a specialized meaning as the technical term to denote the objects to which the techniques of documentation could be applied, how far could the scope of documentation be extended."[49] Buckland is, of course, not writing primarily about digital media; nonetheless, his emphasis on a broader understanding of *document* clearly reflects the fact that we encounter a wider range of media materials anytime we do research into a subject. A simple Google search is as likely to bring up a video clip as it is a written text.

The decision to subsume all of these different media types into the category of "documents" is clearly overdetermined. Buckland sees the textual focus on the term *document* to be an artifact of the history of information, which for a long time—and, particularly, at the time when the modern social sciences were being defined—was overwhelmingly print based. Part of the attractiveness of this way of thinking about computer files is that it provides users with a concrete way of imagining the files they are dealing with. When Microsoft names this central user folder "My Documents," it is defining all computing as a form of writing, just as describing the recording of electrical impulses on a hard-drive platter as "writing" does. These two uses of *writing* are not quite coherent: the computer "writes" to some invisible location within the machine, but the documents that we view and edit on the computer screen are the opposite of this secret storage. Again, Kirschenbaum summarizes the tension insightfully, noting that what we see as a "file" is actually made up of clusters of sections within a track on the disk: "Clusters are not necessarily continuous; larger files may be broken up into clusters scattered over the volumetric interior of the drive. Thus a file ceases to have much meaning at the level of the platter."[50] The written document that we seem to be viewing in our "My Documents" folder has little relationship to the "writing" that the hard drive is doing when it records information.[51]

We should notice one final element of "My Documents." Although the name of this folder is obviously intended to identify the media created or collected by the user, it also draws attention to the broader context of the computer's file system, which is full of files that are not created by the user. The creation of the "My Documents" folder works to make your files easy to find, but it does so by admitting that the vast majority of the computer's files are *not* your documents. This is an irony we have encountered again and again in the definition of computing as writing: for all that writing seems to emphasize the concrete and familiar act of putting words on paper, its institutional and corporate implications surround and complicate the metaphor.

4

The writing metaphor is, then, ubiquitous but uncertain throughout the design of computer operating systems. We can see a similar uncertain importance for writing metaphors in the representation of computers themselves. We might think, for example, about our habits of naming computers, where writing metaphors have become so widespread they are invisible, such as in "notebook" computers. Despite the ubiquity of this language, the writing metaphor in computer design can be traced back only twenty years.

Overwhelmingly, early representations of the computer were based on the model of artificial intelligence. In fact, scholars working on the history of science fiction have noted that, while the imagined futures of these stories are replete with elaborate robots, computers themselves in the way that we use them today for communication, storage, and data analysis have a minor role. Thomas Haigh notes this in Isaac Asimov's *Foundation* trilogy: "Fifty thousand years from now scientists have achieved some miracles of miniaturization, including shrinking nuclear reactors to the size of walnuts for use in atomic powered dishwashers and personal force fields. But they don't seem to have invented computers."[52] In *The Cybernetic Imagination in Science Fiction,* Patricia Warrick locates science fiction in a Promethean tradition: "A pattern that emerges from the study of this large body of fiction creates metaphors of man's relationships with machine intelligence. The images evolve, over the forty-five-year period examined, from the simple to the complex and from optimism to pessimism. Constantly recurring is the Promethean image of man as the creator of a new kind of intelligence through technology."[53] The computers of these stories become intelligent and are defined primarily as decision makers and problem solvers.[54] It is for this reason that so many of these science fiction stories depend on the struggle between human and machine intelligence: "First the machine serves man because he understands how to build it and control it. But the machine begins to dominate. It becomes the *deus ex machina.* Man does not act; he is a passive particle that is acted on. He becomes a robot who can only respond to stimulation and do what he has been programed to do."[55] When the computer is understood essentially as a robot and thus as a kind of intelligence, these conflicts provide easy raw material for stories.

This fascination with robots in twentieth-century science fiction reflects a long tradition of concern for the uncanny nature of the automaton. In his study of the automaton in the European imagination, Minsoo Kang notes that concern can be traced back at least to classical Greece. He goes on to argue that such automata draw our interest because of the way they disturb intellectual boundaries:

> To put it in the most general terms: the automaton is the ultimate categorical anomaly. Its very nature is a series of contradictions, and its purpose is to flaunt its own insoluble paradox. It is an artificial object that acts as if it is alive; it is

made of inert material yet behaves like a thing of flesh and blood; it is a representation that refuses to remain a stable version of the represented; it comes from the inanimate world but has the characteristics of an animate creature; and, finally, it is a manmade thing that mimics living beings.[56]

In this sense, the robot has a natural place within science fiction narrative, since it so easily connects to traditional literary themes about the limits of human intellect, the relationship between imitation and reality, and human pride or hubris. In his introduction to the 1983 story anthology *Machines That Think,* Isaac Asimov links these concerns about automata to attitudes toward human and divine creation: "Robots, because they are usually visualized as at least vaguely human in shape, are perceived as pseudo human beings. The creation of a robot, a pseudo human being, by a human inventor is therefore perceived as an imitation of the creation of humanity by God."[57] Without being anchored in a vaguely human intelligence, it is difficult for novelists and filmmakers to represent computing.

A more mundane but equally important factor in the representation of computers through the 1950s and 1960s was the fact that most of these machines were corporate, and that most people would see only the results of the computer, rather than its operation. This is the case even in science fiction stories that try to imagine everyday interaction with computers in the future. In *2001: A Space Odyssey,* the HAL computer is represented by a glowing red eyelike sensor, but we understand that the computer is integrated seamlessly into the ship, so that it appears in no single location. Likewise in the 1946 short story "A Logic Named Joe," Murray Leinster manages to correctly predict a future with networked computers in the home. But when he represents the individual home computer (referred to here as a "logic"), the machine itself remains hidden and integrated into the house:

> You know the logics setup. You got a logic in your house. It looks like a vision receiver used to, only it's got keys instead of dials and you punch the keys for what you wanna get. It's hooked in to the tank, which has the Carson Circuit all fixed up with relays. Say you punch "Station SNAFU" on your logic. Relays in the tank take over an' whatever vision-program SNAFU is telecastin' comes on your logic's screen. . . . The relays in the tank do it. The tank is a big buildin' full of all the facts in creation an' all the recorded telecasts that ever was made—an' it's hooked in with all the other tanks all over the country—an' everything you wanna know or see or hear, you punch for it an' you get it. Very convenient.[58]

Although Leinster describes a future where individuals own such devices, they remain fundamentally modeled on the inaccessible mainframe.

Likewise, although this device does store information in these "tanks," its primary narrative importance is, like HAL, its sentience: "Joe ain't vicious, you understand. He ain't like one of these ambitious robots you read about that make up their minds the human race is inefficient and has got to be wiped out an' replaced by thinkin' machines. Joe's just got ambition. If you were a machine, you'd wanna work right, wouldn't you?"[59] This story makes clear that the centrality of artificial intelligence and the fundamental else-whereness of the computer are inherently linked: because we have little or no direct physical access to the computer, our interaction with it is frequently seen as speaking (or, more rarely, typing) to an independent entity.

It is only with the rise of personal computers at the end of the 1970s that we are confronted by a need to reimagine the computer and our interaction with it. Early advertisements for "personal computers" were directed at hobbyists, who would assemble the machines by hand (see Figure 1).

The Apple II represented a different approach to advertising, since it was sold already assembled. As a result, Apple emphasized the uses to which the computer could be put and represented it in an everyday, domestic context (see Figure 2). Although it wasn't until the introduction of the Macintosh in 1984 that Apple embraced the concept of the computer as an appliance,[60] already here the computer is represented as one of many familiar domestic devices. IBM's famous Charlie Chaplin campaign with which it launched its PC in 1981 represents a striking contrast, since the computer is placed in a nonspace of minimal white furniture and no background detail (see Figure 3).

The computer here is an element of pure individual work, divorced from any other context. The advertisement's signature single red rose in a vase represents just this minimal individualization of the workspace, and ultimately draws our attention to the blankness of the surrounding space. Although Apple and IBM take fundamentally different approaches to representing computers and how we are to use them, it is clear that the introduction of the personal computer around 1980 brings with it the need to find metaphors and tropes through which we can understand this new technology.

These advertisements are two responses to the challenge in the 1980s to find a way to represent *personal* computers. Such small, distinct devices were slow to arrive in science fiction, as well. A well-known example of the representation of the computer in a science fiction context is the Ono-Sendai "deck" described in William Gibson's 1984 novel, *Neuromancer*. This novel was greeted immediately as a breakthrough for its ability to represent a believable, everyday understanding of future technology.[61] Gibson imagines

Figure 1. May 1975 *Radio-Electronics* magazine advertisement.

Figure 2. Apple II Introduction advertisement. *Byte Magazine*, July 1977.

Figure 3.  Charlie Chaplin advertisement for the IBM PC.
*PC Magazine,* January 24, 1984.

the computer here not as a form of writing, but instead as a kind of mental transportation into another world. As a consequence, characters interface with this computer through "dermatrodes," and we are given no information about the physical actions of characters using this device. We are simply told he "found the ridged face of the power stud" and suddenly he is "in" cyberspace, described as a "chessboard," where information is near or far,[62] and where skillful operation involves finding a way to *move* into different data structures, many of which are walled off by security. Gibson's "deck" is striking today because it reworks the elements that Apple and IBM are using in their ads. Here is an engagement both with the nature of work and personal space. Gibson's hero, Case, is shown traveling around the city, and reference is made to the private space where he will work: "With his deck waiting, back in the loft, an Ono-Sendai Cyberspace 7. They'd left the place littered with the abstract white forms of the foam packing units, with crumpled plastic film and hundreds of tiny foam beads. The Ono-Sendai; next year's most expensive Hosaka computer; a Sony monitor; a dozen disks of corporate-grade ice; a Braun coffeemaker."[63] Like Apple, Gibson locates the computer amid appliances such as the coffeemaker; like IBM, he treats the space in which he works (the matrix) as a purely black plane.

What is striking from today's perspective is that the writing metaphor that Bush depends on is completely lacking in Gibson's deck. This should not be surprising, since Case's use of the deck has little relationship to the kinds of knowledge consumption and production that Bush describes. In the matrix, Case's job is to outwit artificial intelligences that protect commercial and institutional computer storage. In this regard, for all that *Neuromancer* is usually seen as an example of modern science fiction, its tropes for representing computers are firmly rooted in the mainframes and AI models that we see throughout the 1950s and 1960s. His innovative use of electrodes as the basis for accessing this computer space is a metaphorical road not taken in our attempts to imagine what the computer is and how we interact with it—one based on touch and physical contact. Gibson imagines the computer as an object you use through your skin. While many mobile devices today make heavy use of touch and the gestures of fingers across the screen, those elements of the computer have largely remained localized features rather than coming to function metonymically for the computer as a whole.

The intimacy of the computer as an object carried along and kept close to the body is also at the heart of the writing metaphor for imagining computing. This is clearly the case when we describe the computer as a *notebook,* a personal object to be carried at all times. Apple's 1991 PowerBook was the first commercial computer to feature the term in its title, and IBM introduced its similarly bookish ThinkPad line a year later. But the computer-as-book metaphor first emerges in Alan Kay's description of the "Dyna-Book" in 1972, which I mentioned earlier in this chapter. Kay describes his DynaBook in this way:

> The size should be no larger than a notebook; weight less than 4 lbs.; the visual display should be able to present at least 4,000 *printing quality* characters with contrast ratios approaching that of a book; dynamic graphics of reasonable quality should be possible; there should be removable local file storage of at least one million characters (about 500 ordinary book pages) traded off against several hours of audio (voice/music) files.[64]

It is clear here that Kay is drawn to the metaphor of a book because of the size of the object he is describing, but also because, like Bush, he is interested in how this device could be used to access a library of information. The children in Kay's hypothetical description write a computer program by accessing their local library electronically: "As always he had a little trouble remembering what his original purpose was. Each time he came to something interesting, he caused a copy to be send [*sic*] into his DynaBook, so he could look at it later."[65] Kay imagines the DynaBook as a device for programming (like a more traditional computer), a method for accessing library databases, and a book reader.

Although there are many ways in which the DynaBook is prescient, the link between computing and writing is most important to me here. The computer as a notebook pushes Bush's idea of the memex to its logical conclusion, since it embraces this writing metaphor but embodies that in a familiar and concrete physical object designed to be carried along and kept close to the body. It is for this reason, I think, that the term *notebook* (and, less coherently, *netbook*) is used commonly to refer to such portable devices. It is a sign of how thoroughly the computing-as-writing metaphor has taken hold that when Apple launched its touchscreen computer—arguably closer to Gibson's cyberspace deck because of its keyboardless interface—it chose to embrace the writing metaphor by calling it an iPad. Lev Manovich notes the irony of how writing metaphors are not merely carried over into but emphasized in the iPad, "which clearly represents yet another step in migration from the world of physical print to an all-digital environment": "It is as though we are asked to remember and cherish the older media— and erase it at the same time."[66] The name *iPad* has generated a whole set of UI metaphors, such as the built-in "notes" application, which turns the computer into a writing surface modeled on a legal pad. The commercial environment surrounding this product has likewise embraced this metaphor, producing other applications that play on the computer-as-writing-surface metaphor and cases that imitate a printed notebook. We might initially think that the wholehearted embrace of the computing-as-writing metaphor in this touchscreen device is a quirk of Apple's marketing. But a quick survey of the names of competing computing projects quickly reveals an almost uniform emphasis on writing; such computers are called *tablets, slates,* and even *playbooks.* But they are never called a *canvas, portal, screen,* or *window*—even by Microsoft![67] Such names would evoke an entirely different set of metaphors and draw our attention to other qualities of these devices. Although it is no doubt true that portable computers are used for writing and reading, they are also networked, used as part of a professional activity, capable of displaying video and audio, and so on. The writing metaphor mutes all of these elements.

In his recent essay, "What Is Digital Humanities and What's It Doing in English Departments?," Matthew Kirschenbaum suggests that the link between computing and writing has even influenced the organization of academic study. Digital humanities has found a natural home in English departments, Kirschenbaum argues, for several interrelated reasons. Among others is the importance of text to the modern computer: "after numeric input, text has been by far the most tractable data type for computers to manipulate. Unlike images, audio, video, and so on, there is a long tradition of text-based data processing that was within the capacities of even some of the earliest computer systems and that has for decades fed research in fields like stylistics, linguistics, and author attribution studies, all heavily associated with English departments."[68] Within the academy, the English department embodies the close attention to texts that is so central both to digital humanities and to Bush's original vision for the memex. More broadly, we have come to see textuality and writing as central to our understanding of computing in its broadest sense.

I have shown that Bush's vision of the memex is surprisingly modern precisely because it embraces this link between computers and textuality. In the process, it shifts attention away from matters of computation and instead provides an image of what has come to be known as knowledge work. In figuring computing as a kind of writing, Bush brings together the contradictions of work today: the slippery tension between creation and invention, and the question of whether the "trails" discovered in research are produced by the researcher or merely latent within the shared archive of information. As we have seen, writing is uniquely able to articulate these tensions because of its own multiple identity: both a pragmatic part of modern professional life and an embodiment of the private literary aspirations of individual creators. Crucial to writing's ability to serve such a key role in our thinking about computing is its mundane ubiquity: writing moves seamlessly from office to café, from official business documents to a private e-mail to a loved one.

In the next two chapters, I explore these two sides to writing in a computing culture. I begin with the corporate research model in chapter 2 before turning to more literary models for writing in chapter 3.

# TWO

# Writing, Work, and Profession

In chapter 1, we have seen that two definitions of writing circulate through contemporary culture as defined by the computer: writing as a form of social action, pragmatically oriented and shared, often in an academic or corporate context; and writing as literary and creative, often embodied in the lone writer working in obscure or private places using mundane tools. To unpack how these two models of writing operate in our thinking about computing today, I devote the next two chapters to each in turn. I begin with writing as a professional, shared activity, since that is the model to which Bush more explicitly appeals. Already I have evoked scholarship on workplace writing as well as Latour's analysis of the rhetoric of science—both of which emphasize the social agency of actors expressed through writing. We see throughout this chapter, and especially in the next, that this model is under constant pressure from its other, the literary understanding that often accounts for the appeal of the writing metaphor.

As we saw in chapter 1, the central issue in this model of writing is the relationship between the individual and an institutional context, which provides materials and the occasion for action according to professional norms. The work of writing in this context is pragmatic and shared, and we would expect that the texts that result will be more a matter of invention than creativity, to use Steiner's terms from the previous chapter.

## 1

In chapter 1 I noted that Bush's concept of the "trail" created when a researcher moves through an archive raises fundamental questions about the nature of our relation to a prior text. These ambiguities of how new knowledge comes from research into an existing archive might remind us of the problems that undergraduate students seem to have in distinguishing their own thoughts from the sources that they are citing. Having done the work to find the sources and skillfully put them together to form a new paper, a student is shocked to discover that he or she is being accused of plagiarism. I return to the issue of student writers at the end of this chapter, but we should note the broader issue raised here about our position as a writer before the electronic screen, what Christina Haas has called "'the Technology Question': What does it mean for language to become material? That is, what is the effect of writing and other material literacy technologies on human thinking and human culture?"[1] In particular, Bush asks us to think about what it means for language to "become material" in an electronic, networked context. We might invoke Kenneth Goldsmith's description of an explicitly plagiarized essay, "The Ecstasy of Influence: A Plagiarism," published by the novelist Jonathan Lethem in *Harpers:*

> If Lethem submitted this as a senior thesis or dissertation chapter, he'd be shown the door. Yet few would argue that he hasn't constructed a brilliant work of art—as well as writing a pointed essay—entirely by using the words of others. It's the way in which he conceptualized and executed his writing machine—surgically choosing what to borrow, arranging those words in a skillful way—that wins us over. Lethem's piece is a self-reflexive, demonstrative work of unoriginal genius.[2]

Bush's memex essay gives us a prescient description of research and writing in the age of "unoriginal genius"—of mechanical document retrieval and word processing. As Goldsmith suggests, our ideas about writing, creativity, and scholarship are still catching up.

The meaning of new work in relation to an existing body of texts is a question that has baffled more than the writer in first-year composition. In many ways the debate over the value of "theory" in literary study is a struggle with this same issue. We might recall Derrida's complex explanation of the relationship between the text and the deconstructive critic:

> The movements of deconstruction do not destroy structures from the outside. They are not possible and effective, nor can they take accurate aim, except by inhabiting those structures. Inhabiting them *in a certain way,* because one always inhabits, and all the more when one does not suspect it. Operating necessarily from the inside, borrowing all the strategic and economic resources of subversion from the old structure, borrowing them structurally, that is to say

without being able to isolate their elements and atoms, the enterprise of decon-struction always in a certain way falls prey to its own work.[3]

Derrida's passage contains many of the same tensions that we see in Bush's writing. Deconstruction involves inhabiting the text and working with pre-existent materials. Deconstruction is an activity, and yet Derrida is quick to point out that the deconstructive critic adds nothing to the work. Indeed, Derrida's core concept of the *trace* will immediately remind us of Bush's trail:

> It should be recognized that it is in the specific zone of this imprint and this trace, in the temporalization of a *lived experience* which is neither *in* the world nor in "another world," which is not more sonorous than luminous, not more *in* time than *in* space, that differences appear among the elements or rather pro-duce them, make them emerge as such and constitute the *texts*, the chains, and the systems of traces. These chains and systems cannot be outlined except in the fabric of this trace or imprint.[4]

The temporalization of the archive is, indeed, exactly what Bush seems to be describing in the trail, which likewise narrates a movement through a body of texts. And, like the trail, the trace is a way through which meaning emerges. This is an understanding of the critic's movement and the identity of the text similar to that described by Barthes in *S/Z*: "We are, in fact, concerned not to manifest a structure but to produce a structuration. The blanks and looseness of the analysis will be like footprints marking the escape of the text; for if the text is subject to some form, this form is not unitary, architectonic, fine: it is the fragment, the shards, the broken or oblit-erated network—all the movements and inflections of a vast 'dissolve,' which permits both overlapping and loss of messages."[5]

Barthes's pursuit of "structuration" rather than some preexisting struc-ture is precisely what deconstruction's more conservative critics could not accept. When they argued against theory in general, and deconstruction specifically, they did so by ignoring this process of movement through the text—the trace or the trail. For example, in *Against Deconstruction* John Ellis is unable to distinguish between deconstruction and reader-based theories in general, and faults them all for giving the reader a fundamental role in interpretation: "Sometimes the reader is said to *discover* the text's range of meanings, sometimes actually to produce and *create* meanings, but com-mon to all versions of this point is the assertion that the critic is far more important and creative than criticism has assumed him to be. The reader is no longer the humble servant of text and author, and advocates of this view speak scornfully of the false humility of a subservient role for critics and readers of texts."[6] Ellis's framing of this issue is simplistic, but he gets at one of the central features of deconstruction that caused anxiety in many critics: the increased role of the critic in inhabiting the text and producing an interpretation that is not simply an approximation of the original authorial intention but rather an independent text in its own right. This shift in attitude toward the critic's contribution to the text is reflected in the often-disproportionate length of some of Derrida's analyses, such as his book-length study of Husserl's brief "Origin of Geometry" or his thirty-eight-page essay "*Ousia* and *Grammē*," which he wryly subtitles "A Note on a Note from *Being and Time*."[7]

Critics and commentators have tended to see the issues raised by deconstruction as a way of rethinking the nature of textuality and meaning; much of the celebration and hand-wringing about deconstruction in the 1980s focused on the slippage and deferral of meaning captured by *différence*. Underappreciated here is something that Bush's memex allows us to see more clearly: that these kinds of texts imply a different understanding of an individual's work in relation to the text. We can see a similar neglect of the issue of work in the first wave of commentary on computing culture in the 1960s and 1970s, which often reinterpreted the memex not as a meditation on work and individual activity but as a new model for the human mind. When he looks at Bush's essay, Theodor Nelson sees a new model for textuality, which he claims we need to "generalize" by separating it from the particular device:[8]

> As Bush pointed out in his own terms, we think in hypertext. We have been speaking hypertext all our lives and never known it. It is usually only in writing that we must pick thoughts up and irrelevantly put them down in the sequence demanded by the printed word. Writing is a process of making the tree of thought into a picket fence.[9]

Nelson's treatment of Bush in this passage is particularly rich, since he reworks Bush's trails into an associative pattern inherent to the human mind while at the same time removing the key issue of writing from the equation. Bush takes exactly the opposite approach: he makes few claims about the nature of the human mind or even the shape of the profession and instead focuses on the material act of adding documents to archives. Although Bush's physical device leaves many questions unanswered, Nelson's attempt to universalize hypertext into a description of the human mind only serves to make these questions invisible. The same relative blindness to the issue of work is evident in the next generation of commentators writing in the

1990s. When, for example, George Landow sees in the memex a proto-deconstruction, he grasps the changing nature of the archive and our ability to follow links to other texts, but he gives the changing relationship between a researcher and a body of texts on which he or she works only passing attention.[10] It is the issue of *work* that is central to Bush's memex and to his appeal to writing as its implicit basis.

## 2

Although Bush's memex has been connected to academic criticism by writers like Landow, his essay arises from a much broader cultural change in the idea of work. As I noted in chapter 1, Bush embraced the role of the expert. He was also a strong advocate for close relations between university research and the military. Bush's biographer notes that his return to MIT in 1919 marked a time during which these relations were rapidly expanding: "The Institute's embrace of corporate values was a sign of the times. In the decade following the end of the war, society's most vital force was found in the marriage of technology and corporate capitalism,"[11] including electrification and Ford's mass production of the automobile. Bush embraced these values, and pushed for greater military funding for university research. As Zachary explains, "Anticipating the expansion of what would later be called the 'military-industrial-academic complex,' Bush envisioned a partnership of three sectors—the military, industry, and the universities."[12]

Needless to say, such an expansion was not without controversy. A particularly clear counterpoint is articulated by Bush's friend and sometime collaborator Norbert Wiener. Best known for coining the term *cybernetics,* Wiener's interest in communication, machines, and organization increasingly lead him into direct conflict with Bush's embrace of the military-industrial-academic complex. Wiener's focus on the human implications of these vast changes in corporate organization is embodied in his 1950 *The Human Use of Human Beings.* He writes at the outset:

> It is the thesis of this book that society can only be understood through a study of the messages and the communication facilities which belong to it; and that in the future development of these messages and communication facilities, messages between man and machines, between machines and man, and between machine and machine, are destined to play an ever-increasing part.[13]

Wiener's work on cybernetics is usually remembered today as the origin of information theory, and for laying the groundwork for human–computer interface design. But it is very clear in this book that he is also concerned with the relationship between individuals and the social, intellectual, and corporate institutions with which they communicate. He frames this as a link between communication and control: "The commands through which we exercise our control over the environment are a kind of information which we impart to it. Like any form of information, these commands are subject to disorganization in transit. They generally come through in less coherent fashion and certainly not more coherently than they were sent. In control and communication we are always fighting nature's tendency to degrade the organized and to destroy the meaningful."[14] Here communication is linked to control; to be able to send a message reliably is to be able to control elements of a system—a machine or an army division, for example—effectively.

Wiener is well aware that any organization involves communicating with its members, and in this sense with exerting control over them. Later in the book he examines the model of the ant community, where "each worker performs its proper functions" and worries about the "aspiration of the fascist for a human state based on the model of the ant": "I am afraid that I am convinced that a community of human beings is a far more useful thing than a community of ants; and that if the human being is condemned and restricted to perform the same functions over and over again, he will not even be a good ant, not to mention a good man being. Those who would organize us according to permanent individual functions and permanent individual restrictions condemn the human race to move at much less than half-steam."[15] This issue of the organization of individuals within a society is one that Wiener struggled with throughout his career; as his biographers Flo Conway and Jim Siegelman note, Wiener "was not a company man, but he wasn't a loner either. Deep down, he longed to be a factor in some larger matrix of minds."[16] This urge toward a meeting of the minds drew him to interdisciplinary endeavors like the Macy conferences, which began in 1942 and brought together scholars working at the junction between psychology and brain science. It also brought him into direct conflict with the military-industrial-academic complex, as when he published an article in 1947 in the *Atlantic* appealing to his fellow scientists' conscience and attacking the scientific community's support for "irresponsible militarists."[17]

Of course, Wiener wasn't alone in questioning the role of social organizations and corporate institutions in shaping individual lives, especially after the Second World War. Herbert Marcuse's 1964 *One-Dimensional Man* resonates particularly well with Wiener's critique of social control. Like Wiener, Marcuse emphasizes the way that technology has transformed human life. And, also like Wiener, Marcuse sees society's ability to control its members not as a simple process of repression but rather as a complex system of communication:

> This repression, so different from that which characterized the preceding, less developed stages of our society, operates today not from a position of natural and technical immaturity but rather from a position of strength. The capabilities (intellectual and material) of contemporary society are immeasurably greater than ever before—which means that the scope of society's domination over the individual is immeasurably greater than ever before. Our society distinguishes itself by conquering the centrifugal social forces with Technology rather than Terror, on the dual basis of an overwhelming efficiency and an increasing standard of living.[18]

Marcuse shares Wiener's concern with the way that society organizes its individuals according to ant-like functions: "In this society, the productive apparatus tends to become totalitarian to the extent to which it determines not only the socially needed occupations, skills, and attitudes, but also individual needs and aspirations" (xv). Power here is "over the machine process and over the technical organization of the apparatus" (3). The result is "one-dimensional thought": "We live and die rationally and productively" (145). Both thinkers define contemporary society by how it is organized through information and control. Both, likewise, see the definition of knowledge as central to this control. For Wiener, this knowledge is that of the scientific community; for Marcuse, it is the "totalitarian universe of technological rationality" (123). For both, organization operates through professional identity. As Marcuse writes, "To the extent to which the machine becomes itself a system of mechanical tools and relations and thus extends far beyond the individual work process, it asserts its larger dominion by reducing the 'professional autonomy' of the laborer and integrating him with other professions which suffer and direct the technical ensemble" (27–28).

Marcuse, Weiner, and Bush are all responding to fundamental changes that took place in the middle of the twentieth century regarding the relationship between work, professions, and corporations. The rise of what Harold Perkin calls "Professional Society" is traditionally associated with the end of the nineteenth century, and it brings with it a fundamental change in the nature of social organization and hierarchy:

> We live, in fact, in an increasingly professional society. Modern society in Britain, as elsewhere in the developed world, is made up of career hierarchies of

specialized occupations, selected by merit and based on trained expertise. Where pre-industrial society was based on passive property in land and industrial society on actively managed capital, professional society is based on human capital created by education and enhanced by strategies of closure, that is, the exclusion of the unqualified.[19]

Perkin notes that this is a shift in social ideas, from the "aristocratic ideal based on property and patronage" to one based on "trained expertise and selection by merit."[20] Others, however, have noted that it is precisely the growing power of the corporation over the course of the twentieth century that has diminished the influence of the professions themselves. As Elliott Krause argues, "Gradually . . . the key professions in the United States began to lose guild power, and in the years since 1970 their control has increasingly been shared with capitalism and the state."[21] These seemingly contradictory statements about the role of professions are not quite as at odds as they may seem, since the ideal of professionalism can gain in power even while individual professions lose the ability to regulate themselves. Nonetheless, it is clear that our ideas about what it means to *work* in the context of our contemporary corporate information economy are particularly complex.

Many have suggested that the meaning of work has changed fundamentally in the later part of the twentieth century. Michael Hardt and Antonio Negri summarize the common three economic paradigms since the Middle Ages: "a first paradigm in which agriculture and the extraction of raw materials dominated the economy, a second in which industry and the manufacture of durable goods occupied the privileged position, and a third and current paradigm in which providing services and manipulating information are at the heart of economic production."[22] Richard Florida's 2002 *The Rise of the Creative Class* is probably the most explicit articulation of the idea that contemporary occupations have blurred the line between technical and creative activities. Florida conveniently contrasts the state of work today to that described by William Whyte in his classic 1956 analysis of modern corporate work, *The Organization Man*. According to Florida, Whyte describes a world of stifling organization and bureaucracy, in which even one's home time, defined by the suburban communities, "exert strong pressures of their own for social adaptation and conformity."[23] In contrast, today:

> The new employment contract could not be more different. Creative people trade their ideas and creative energy for money. But they also want the flexibility to pursue things that interest them on terms that fit them. Thus they trade

security for autonomy, and conformity for the freedom to move from job to job and to pursue interesting projects and activities. The shift to self-motivation and personal autonomy in the workplace is bound up with the fact that we no longer take our identity from the company we work for, but find it in the kind of work we do, our profession, our lifestyle interests and the community we live in.[24]

The kinds of jobs that Florida lists as belonging to the "creative economy" include research and development, publishing, software, design, music, architecture, and video games. For him, the economy that results reflects not just a shift in available employment but also a change in the places and conditions under which members of this class live. The creative class gravitates toward "the economic winners of our age," where they fund communities with "abundant high-quality amenities and experiences, an openness to diversity of all kinds, and above all else the opportunity to validate their identities as creative people."[25] Florida's link between creativity and the contemporary economy will be especially important in chapter 3, where we will look at literary models of writing as they are applied to computing.

This theory of the creative class is based on earlier analysis of changes in work and the rise of what Robert Reich has called the "symbolic analyst." Reich identifies this job category in his 1991 book *The Work of Nations,* and defines it as including "the problem-solving, identifying, and brokering of many people who call themselves research scientists, design engineers, software engineers, civil engineers, biotechnology engineers, sound engineers, public relations executives, investment bankers, lawyers, real estate developers, and even a few creative accountants."[26] Reich's list of professions attributed to the symbolic analyst is more technical than Florida's understanding of the creative economy (which emphasizes designers), but both recognize a kind of creative activity that is built around "manipulating symbols" (178) rather than working with physical materials. Reich notes that symbolic analysts often have trouble explaining what they do, "because symbolic analysis involves processes of thought and communication, rather than tangible production" (182). And like Florida, Reich puts creativity at the center of this activity: "Symbolic analysts often can draw upon established bodies of knowledge with the flick of a computer key. Facts, codes, formulae, and rules are easily accessible. What is much more valuable is the capacity to effectively and creatively *use* the knowledge" (182). This merger of technical knowledge and creative production is exactly the shift that we see in the representation of computing as a form of writing. Writing in 1987 about the philosophical implications of the increasingly ubiquitous use of word-processing programs for writing, Michael Heim notes that the coming "paperless society" transforms information into something to be managed:

> The shift in economics is inseparable from a different apprehension of truth. Today, what is true presents itself within the drive toward greater productivity, better management and control, and increased organization through technology. Things present themselves first and foremost as things to be managed, organized, and scheduled. When reality is apprehended under the guise of Total Management . . . then thinking too falls under the heading "knowledge productivity."[27]

For Heim, the shift of writing onto the computer is part of a larger change in contemporary work that focuses on the organization and manipulation of what Reich calls "symbols."

This changing nature of work has led some to conclude that professional norms have weakened, and that our creative activities are freer than they have been in the past. This has especially been the case when talking about the expanding access to the identity of *author*. One response to the changing image of work and writing has been a facile notion of writing today as an opportunity for simple, unfettered creativity. As John Blossom asserts:

> Sent an email lately?
> You're a publisher
> Posted a photo, a video, a comment, or a vote on a Web site?
> You're a publisher.
> Keyed in a text message to friends on your cell phone?
> You're a publisher.[28]

Like Bush's memex essay, this simplistic model of publishing fails to explain where new knowledge comes from: everything ever typed or uploaded seems to be a new thing once we start describing this process as *publishing*. Others have gone to the opposite extreme and described "remix culture" as a form of cultural circulation without origin: "the lines between media consumption and media production are porous in digital spaces."[29] Dennis Baron frames these changes in terms of professions and guilds: "thanks to the internet, that gap [between the number of readers and writers] may be narrowing dramatically. Each new stage in the history of writing technologies tends to expand the authors club, and the digital explosion seems to have opened that guild up to something approaching universal membership, at least so far as the universe of computer users goes."[30] Barron doesn't pursue what happens culturally once a guild adopts universal membership, nor does he explain how our notion of work changes when writing becomes ubiquitous. In *The Laws of Cool,* Alan Liu has unpacked the implications of this shift for our thinking about the kind of creative activity that we associate with writing. For Liu, knowledge work "has no true recreational outside":

> But today it is producer culture that governs work life and home life alike in the name of a ubiquitous new regime of knowledge: not just company-mandated "lifelong learning," but also the "home office," "telecommuting," "edutainment," "investment clubs," and, as Paul A. Straussmann has observed, the thousand and one other routine jobs that have shifted to, or created ex nihilo, within leisure time.[31]

The rise of the "creative economy" is not just a matter of a changing understanding of work. It is also a matter of transforming (or, perhaps, as Liu suggests, destroying) the line between work and nonwork. In this context, the role of writing will be crucial. As an image of work that is also connected to leisure and creativity, associating writing and computing is a complex social act.

## 3

Being a writer has always had a complex relationship to professions. Literary historians often go back to Thomas Carlyle's 1840 essay "The Hero as Man of Letters" as a signal of this emerging figure. William Paulson notes that the modern image of the writer emerges in the eighteenth century by breaking from rhetorical culture: "The writer . . . came increasingly to be seen as a specific, original, creative figure, not just a particularly skilled practitioner of a rhetorical culture shared by his readers, but someone distinctively inspired or gifted."[32] In particular, Paulson notes, the writer is "emancipat[ed] from the control of church, court, or patron" while at the same time increasingly dependent on the "growing importance and specificity of the literary market."[33] By the nineteenth century, the writer takes on a particularly complex role within the emerging structure of modern professions, which W. J. Reader has argued is "very much a Victorian creation."[34] Clearly, the profession of writing is part of a larger shift that I already noted toward "professional culture" in the late nineteenth century. In fact, writing is a particularly good example of the way that professions claim a broader cultural importance. In her analysis of the sociology of professionalism, Magali Sarfatti Larson notes that a certain material self-lessness is part of a profession's traditional definition: "professions are occupations with special power and prestige. Society grants these rewards because professions have special competence in esoteric bodies of knowledge linked to central needs and values of the social system, and because professions are devoted to the service of the public, above and beyond material incentives."[35] Mary Poovey notes this careful handling of the economics of writing in Victorian culture: "Writers' claims to merit more respect than they felt they currently received almost all addressed the issues of work and money directly. Frequently, they conceptualized their work as contributing inestimable benefits to society; part of this representation was the image of the selfless writer, whose altruism generously canceled the 'debt' his grateful readers incurred."[36]

Writing has an uneasy relation to professions' emphasis on training. As Jennifer Ruth has recently argued, writing emerges out of a Victorian culture in which professions are associated with natural gifts. In other words, one becomes a writer not just by writing but by allowing an innate ability to emerge: "this tension between doing and being structures the text's production of a credible (and credentialed) professional."[37] This same tension has continued today, as the rise of creative writing programs have sent mixed messages about the degree to which this skill can be taught. In his history of creative writing programs, Mark McGurl calls these "the simple but difficult questions that have haunted creative writing programs since their inception."[38] Writing is the most "professional" of the arts, and thus the profession that best balances the appeal to innate talent and trained skills. Writing also has a complex relationship to physical labor. Generally professions depend on "their relative superiority over and distance from the working class."[39] Poovey likewise notes that writing is often seen as a form of un-alienated labor, a kind of activity that is inherently connected to the personality of the individual and thus not work at all: "Dickens displaces the material details and the emotional strain of labor onto other episodes—thereby conveying the twin impressions that some kinds of work are less 'degrading' and less alienating than others and that some laborers are so selfless and skilled that to them work is simultaneously an expression of self and a gift to others."[40] At the same time, however, these material concerns are never far beneath the surface:

That the literary man was viewed both (or alternately) as a disinterested sage and a mannerless miser points to the decidedly mixed lineage of the Victorian image of the writer. On the one hand, the Victorian writer could claim as ancestors leisured men of letters, those medieval court scribes and Renaissance intellectuals whose education marked them as privileged men, even if their daily meat came from patrons. On the other hand, the professional writer was descended from the early and mid-eighteenth-century hacks who sold ideas by the word and fought off competitors for every scrap of work.[41]

Writing, then, reveals tensions between the market and professionalism in particularly clear ways.

Writing likewise resists professions' notion of communally certified authority. As Perkin explains, "Specialization leads directly to professionalism. Specialists rapidly form guilds, associations, clubs or union to enhance their status, protect their skills from competition, and increase their incomes."[42] Writers, however, are marked by their individuality. Poovey notes the contradictions surrounding the individualization of the author, which emerged during the Victorian period in part as a means of "the commercial marketing of books by linking a writer's name to a unique and recognizable image": "On the one hand, by its very nature, the successful promotion of a marketable 'name' depended on distinguishing between this writer and all other competitors. But on the other hand, arguments advanced to discriminate a writer's personality so as to enhance the value of his work often referred to his ability to appeal to or represent the taste of all his readers—to be, in other words, like everybody else."[43] This is still true today. Even though we think of a novelist (for example) as a "professional writer," we tend to imagine that profession is based on inborn talent or drive rather than something learned.[44] Indeed, our images of novelists at work are resolutely those of solitary activity, and we are often fascinated by the quirks of individual authors' writing practices.

The problem of work has been a theme in the popular use of the writer figure in film and television—from the frightening pointlessness of the repeated typing in *The Shining* to the light comedy of Michael Chabon's stalled novelist in *Wonder Boys*. The ironies that surround the profession of writing and the nature of its labor are the basis for Paul Auster's well-known postmodernist novella, *City of Glass,* which provides an insightful description of the way that Victorian tensions between writing and related professions manifest themselves today. Auster's central character is Daniel Quinn, a writer whose recurring protagonist is detective Max Work. Auster's story opens with a tidy description of writing as the representation of work, but over the course of this metafictional narrative the lines become blurred. Quinn has lost himself not merely in the character of his detective but in the work of writing: "He had, of course, long ago stopped thinking of himself as real. If he lived now in the world at all, it was only at one remove, through the imaginary person of Max Work. His detective necessarily had to be real."[45] Quinn is drawn into a mystery of his own when he receives a telephone call asking for Paul Auster of the "Auster Detective Agency."[46] Quinn eventually takes on the role of Auster and begins the detective work that he has in the past only written about through his fictional character. Jeffrey Nealon articulates the implications of this convoluted play with identity: "Here we see Quinn's conception of Work collapsing: his extratextual job or quest becomes text; his attempt to withdraw from the uncertain space of the artistic work into the productive economy of metaphysical work fails."[47] Nealon sees this representation of the writer's work as reflecting a postmodernist attitude toward the text: "the thing produced by the writer remains unmasterable, refuses to pass into work."[48] But the anxiety about the nature of writing and its relationship to labor is well established in the eighteenth century, and it may be that the history of writing affords the writer an unambiguous relationship to the marketplace of goods and labor only in rare cultural moments.

As Nealon's reading of Auster suggests, writing has functioned as a powerful metonymy for our thinking about creativity and work. Clifford Siskin's *The Work of Writing* articulates the special cultural role of writing as a place where modern disciplines are negotiated. Siskin argues, "In representing itself as a type of labor, writing played a crucial role in valorizing and hierarchizing other kinds."[49] Siskin locates writing in relationship to professions as "the technology whose proliferation helped to elicit disciplinary and professional control" (37). The key term in Siskin's account is *novelism*. He describes novelism as "the now habitual subordination of writing to the novel" (172). The novel is the privileged incarnation of writing, through which we imagine what it means to write; it is, for this reason, that we have the "common assumption that a would-be 'writer' is an aspiring 'novelist'" (173). For Siskin, the novel becomes a tool by which we think about writing and its place within the professions: "By ordering our experiences with and understanding of writing, novelism—as the discourse of and about novels— produces and reproduces private, public, and professional norms" (173). Siskin captures well the way that the writing of the novel has been "naturalized" (174) by being integrated into stories of everyday life. One concrete example of this kind of naturalization is the common question asked of novelists by interviewers of the *Paris Review* school: Do you keep to a schedule for writing? Do you keep a notebook? Do you research specifically for your fictional writing? These mundane questions link writing to the rhythm of day and week, and they suggest more broadly that writing is not a specialized activity. *Literary* writing depends on its closeness to the mundane work of everyday life, even though it is also special. These interviews are a particularly good example of novelism because they are self-reflexive and part of a discourse that *surrounds* the novel: "By seeing the critical as not just a supplement to, but a constituent part of, that Authorial output we can begin to distinguish between the *novel,* as an autonomous aesthetic object in the category of Literature, and *novelism* as the discourse of and about novels" (176).

Siskin's focus is on the eighteenth century, but he notes that the place of writing may be going through another change today. With the rise of celebrity culture surrounding authorship in the middle of the twentieth century, writers were represented in a way that emphasized a subtle difference from everyday life. The typewriter frequently functions as the embodiment of this difference, and magazines like *Life* loved images of writers showing them hard at work on their typewriter in otherwise domestic or inappropriate environments (see Figure 4).

The typewriter has continued to play this role even as it has faded into obsolescence. Darren Wershler-Henry notes this ghostly existence at the outset of his history of the typewriter:

> Even in our image-saturated culture, the iconic value of the typewriter looms large. Artfully grainy, sepia-toned close-up photos of its quaint circular keys grace the covers of tastefully matte-laminated paperbacks, announcing yet another volume extolling the virtues of the writing life. . . . On radio and TV, the rapid clatter of type bars hitting paper signals the beginning of news broadcasts. We all know what this sounds means: important information will soon be conveyed.[50]

The typewriter has retained its symbolic power in culture because it performs such a crucial role in identifying the nature of work. The typewriter in these images represents the writer's peculiar position within the culture: different and yet not so different. The purchase of a typewriter signaled serious aspirations in writing, but the domestic and personal environment of these images emphasized that the writer did not occupy a formal business space in which the typewriter would be a common feature. The personal typewriter embodied the writer's subtle difference from others who merely wrote private letters by hand or business letters in an office. This is a crucial part of how writing operates as a commentary on professions: writing seems to be a point at which professional activity is not just that. We see in chapter 3 that this kind of mundane quality is a crucial linchpin connecting the various uses of writing to computing. Writing is so powerful a metaphor

Figure 4. William Faulkner in Hollywood, for *Life,* January 1, 1943. Photo by Alfred Eriss. The LIFE Picture Collection, Getty Images.

for computing because it seems to be the point at which the personal and the professional connect. As Liu argues, it is this erasure of the line between work and leisure that is characteristic of the contemporary information economy.

Writing, then, has a conflicted relationship to models for work current through the nineteenth and twentieth centuries. It has been linked to professional societies and is a central example of modern knowledge work, but it is also mundane and accessible to everyone in a way that other examples of knowledge work produced by "symbolic analysts" generally are not. It is easy to see, I think, how these complex and even contradictory definitions of writing help to make it central to computing culture.

## 4

Having unpacked the role of writing in relationship to work and profession, I would like to close this chapter by turning to a crucial moment of professionalization where these tensions are especially clear—in the teaching of writing in the university. The ambiguity about the relationship between new work and an existing archive of prior research that Bush creates in his description of the *trail* is evident when scholars and teachers discuss student research and writing, since that circumstance particularly demands that they be able to articulate the relation between individual and the larger professional community clearly. Tellingly, in such circumstances, critics writing about engagement with prior texts are most likely to resort to *oral* models rather than to the written ones with which Bush is struggling. This kind of language is especially clear in the ubiquitous metaphor of *conversation* in reference to writing in the first-year composition classroom. The widely used textbook *The Informed Writer* opens by announcing "A Writer Is Never Alone" before launching into a discussion of "the Written Conversation."[51] In a handbook on composition instruction, Sue Dinitz says, "The act of writing can be viewed as a conversation carried on by the writer with his or her text, and as a conversation that is facilitated by other conversations with trusted readers and with other texts. These conversations, in turn, helped students see writing as connected to their own interests and the world around them."[52] Likewise, Mark Gaipa applies this conversation metaphor to scholarship in the literature classroom as an alternative to the "Malthusian" view in which students compete ruthlessly for scarce original ideas: "It is precisely this metaphor—of criticism as a conversation—that I use to induct students into the world of scholarship."[53]

It's difficult to overestimate how common the language of *conversation* is in composition scholarship. The popularity of this framework for talking about writing can be traced back to the influence of Mikhail Bakhtin's description of writing as dialogue, which entered into composition study during the later 1980s. It is ironic that such an oral model of writing should emerge so strongly at the precise moment when Derrida's call for grammatology was urging an embrace of writing without subordinating it to spoken language. In *Applied Grammatology,* Gregory Ulmer goes further and invokes George Steiner's *Language and Silence,* which argues that modern scientific language is not based in oral or "vernacular" statements but instead in mathematics:

> Chemistry uses numerous terms derived from its earlier descriptive stage; but the formulas of modern molecular chemistry are, in fact, a shorthand whose vernacular is not that of verbal speech but that of mathematics. A chemical formula does not abbreviate a linguistic statement; it codifies a numerical operation.[54]

Steiner sees this shift not merely in the sciences but also in symbolic logic that he traces back to Leibniz, which "constructs a radically simplified but entirely rigorous and self-consistent model" whose syntax is "freed from the ambiguities and imprecisions which history and usage have brought into common language."[55] In all of these cases we see a "retreat from the word" toward an abstract mathematical system that has no basis in oral speech. Bush's image of moving through the memex seems a significantly better description of interacting with such written texts than the metaphor of a conversation.

The conversation metaphor also has some immediate, practical limitations. Joseph Comprone summarizes: "writing is very much *not* conversing, and we may, by too easily embracing the 'ongoing conversation' metaphor (for it *is* a metaphor), diminish the important distinctions between oral and written text-making."[56] In particular, this metaphor makes it difficult to discuss the actual tools and artifacts that the writer encounters in this "conversation." A good example of this limitation is the problem that writing instructors have with discussing plagiarism. Most commonly plagiarism is treated as a moral failure, in which the student simply refuses to do the honest work of writing his or her own paper. Occasionally it is handled as a failure of disciplinary orientation, in which the student has not been given the information necessary to use sources properly. But Rebecca Moore Howard has written suggestively about plagiarism as a strategy. She describes what she calls "patchwriting" as "a composing phenomenon that may signal neither a willing violation of academic ethics nor ignorance of them, but rather a healthy effort to gain membership in a new culture."[57] Specifically, she describes patchwriting as a response to an assignment to summarize a scholarly text:

> When recapitulating the source material, these writers "borrowed" phrases, patched together into "new" sentences; they "borrowed" whole sentences, deleting what they consider irrelevant words and phrases; and they "borrowed" a hodgepodge of phrases and sentences in which they changed grammar and syntax, and substituted synonyms straight from *Roget's*. (235)

Howard goes on to argue that patchwriting is actually a strategy rather than a mistake or moral failure: "copy-deletion, or what I prefer to call 'patchwriting,' may be a preliminary way of participating in unfamiliar discourse, of finding a way into it" (239). She notes that the students guilty of this form of plagiarism were "in foreign discourse territory. None of the concepts contained in [the text for analysis] had been previously introduced or discussed in class" (239).

What is especially relevant about Howard's concept of patchwriting is that it identifies a failure of the conversation metaphor for describing research writing. These students are trying to "enter a conversation" but lack the knowledge and context necessary to participate. In particular, they are encountering texts and do not have the tools necessary to respond to them as they would in a conversation. The strategy of patchwriting that they adopt grows directly out of their material encounter of these texts. In fact, it is easy to see that patchwriting will become even more common as students increasingly encounter electronic texts, from which it is so easy to copy and paste phrases and sentences. Much of our thinking about plagiarism is rooted in a predigital age, when passing another's writing off as one's own involved the work of retyping a passage from another's text. As we move into an increasingly networked world, where others' writing resides on the computer screen beside the "new" writing that the student is producing from those sources, this predigital model seems increasingly irrelevant. This is a point that Howard makes herself in another essay. In a "post-Gutenberg" world, "the technological innovation of the computer is precipitating and accompanying shifts in textual values that may be as profound as the modern emergence of the normative autonomous, individual author."[58] In particular, hypertext "makes visible what literary critics have theorized: the cumulative, interactive nature of writing that makes impossible the representation of a stable category of authorship and hence a stable category of plagiarism."[59] For students, the conversation metaphor provides them with little guidance about what it means literally to take parts of a text and reuse them in their own. Indeed, the idea of reuse makes little sense in the context of oral conversation, where the repetition of another's words is both difficult and has little strategic value—except perhaps as a form of parody.

Our position relative to prior statements in oral communication is entirely different.

Some of the most sophisticated work in composition operating within the conversation model negotiates this problem by locating reading as a stage preliminary to writing. In her analysis of Bakhtinian composition theory, Kay Halasek describes the problems of a form of discourse that has been read but not sufficiently digested so that writers can use that source material dialogically: "When a reader reads a text authoritatively, that reader's voice, authority, and subjectivity are undermined. This model of reading valorizes the text and the power of the author and establishes a seemingly objective meaning. Those who read authoritatively do not achieve a dialogic understanding of a text."[60] Although Halasek's description of authoritative reading can apply to spoken as well as written contexts, it is easy to see that the printed text—and, indeed, the vast body of what we call *literature*—poses particular challenges for adopting such a dialogic position precisely because this body of texts transcends the immediate conversational moment.

We might articulate these problems by turning to Bruno Latour's aptly titled chapter "Literature," in his influential study of scientific rhetoric, *Science in Action,* whose action-based model of writing I invoked in chapter 1. In some ways, Latour seems to repeat the conversational model that I have been criticizing. Latour inserts images of individuals with speech bubbles summarizing their responses to a scientific text: "It is a good paper"; "It's all wrong"; "I would not quote"; and, most tellingly, "I am an isolated author"[61] (see Figure 5).

Here scientific inquiry is translated into a dialogue, and position taking is treated according to a fundamentally oral model. But Latour's analysis is more sophisticated in practice than this cartoon suggests. He describes a complex rhetorical situation in which new truth claims can qualify prior statements in different ways. Some statements accept the validity of those prior claims and lead the reader "downstream" toward implications; others lead the readers "upstream" by questioning the accuracy or motivation of the original claim.[62] As science moves further and further downstream, these original statements become an increasingly unstated part of the field. Latour notes that these claims eventually become assertions without any modality ("A is B"), and can develop further into tacit knowledge that does not need to be articulated at all. Eventually, in its least modalized state, this knowledge is incorporated into the instruments that the scientific field uses to produce new knowledge. Latour's articulation of the rhetoric of science is an important counterbalance to the dialogic model that emphasizes the voice of the student writer. In the Bakhtinian model, writers take all

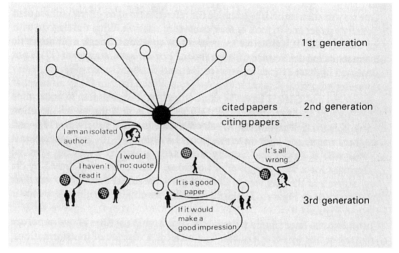

Figure 5. Dialog as a metaphor for engaging in research in Bruno Latour's *Science in Action*.

statements to be operating dialogically and recognize the possibility of changing the conversation. Latour reminds us, however, that any field is made up of many kinds of statements, some of which are so implicit that they are not available for dialogic transformation. More broadly, writing (rather than speaking) makes especially clear the sedimented nature of the environment in which individual actors operate.

5

Throughout this chapter I have examined writing as a component of professional activity broadly conceived—that is, as it engages with research, is situated within corporate and academic institutions, and participates in the symbolic analysis that is the basis of knowledge work. My emphasis has been primarily on invention instead of creativity—to use Steiner's terms from chapter 1—and I have been primarily concerned with how individuals operate within a shared space of resources rather than creating something that they own themselves. In the process of investigating this professional writing, however, we have seen again and again that an alternative understanding of writing haunts us. The writer is *not* just a figure of adaptation to professional norms and institutions. For all that writing is linked to the corporate activity of knowledge work, writing nonetheless also appeals to the mundane, the individual, and the personal—to the image of the writer sitting alone jotting notes in a private journal or typing beside the pool. When that private journal turns out to be a networked iPad, the tensions between invention and creativity, the individual and the shared, and the professional and private are made especially clear.

In chapter 3 I turn to images of writing in a computing context that embrace the other side of this equation—the programmer as a kind of creative writer, with literary goals and a personal vision for individual action.

# THREE

# Programmer as Writer

Having examined writing as a form of professional action often involving a research archive in chapter 2, I would like to move on to another understanding of writing common throughout computing culture, one drawn from literary rather than research models. Already in chapter 2 we have seen that our thinking about the profession of writing frequently depends on these literary ideas, even while foregrounding the institutional and corporate.

Geoff Cox and Alex McLean have recently argued that we should see programming as a form of expression: "programmers express themselves through the use of program languages . . . in ways similar to other human communicative expression through language and gesture."[1] Chapters 1 and 2 should suggest that I am quite sympathetic to this reading of programming, since we have seen again and again appeals to programming as a personal, expressive act. Cox and McLean, however, take as their model spoken language: "program code is like speech inasmuch as it does what it says."[2] In this chapter we see that the personal, expressive understanding of programming code is routinely articulated as a form of writing in a literary context, and that this literary context is essential to understanding the place of computing in the contemporary imagination. We find again and again that appeals to literary writing when thinking about computing end up also invoking a corporate, professional context, and that these two ways of understanding writing are deeply entwined in contemporary culture.

1

*The Social Network* achieved most of its notoriety because of its gossipy account of the origins of a ubiquitous part of popular culture—the social networking site Facebook. But the film is also important for marking a change in the way that computers and, especially, programming are represented in U.S. popular culture. As I noted in chapter 1, the computer has played a narrow range of roles in film. Usually it is threatening, an inhuman machine that is at best unconcerned about individual people, and at worst explicitly hostile toward them. The *Matrix* films of the late 1990s embody this approach, where humans are locked in a war against machines and the computer programs that enslave them. The computer is almost always a corporate entity and part of a larger industrial culture in which humans are insignificant. This is the approach taken by the Cold War thriller *War Games,* the comedy *Office Space,* and even the recent *Tron* remake.[3]

What makes *The Social Network* so distinctive in this tradition is that computing here is creative, social, and individual. As the story of Mark Zuckerberg's creation of the Facebook site, *The Social Network* approaches programming in a way that is fundamentally different from the threatening machines of *The Matrix.*[4] Of course, in doing so writer Aaron Sorkin and director David Fincher are merely recognizing the realities of computing today: for all that the PC in our office might be frustrating and impersonal, much of our private lives involve social connections and creative activities made possible by computing. In representing computing as a creative activity, *The Social Network* is introducing a completely different set of story motifs and metaphors for talking about computing and engaging in a complex process of articulating the place of the computer in our lives. And yet, at the same time, it *is* a story about corporations. As we see in this chapter, *The Social Network* is fascinatingly poised between an urge to see programming as an individual creative act and a recognition that computing is fundamentally a corporate, bureaucratic activity. We have seen this same ambiguity to be central to Bush's memex, whose user is solitary and yet immediately connected to a universal scholarly community.

To unpack what makes *The Social Network* so different, I want to turn to a film for comparison that might seem like an odd choice, the 1957 romantic comedy *Desk Set,* starring Spencer Tracy and Katharine Hepburn.[5] What makes the dialogue between these films interesting is not merely their historical differences but also their focus on the relatively mundane place of the computer in our lives. In contrast to futuristic representations of computing like *2001* or the *Matrix* films, these two narratives are resolutely focused on familiar social and commercial environments. Although it seems as though *Desk Set* should be dated in its understanding of computing, in fact it articulates the underlying assumptions about the human encounter with computing that remain in place largely until *The Social Network* shakes up our metaphors and plots a half century later.

*Desk Set* takes place in the reference library for a fictionalized version of NBC. The head librarian is Bunny Watson (Katharine Hepburn), whose staff becomes anxious when Richard Sumner (Spencer Tracy), a computer engineer, appears and begins making plans to install an EMERAC computer. Although Bunny and the other women who make up her library staff assume that the EMERAC will replace them, the computer proves to be worthless without skilled operators to query it in the right way, and at the end of the film we discover that Sumner had never intended to reduce or eliminate the library staff. Even this brief summary of the film makes clear that the threatening and inhuman nature of the computer is already well established in this early story. In fact, *Desk Set* is really about the narrative expectations of the threatening computer—the assumption that all the librarians make that the coming of the computer will mean the end of their jobs. (It should be no surprise that the film thanks the IBM corporation for its assistance in production; the story reads like an apology for the coming of the computer to the office.) The film works against fears about the computer, but the conventional assumptions about the nature of computing are clear here. Although we are supposed to see him as sympathetic and ultimately concerned about the lives of the women who work in the library, Sumner's preparation for the installation of the EMERAC computer focuses entirely on the physical space of the room. His early interaction with the women in the research department is designed to create a sense of mystery and suspense, as his focus on the width of the room and the height of its ceiling runs completely counter to the women's understanding of their jobs. We are to understand that Sumner's attention to this space is strange precisely because the women have become so used to the routine of their lives that they are unable to see their surroundings. The role of routine is established early in the film, even before Sumner begins his measurements, by a romantic subplot in which Bunny has been strung along for seven years by a boyfriend who refuses to propose marriage. In both his professional and romantic roles, Sumner is someone who shakes up established patterns and habits.

Once the computer has been inserted into the research room, several narrative possibilities present themselves. The computer brings with it strict environmental requirements—the women are no longer allowed to smoke and must keep the door to their office closed at all times. As they hang around waiting to be fired, they flirt with the idea of sabotaging the machine (one blows smoke at the computer when the operator's back is turned), especially once they (mistakenly) all receive pink slips in their paychecks firing them. To crash the computer the women do not need to take any drastic action, however; merely refusing to help the technician results in a barrage of poor search queries and an overwhelmed system. For a moment, *Desk Set* seems very much a member of the hacker model of computing films, in which a group of renegades destroys or at least disrupts an oppressive machine. This is the plot of *Office Space,* where alienated programmers from the Initech introduce a virus into their corporate network to steal money through unnoticed small transactions. In *Desk Set,* this anarchic vision only lasts for a few minutes of film time. The happy ending around which the film is built asserts that it is the social and professional context in which the computer is used that matters. Technical speed of calculation or the ability to store vast amounts of information is worthless, we learn, if the human operators searching for answers do not understand the nature of the question and the resources to be used to answer it.

What *Desk Set* and films in the hacker tradition share is an understanding of the computer as a monolith that must either be resisted or accepted as a whole. This is especially evident in the emphasis that *Desk Set* places on the physical space of the machine: here the computer is literally a huge box dropped into the middle of an established space. It has no inside. Even when Sumner must halt its meltdown by repairing it with one of Bunny's hairpins, the access involves opening a simple glass front panel and prodding an exposed circuit. Nothing about the computer can be changed, and there appears to be nothing behind the facade that can be investigated. We see no programming or design activity, and the only work done to make the computer operate within the space of the research department is to translate reference books into punch cards, which are then fed into the computer. When the computer breaks down, it is not because of a flaw in its design or because its programming must be altered. Instead, the people into whose lives it has come must change so that they can feed it appropriate questions. At one point the librarians bristle when Sumner asserts that the only way the computer can make a mistake is if its operators make one first, but the film bears out this assertion: the computer's eventual breakdown is the result of operator error. Overall, it is clear here that computers do not change; instead, humans must adapt to them. In this sense, the dark vision that the film invokes and then dismisses once the librarians learn that they are not to lose their jobs is ultimately still relevant: computers are unchangeable objects that will transform your life, rather than the other way around.

Described thematically, *The Social Network* and *Desk Set* might seem quite similar: both are about the social changes produced by computing technology. And yet computing plays a fundamentally different role in this more recent film—precisely because the computer is no longer treated as an unchangeable monolith that drops into the lives of the characters. Instead, computing in this film—and it is appropriate to refer to computing more than to specific computers, which only appear on-screen in passing—is fundamentally treated as something to be adapted and improved by its designers. Framed in this way, it is shocking to consider just how few films represent programming as a creative rather than destructive activity. *The Matrix* includes a brief allusion to programming when Mouse (Matt Doran) is credited with creating a training simulation in which the hero, Neo, will learn to push the boundaries of physics. One of these programs stars an attractive woman in a red dress, who has been added to test Neo's resistance to distraction. The woman is clearly the product of Mouse's creative and libidinal activity, although we never see him actually writing the code. A more telling example is the original *Tron,* where the title character is actually the creation of a programmer Alan Bradley (Bruce Boxleitner) but we do not see him working on the project itself.[6] In fact, the most concrete interaction between programmer and computer in this film is the attempt by Bradley and the main protagonist Kevin Flynn (Jeff Bridges) to gain access to their programming code stored on the corporate mainframe, which we see represented as typing commands. Here attempting to hack into the system functions as a metonymy for programming.[7]

The fundamentally different role of programming in *The Social Network* is especially evident in the opening scenes, which concisely narrate the origins of Facesmash, the proto-Facebook website that draws the attention of the Harvard community and sets in motion the financial and personal entanglements that make Facebook's success the basis for legal wrangling. The film opens with a dialogue between Zuckerberg and his girlfriend Erica Albright that foregrounds his insecurities about social acceptance and status. In the course of their exchange, Zuckerberg offends Erica by insisting on the importance of social status and by belittling her studies at Boston University. Erica dumps him, and Zuckerberg returns home to drink and blog bitterly about her. The posts begin with simple insults about her body and name, but become more introspective as Zuckerberg admits that she "has a nice face" and "I need to do something to help me take my mind off her." He comes up with the idea creating a voting site where the pictures from his dorm's "Face Book" are compared against one another. This requires a large number of pictures from across the university, and since there is no public database from which he can draw them, he announces, "Let the hacking begin." What follows is the film's longest sustained use of technical language, as Zuckerberg describes how he will access these pictures using a variety of techniques for gathering the information from different dorm sites with different indexing and security systems. This initial phase of the film ends when Zuckerberg's roommate Eduardo returns and provides him with an algorithm that he developed to rank chess players, which is then used to organize his ranking of the female student pictures that have been gathered together. The result is the Facesmash site, which becomes an instant phenomenon across campus.

In just the first fifteen minutes of the film, we see a fundamentally different approach to thinking about computing and programming. The computers of this film are located in intimate spaces. We see few computer labs or offices; instead computers appear mostly in private spaces—above all, individual dorm rooms where students have gathered in groups of two or three. At first we might think that the changes in the representation of computing are simply the result of material changes in the computers that we use. The computer in *Desk Set* is a mainframe located in a corporate space, rather than the PCs that we see in the dorms of *The Social Network*. But the latter film works to undermine exactly this distinction. Facesmash overwhelms the campus computer network and leads to an administrative board hearing about this breach of security and copyright violation. The remainder of this film is concerned with Facebook as a corporation, whose controlling ownership by Zuckerberg seems to depend on excluding other people (like Eduardo) who have contributed to the site as it was being developed. Facebook *is* a corporation in exactly the same way that the fictional NBC is in *Desk Set,* even though on the surface it might seem to be very different. Ultimately, this is what makes *The Social Network* such an important film for thinking about the nature of computing in contemporary culture, since it refuses to set up a simple opposition between programmer and system.

Even more striking here is how the origins of Facesmash and, eventually, Facebook are narrated: by appealing to the biography and individual quirks of its author. Facesmash arises out of a personal (albeit minor) trauma, which in turn depends on character flaws like envy and cliquishness in its creator. Facebook, we come to understand, has the impact that it does in large part because it taps into universal human weaknesses. At one point, for example, an encounter with a student in a computer lab prompts Zuckerberg to realize that "relationship status" is what drives life in college—"Are you having sex or aren't you." It is hard to imagine a greater contrast to films like *Desk Set,* where the computer is an unchanging object to which everyone else must adapt. Here, we understand, is a program that gets its power from the unique qualities that Zuckerberg has instilled in it because of this biographical trauma. The film insists on this uniqueness at several points— once during the creation of Facesmash, where it is compared with the less effective hotornot.com. Although *Desk Set* suggests a personal history in Sumner—he broke up with his last girlfriend because she was a poor letter writer, a fact that I discuss in a moment—that history has no effect on the computer that he installs, only on the way that it is implemented in the corporation. We understand that Sumner is a well-rounded person and not some bland technician, and as a result he is able to install EMERAC in a way that insists on the importance of the research librarians in feeding the appropriate search queries to the machine. But, ultimately, nothing in his biography becomes part of the machine itself.

Although the biographical narrative that is the basis for Facebook's design and success is an anomaly in the history of films about computers, it is very familiar from another type of film: those about great artists. Typical of the genre is *Amadeus,* which gets much of its energy from the contrast between the immature personality of Mozart and the beauty of his music.[8] The unfairness of the vulgar Mozart's great skill is what prompts our narrator, Antonio Salieri (F. Murray Abraham), to plot his downfall. "Why," he asks, "would God choose an obscene child to be his instrument?" But it is late in the film where the parallel to *The Social Network* becomes especially apparent, when Salieri disguises himself as Mozart's deceased father and commissions a requiem mass. As Mozart struggles to complete the mass, he is pushed to the point of exhaustion, and we recognize that Mozart is writing his own funeral music. In this final phase of the film the link between biography and art is especially clear: Mozart's late work, we are meant to feel, gains its depth because of the great emotional struggle that animates his life at the time. The gap between Mozart's artistic skill and his personal superficiality is closed, and his suffering is translated directly into the music that he produces. This is the core appeal of films about artists; we are promised that the qualities of the artwork are ultimately explained by the biographical details of their creator's lives. Hugh Kenner described this as the biographical fallacy when reviewing weighty biographies about Beckett and Joyce: "the assumptions such books cater to, notably the assumption that a writer's life and his work are related as truth to fiction, truth being—surely?—the substantial quiddity, fiction its image in unstable water."[9]

*The Social Network* borrows, then, narrative tropes usually used to describe the origins of works of art to represent the design and programming of an influential social media service. The computer is no longer a monolithic object that must be resisted or accepted wholesale, but is now a medium through which individuals can express their insights and personal experiences. And just as in *Amadeus,* the smallest differences in the nature of the work that results define its success. Salieri writes a "March of Welcome" in Mozart's honor, and Mozart shows his great musical gifts by playing it from memory later in the scene. As he plays it, he begins to insert small variations because he discovers a spot in the melody "that doesn't really work, does it?" These offhand and seemingly small revisions to the song fundamentally transform it, making Salieri realize bitterly the limits of his skills. Likewise, in *The Social Network,* the program that Zuckerberg creates is not some finished object that springs into the film's world as a whole; instead, it is refined by small insights and variations based on its creator's experiences.

## 2

From chapters 1 and 2 of this book, it should be no surprise in *The Social Network* and *Desk Set* writing metaphors are an important but conflicted way of thinking about how we interact personally and creatively with computers while negotiating their corporate origins. Initially, writing would seem to play a tangential role in both films. Writing figures in *Desk Set* as a sign of Sumner's humanistic inclinations. Later in the film, when romantic chemistry has developed between the two, Bunny asks Sumner why he has never married. He explains that he was engaged to a model named Caroline but got cold feet because the letters that she wrote to him during the war were boring and trivial. The romantic scene culminates when Sumner declares, "I bet you write wonderful letters." Bunny's proficiency with literary language is confirmed later in the film. EMERAC is asked if, in the film *King Solomon's Mines,* the king of the Watusis drives an automobile, and the operator seems unable to understand how to parse such questions about fictional narratives. A similar failure occurs minutes later. Asked about the island of Corfu, the operator mistakenly thinks the question concerns curfews, and eventually the computer begins printing the narrative poem "Curfew Shall [*sic*] Not Ring Tonight." While chaos engulfs the research room, as multiple searches are confused and calls continue to come in, Bunny gleefully and dramatically recites the poem from memory, as EMERAC senselessly continues to print out the entire text of the poem. Bunny's facility with books, and, in particular, her understanding of the narrative context of the raw data that EMERAC has simply stored, is the crux of this scene. The contrast here is the same one implied in Sumner's boring letters from Caroline: the difference between raw data and the literary meaning of the words.

Writing plays a key role, then, in this film's representation of the difference between personal and statistical information. The thematic spine of the film is the necessity of an ongoing, human context for the raw data that computers can so quickly store and retrieve. The film could have dramatized this theme in any number of ways, and initially this detail of characterization might seem arbitrary. Writing is simply one way to embody the fundamental attractiveness and humanity of Bunny, but after making the simple point that Bunny is a writer and the computer is a data storage device, the film has the computer begin writing, undermining the very point that Bunny's letter-writing skills just demonstrated. We see this pattern many times throughout this book: writing has a seemingly simple and almost incidental appeal as one metaphor among others, but inevitably this appeal is undermined by a kind of uncanny complexity. The film might have embodied such personal knowledge in some skill unrelated to computing—such as making Bunny a wonderful singer or giving her a talent for painting or sculpture—and in the process emphasized the fundamental difference between two kinds of knowledge. Instead, *Desk Set* uses writing to convey both. Even though EMERAC can print out texts, it does not understand what it is doing, nor can it provide context or meaning to the words that it prints. In the film, the ability to write "wonderful letters" stands in for just these abilities. But by making EMERAC ultimately a writer just like Bunny, the film insists on how close rather than how far apart these two ways of knowing the world are.

As this example makes clear, part of the power of writing in stories about computers is the ambiguity of this relationship between its literary and corporate uses. While *Desk Set* uses writing to embody what the computer cannot do, it is obvious even in the scene of Bunny's narration that the computer can, indeed, write. In fact, EMERAC's problem is that it writes constantly and without reasonable limits. When Sumner praises Bunny's ability to write, he is not pointing to some physical ability but rather noting the place of that writing within a whole identity. The difference between the computer's and Bunny's writing is not the physical artifact—he misspeaks when he says that the letters themselves will be beautiful—but instead the way that writing mediates social relationships. This is just how Bush uses writing in his memex essay: to describe individuals taking their place within a scholarly community. The difference introduced by these new technologies ironically has nothing to do with writing itself, and in many ways the new technology undermines the link between writing and computing. The computer produces more rather than less writing than its skilled counterpart does, while Bush's memex owners may actually spend less time physically writing than they would have in the days before acquiring this new technology. Writing here embodies the ambiguous relationship between the new technology and the social environments into which it intrudes—whether personal or corporate.

This ambiguity helps explain why writing returns in such a powerful way when *The Social Network* reworks programming as a creative act. The opening scene that I described already makes the centrality of writing clear: the film seamlessly transitions from Zuckerberg's blogging about his experience to writing the code that then posts these images on the Web and sets up the rating system. The film cleverly uses voice-over narration to accomplish this so that, at times, we simply hear what Zuckerberg writes on his blog and, at other times, we apparently hear Zuckerberg narrate what he is doing in bypassing the security surrounding these images. At this point the film feels more like Zuckerberg writing a novel about his experience than a programmer writing code to pull images from university databases. Programming here is indistinguishable from what we would normally think of as more literary, introspective writing.

Although I have been suggesting that the uses of writing in *The Social Network* have rhetorical and narrative power, we should recognize that programmers themselves have made the equation between writing and programming in a more direct and literal way. In his well-regarded guide to software development, Steve McConnell analyzes the "confusing abundance of metaphors [that] has grown up around software development."[10] The first one he considers is "writing code": "The most primitive metaphor for software development grows out of the expression 'writing code.' The writing metaphor suggests that developing a program is like writing a casual letter— you sit down with pen, ink, and paper and write it from start to finish. It doesn't require any formal planning, and you figure out what you want to say as you go" (ibid.). McConnell is dismissive of this way of thinking about software development, which he feels requires considerably more planning and management. He exaggerates the narrowness of the writing metaphor by taking as his instance the writing of a letter. If, instead, he used as his example the writing of a novel—which requires the orchestration of many characters, plot details, and changes in perspective—the contrast that he is trying to articulate would not be so stark. The term *software development* embodies this contrast, since it represents the creation of a program as an ongoing process in which many people are involved.

McConnell argues so energetically against the writing metaphor for software development in large part because it articulates something that is fundamentally true about programming. Frederick Brooks's famous 1975 critique of software development, *The Mythical Man-Month*, clearly explains why programmers so often think of themselves as writers rather than members of a development team: "The programmer, like the poet, works only slightly removed from pure thought-stuff. He builds his castles in the air, from air, creating by exertion of the imagination. Few media of creation are so flexible, so easy to polish and rework, so readily capable of realizing grand conceptual structures."[11] Brooks goes on to argue that the creation of software departs fundamentally from most construction projects, where adding more workers shortens the time to complete the task. He offers the following "law": "Adding manpower to a late software project makes it later" (25). He explains:

> The number of months of a project depends upon its sequential constraints. The maximum number of men depends upon the number of independent subtasks. From these two quantities one can derive schedules using fewer men and more months. . . . One cannot, however, get workable schedules using more men and few months. More software projects have gone awry for lack of calendar time than for all other causes combined. (25–26)

In a more recent casebook on software development, Scott Rosenberg concisely summarizes the implications of Brooks's law: "Brooks's Law implies that the ideal size for a programming team is one—a single developer who never has to stop to communicate with a colleague. This approach streamlines everything, and it also provides insurance that the project will retain what Brooks calls 'conceptual integrity': the alignment of all its parts toward the same purpose and according to a harmonious plan."[12] This explanation makes clear that ultimately programming does have a great deal in common with large-scale writing projects, which likewise involve being able to keep coherent a series of relatively independent contributing elements. Rosenberg goes on to note that developers themselves often prefer sitting down and writing code to project planning, and that "programmers are motivated and led toward their best work by a desire to accomplish something that pleases them or fulfills a personal need."[13] The urge simply to sit down and begin writing code runs throughout the profession. Addressing the issue of reusing code from other projects or from standard libraries, Larry Constantine notes that "most programmers like to program. Some of them would rather program than eat or bathe. Most of them would much rather cut code than chase documentation or search catalogs to try to figure out some other stupid programmer's idiotic work. . . . Other things being equal, programmers design and build from scratch rather than recycle."[14] As a result, many programmers feel that their real work is sitting down before a computer and writing code, rather than engaging in development planning or orchestrating their work with others. In this sense, the fundamental image of what it means to be a programmer does not seem all that different from what it means to be a writer: both involve sitting in front of a computer and putting words onto the screen.[15]

Even the tools that programmers and writers use overlap to a surprising degree. Although people outside the industry may imagine programming to involve highly specialized software, most of the nuts-and-bolts work of producing programming code is done using a simple text editor of some sort. In fact, because programming involves staring at a screen for extended periods of time, and also because overlooking tiny typos can cause an entire program to crash, software developers often have strong opinions not just about the best text editor to use when writing code but also which font is the best for programming. A simple Google search will produce dozens of surveys of developers, which inevitably prompt discussions that go on for many pages, and that attend to the smallest elements of design: Are each of the letters clear, especially the zero and letter *O*? Are the curved brackets clearly different from the parenthesis? Is the number one clearly different from the letter *l*? These are the kinds of debates that we would expect from book designers, rather than programmers. They have resulted in a lively business for general text editors designed specifically for programmers; in the Apple design environment, for example, programs like BBEdit or Text-Wrangler have loyal followings.[16]

A good example of the evolution of programming toward traditional writing models is the markup language created by John Gruber and Aaron Swartz called Markdown. Markdown provides a minimal set of tools for easily formatting text for use in web browsers. In contrast to handwriting HTML code, or using graphical interfaces to produce What You See Is What You Get (WYSIWYG) text that looks exactly like it will when displayed online, Markdown is designed to provide a low-friction way to insert common formatting into text on the fly. For example, Markdown will translate any text preceded by a number sign (#) as a header: "# title" would be translated into a first-level header, while "### title" would be translated into a third-level title.[17] An unordered list can be created simply by typing items that each begin with an asterisk, while strong or bold text can be created simply by surrounding the word or phrase with double asterisk (**make this bold**). What makes Markdown so popular among many writers working on the Web is that it allows formatting to take place without having to depend on particular mechanisms and commands native to an application. Markdown text can be written using any text editor, and text can simply be moved by cut-and-paste from one document or application to another. More significantly for our thinking about writing and computing, Markdown turns writing for the Web into the creation of simple text that depends on very common, typewriter-era keyboard symbols. As John Gruber explains, "The overriding design goal for Markdown's formatting syntax is to make it as readable as possible. The idea is that a Markdown-formatted document should be publishable as-is, as plain text, without looking like it's been marked up with tags or formatting instructions" (ibid.). Here web design seeks to disappear into writing in this simplest state.

This interest in text entry and editing among programmers results in subtle changes in the nature of writing in contemporary culture in general. Ben Yagoda recently argued in the online magazine *Slate* that the growing popularity in the United States of the British way of placing commas and periods outside of quotations marks—what he refers to as "logical punctuation"—actually reflects the influence of programming: "[one reason] is a byproduct of working with computers, and writing computer code. In these endeavors, one is often instructed to 'input' a string of characters, and sometimes (in the printed instructions) the characters are enclosed in quotation marks. Sticking a period or comma in front of the closing quotation marks could clearly have bad consequences."[18] It is certainly the case that, as more people become familiar with varieties of coding—such as the accessible HTML that might be part of a blog—expectations about writing are shaped more by the requirements of programming languages. This is the case even for less technical users of digital media; everyone has had the experience of mistyping a URL address in a web browser because of a seemingly trivial mistake in a slash mark, period, or underline symbol. This is a form of interaction with language that puts a great deal of emphasis on the precise use of punctuation in a way that is unprecedented before the twentieth century. In fact, James Gleick has recently noted that until the sixteenth century "few had any concept of 'spelling'—the idea that each word, when written, should take a particular predetermined form of letters."[19] The rise of printing led to alphabetical forms of organization and the standardization of spelling that we now take for granted. It seems clear that our routine interaction with websites and e-mail addresses has pushed this standardization further, so that users understand the difference between a hyphen and an underline, between a forward and a backward slash.

3

Just as our everyday writing has become more like programming, so too have programmers argued that we should see writing code as ultimately a literary activity. Donald Knuth has been one of the most outspoken advocates for viewing programming as a literary activity. His central argument is that programming should be best thought of as a form of communication between people rather than as a simple set of instructions for a machine: "Literature of the program genre is performable by machines, but that is not its main purpose. The computer programs that are truly beautiful, useful, and profitable must be readable by people. So we ought to address them to people, not to machines."[20] The crux of Knuth's argument is that code should be written in a way that makes the design and purpose of the program as obvious as possible. Good programming not only works efficiently; it is also easy for other programmers to understand whenever it must be adapted to another context. Knuth explains:

> The practitioner of literate programming can be regarded as an essayist, whose main concern is with exposition and excellence of style. Such an author, with thesaurus in hand, chooses the names of variables carefully and explains what each variable means. He or she strives for a program that is comprehensible because its concepts have been introduced in an order that is best for human understanding, using a mixture of formal and informal methods that nicely reinforce each other. (99)

Knuth offers this definition of literate programming as having practical benefits—he notes that this is a way to solve "all the major problems associated with computer programming" (ix)—like portability and maintainability—but I think that this claim is more important for how it redefines the nature of writing as a creative activity in much the same way that we see in *The Social Network*. But Knuth also makes clear that this redefinition of programming allows him to conceptualize the basic tasks of code development, as well. He explains, using language that seems appropriate to creative writing: "Programming is a very personal activity, so I can't be certain that what has worked for me will work for everybody. Yet the impact of this new approach on my own style has been profound, and my excitement has continued unabated for more than two years" (100). Knuth describes the attempt to think about the activity of programming in a new way and how this affects his day-to-day work. Although not widely known outside programming circles, his work has spawned what some describe as the "literate programming movement." The claim that we should think of the writing of code as a form of creative writing is frequently entertained by programmers from a variety of development platforms. Rosenberg cites Richard Gabriel about the training of programmers:

> My view is that we should train developers the way we train creative people like poets and artists. People may say, "well, that sounds really nuts." But what do people do when they're being trained, for example, to get a master of fine arts in poetry. They study great works of poetry. Do we do that in our software engineering disciplines? No. You don't look at the source code for great pieces of software. Or look at the architecture of great pieces of software. You don't look at their design.[21]

Although Gabriel is not thinking about the readability of code in Knuth's sense, it is clear that both share an interest in code as a creative activity imagined as a form of writing.

Given the fact that writing has played such a complex role in the films that I have discussed thus far, we should consider what work *literature,* rather than any other form of art to which Knuth might have compared programming, does for his argument. Obviously, literature seems like a natural term for him to use since programmers are writing code, but their interaction with the computer also involves many visual and iconographic elements that are ignored when we treat this all as a form of writing. But even if we leave aside these visual elements as secondary, Knuth's focus on literature has some additional implications that resonate with changing conceptions of the computer. First, it allows him to move into the background all those elements of his work that depend on corporations. This, after all, is the basis of McConnell's critique of "writing code" as a metaphor for software development—it fails to recognize the process and institutional context in which the writing occurs. But for Knuth, writing is *personal* rather than part of a larger bureaucratic organization. He makes no mention, for example, of the company for whom he is developing, the institutional bodies that define the standard library of coding functions, or the patents under which he is working. Much as Constantine observes, for Knuth creating a program involves sitting down and writing from scratch. He seems to envision the life of the programmer in terms appropriate to the novelist: "I find myself unable to resist working on programming tasks that I would ordinarily have assigned to student research assistants; and why? Because it seems to me that at last I'm able to write programs as they should be written. My programs are not only explained better than ever before; they are also better programs, because the new methodology encourages me to do a better job."[22] Programming in this passage is introspective and makes all the institutional context of his work—especially, his use of research assistants—irrelevant. I noted the same thing in chapter 1 in Bush's description of the use of the memex as a solitary activity. This description of his newly energized activity could apply just as easily to the novelist sitting in the coffee shop. The second thing that is striking about Knuth's definition of coding as literature is that it emphasizes communication. This issue of human connection and communication has been an element of both films that I have discussed, as well. In *Desk Set* the computer is fundamentally inhuman but can be used effectively as long as the corporation installs it appropriately and builds an appropriate personnel framework for its use. In *The Social Network*, conversely, computing is inevitably social. Zuckerberg's programming naturally arises out of his blog, which in turn is a way of communicating his resentment of Erica to the world. Knuth makes the same point: by treating programming as a form of literary writing, he insists on the communicational function of the computer. This communicational function is one that Knuth invokes at the very beginning of his book: "Computer programs are fun to write, and well-written computer programs are fun to read. One of life's greatest pleasures can be the composition of a computer program that you know will be a pleasure for other people to read, and for yourself to read."[23]

These two qualities of the computer are, if not quite contradictory, at the very least strongly in tension with each other. The writer of code and user of the computer are in some ways represented as self-reflexive individuals independent of any outside responsibilities; at the same time, writing emphasizes that the computer is a means of communication and social contact. This is the same irony that we saw throughout Bush's memex: the user is alone and yet not alone. These two ideas have always been implicit in our image of the artist and, especially, the writer. Loren Glass has noted that the issue of literary celebrity arose powerfully out of the changing conditions of book publication and advertising in the nineteenth century. He takes as an example of the anxieties these changes produce a satirical essay published in *Bookman* in 1901, "An Interview with Nobody," who (we find out) was "born and erased in Nowhere, New Jersey" and has "no methods, no style, no knowledge."[24] Glass notes that his "pure, empty generality functions as a revealing caricature of literary celebrity, which clearly is perceived here as having nothing to do with authorial identity or individual talent. Rather, Mr. Nobody is simply a new form of corporate property" (12). He can sell "'more copies [of the book] before than after publication,' confirming that the value of the book corresponds to the economic investment in its promotion" (ibid.). Glass goes on to trace how this anxiety about authorship manifests itself through the late nineteenth and most of the twentieth century. He notes, for example, that the popularity of authorial autographs "provided a way of achieving an intimacy with authors that seemed unavailable in the public sphere of print" (41).

Hemingway's career provides the best example of the changing relationship between the author and the marketplace. Glass notes that Hemingway's masculinity is explicitly represented as a break from the marketplace, which is equated with a mass female readership: "The terse minimalism that originally established Hemingway's literary reputation has been widely understood as a specifically masculine response to feminine genteel literary conventions, a way of making literature safe for real men" (139). Leonard Leff makes a similar point about the literary culture that surrounded Hemingway: "Authors generally wore the carping of Middletown reviewers as a badge of honor. The authors insisted they wrote books for neither critics nor readers but, as William Faulkner said, 'for the sake of writing the books.'"[25] Hemingway's mass popularity is, however, considerably more complex, since he was able to use this persona to market his writing: "In the 1930s, Hemingway found himself straddling a divide between modernism and mass culture that literary critics would understand as an almost-heroic struggle between the ascetic demands of the 'style' and the worldly temptations of the 'personality.'"[26] Glass sees the same irony in other modernist writers, like Stein, who says (famously), "You are you because your little dog knows you, but when your public knows you and does not want to pay for you and when your public knows you and does want to pay for you, you are not the same you."[27] Glass summarizes: "The transformation of the literary value of a text in turn transforms the identity of the author who wrote it. Now that Stein was the world-famous writer she had always known she would become, she felt strangely as if she had become someone other than who she had been before."[28] Celebrity here depends on the biographical basis for art, but at the same time seems to invert it, making the celebrity the genuine source of the writing and biography.

Celebrity is clearly an element of *The Social Network*'s popularity, since audiences come to the film because of the fame of Facebook, and much of the publicity of the film depended on the public identity of Zuckerberg as its subject.[29] In fact, Facebook itself explicitly raises the relationship between personal and public identity. But it is also clear that when the film treats programming as a kind of writing, it is drawing on these hidden tensions that run throughout the twentieth-century representation of writing. Is Zuckerberg the sole originator of Facebook, or do the people in his life that prompted his creation of this site deserve some of the credit (and windfall) for the project? The film is, of course, explicitly concerned with the legal wrangling over the value of stock that some contributors received, but underneath these events is a broader interest in accounting for how much a writer owns the product of work. Although the film explicitly embraces the traditional romantic search for biographical sources of creativity, it complicates this by locating this creative activity in a corporate context. This is what we find again and again when programming is defined as writing: an ambiguous and conflicted attempt to emphasize the concrete and individual actions of the creator, which nonetheless constantly makes reference to all of those institutional and corporate forces that stand behind the process.

## 4

In chapter 2 I noted the rise of what Richard Florida calls the "creative economy," Robert Reich describes as the work of "symbolic analysts," and Alan Liu analyzes as "knowledge work." Software development is in many ways a particularly clear example of this new form of work. Google's unconventional workspaces are legendary for their mixture of leisure and work, but Florida and others often fail to appreciate the individuality that has emerged in software development, and how strongly it has shifted away from a traditionally corporate model in the decade after his book was published. Florida uses software development as an example of the dependency of creative individuals on corporate support: "Whereas one person can write brilliant software, it takes large organizations to consistently upgrade, produce, and distribute that software."[30] In his book on the software development industry, Rosenberg notes important exceptions to this, such as the intentionally limited scope of the development studio 37 Signals, who assert that "constraints . . . are your friends."[31] This small-scale approach to development has become even more common with the introduction of Apple's App Store first for its mobile and then for its desktop devices. By hosting the software and managing the store and payment, Apple makes it possible for individual developers to create small applications that can nonetheless be extremely successful. Stories of individual programmers who became millionaires as the result of a single program developed in their spare time are common (if perhaps exaggerated). A 2009 *New York Times* story about Ethan Nicholas is typical of the genre: "For six weeks, he worked 'morning, noon and night'—by day at his job on the Java development team at Sun, and after-hours on his side project. In the evenings he would relieve his wife by caring for their two sons, sometimes coding feverishly at his computer with one hand, while the other rocked baby Gavin to sleep or held his toddler,

Spencer, on his lap."[32] The story goes on to describe Nicholas's success (at one point earning thirty-five thousand dollars in a day) and how he eventually quit his job at Sun. Such accounts invoke familiar stories about the overnight success of an actor, singer, or novelist more than our traditional models of program development. The focus on the individual developer treats programming as an expression of individual creativity and hard work, rather than the result of corporate development cycles. Given the cultural power that these kinds of stories have, it should be no surprise that they have exerted an oversize influence on our ways of thinking about what programming means today.[33]

More broadly, the issue of design and creativity in software development has increasingly expanded the tools and circumstances that can be considered "programming." Early writing for the Web in HTML depended on relatively simple forms of markup that indicated italics, bold, headings, and paragraph breaks. This itself was a change from the preparation of print manuscripts. As Bradley Dilger and Jeff Rice note, "In the age of new media, markup is the process of writing, whether on a word processor, which hides the markup completely, or on the Web, where markup is easily accessible. We can no longer distinguish our writing from the markup we use to situate that writing within its given spaces."[34] Some of the new language features added to later versions of HTML remained within the general style of print markup, such as the introduction of frames by Netscape in 1995. But with the advent of JavaScript and the transition toward dynamic websites that change based on context or user action, more of the work in website development has moved from static layout to designing forms of interaction. Alan Cooper makes this point in his guidebook to website design:

> The first edition of *About Face* described a discipline called software design and equated it with another discipline called user interface design. Of these two terms, user interface design has certainly had better longevity. We still use it occasionally in this book, specifically to connote the arrangement of widgets on the screen. However, what is discussed in this book is a discipline broader than the design of user interfaces. In the world of digital technology, form, function, content, and behavior are so inextricably linked that many of the challenges of designing an interactive product go right to the heart of what a digital product *is* and what it *does*.[35]

Cooper makes clear that the nature of design has broadened to include things like "information architecture" on the Web. As a matter of day-to-day work in website development, the line between writing and programming is tenuous indeed.

As a consequence, *writing* has become an increasingly ubiquitous term for thinking about work in all its forms. Although we would think that an interest in work would carry us back to the corporate model of social action that I discussed in chapter 2, the mundane and individual nature of writing as a literary activity is just as often central to our thinking about work. Let us take the example of the emergence of the idea of "electronic literature" in Michael Joyce's early writing, which I touched on briefly in my preface. I am especially interested in the first wave of what are usually described as literary hypertexts—narratives like Joyce's *afternoon* (1987), either published on the Web or through stand-alone authoring systems like Eastgate's Storyspace. In 2007 Astrid Ensslin wrote *Canonizing Hypertext* as an inquiry into how hypertext narrative can be studied in a literary context and how it can be used in the literature classroom.[36] But even at the very moment of its origin, few people stopped to consider whether such literary hypertexts *should* be canonized as literature. Joyce implies this when he uses the term *hypertext* "where *hypermedia* would do as well, since nearly all hypertext systems involve other media, and I know of no hypermedia systems that use no text."[37] That is, almost from the moment that Joyce published his electronic story critics have accepted this work as a natural extension of literary activity. But recently this definition of new media as literary has emerged as the subject of a vigorous debate. Partially this was prompted by the work of self-described ludologists like Espen Aarseth interested in defending the unique qualities of games against an insistence on seeing them as a form of storytelling.[38] This debate also reflects the fact that recent work often depends more heavily on other media such as sound, video, and images.

What is interesting to me is that these kinds of reservations have only emerged recently, and that the initial inclination of critics was to see the electronic work as primarily a literary matter. A good example of this is the publication of the *Electronic Literature Collection Volume 1* in 2007. One of the collection's editors, Katherine Hayles, frames this collection in unambiguously literary terms. She describes her companion book *Electronic Literature* as "intended to help electronic literature move into the classroom. For someone teaching a course on contemporary literature, for example, it can be used along with a unit on electronic literature as an increasingly important part of the twenty-first-century canon."[39] Although the works contained in this collection are quite heterogeneous and frequently use words as merely one component—probably Kate Pullinger's *Inanimate Alice* is the most striking case of this—Hayles sees the overarching category in which they belong to be literature.[40] More broadly, I think we can say that Hayles assumes that our creative interaction with the computer is first and foremost a matter of writing rather than any other art form. Hayles's assumption that computing is a form of writing seems natural, since we have seen the same equation made throughout this book.

These contradictory ideas about writing come together in Michael Joyce's *Of Two Minds,* a book advocating electronic textuality framed in largely literary terms. The collection itself was published in 1995 but reprints material from the late 1980s, thus conveniently providing a framework for thinking about the link between computing and writing as this electronic literature was emerging. We can start with Joyce's retrospective essay "What I Really Wanted to Do I Thought," which narrates the origins of his electronic writing and the Storyspace software that he helped develop with Jay Bolter. The story adopts a structure that will be familiar from interviews and memoirs of novelists and poets. It begins with Joyce having "published a prize-winning small press novel." "Like any novelist," Joyce knew that having to retype successive drafts of a story was a burden on himself and those who supported him, and so he was interested in buying a word processor. The essay defines Joyce's discovery of electronic literature as the result of the traditional struggles of the novelist. He tells a familiar type of story about the writer who sets out to do one thing, but in the process discovers an entirely different goal that he or she did not grasp before: "Immediately, I discovered that what I *really* wanted to do was something else. What I really wanted to do, I discovered, was not merely to move a paragraph from page 265 to page 7 but to do so almost endlessly. I wanted, quite simply, to write a novel that would change in successive readings."[41] Framed in this way, the computer is merely a vehicle for doing an absolutely conventional activity of the novelist: to explore aesthetic yearnings and create his next story. It is no surprise that he sees his work on the computer as a form of writing. In fact, Joyce's brief account of *afternoon* could serve as an emblem of the way that computing has been naturalized into a form of writing that we have seen throughout this book.

What makes Joyce's *Of Two Minds* especially valuable for understanding the redefinition of writing in a computing environment, however, is how he links these specifically literary concerns to his work as a writing teacher. Joyce's story about a novelist discovering his next book could have become the basis for expressing his artistic uniqueness, but instead it is connected to the most mundane of all university activities: the teaching of first-year composition. In particular, Joyce describes using his Storyspace system to teach the organization of knowledge that is the basis for writing:

It is a critical test in judging whether courseware authored with hypertext tools engages learners in looking at material in new ways or merely looks like a new way of learning. In many ways, of course, this kind of test is not new to us. Understanding, plotting, navigating, and recreating knowledge structures is the essence of learning. As current critical thinking across curriculum attests, however, we are less and less certain of our ability to convey these skills. (43)

Joyce describes the Storyspace system as a method by which students can organize their thoughts and shift between conflicting perspectives and sources of knowledge. For him, the system is especially powerful because it enables students to grasp all of those structures that surround the text itself. He tells the story of the students in his class who discover "their ability to perceive and express . . . the existence of information below the surface of a writing and to use that awareness of structure in commonplace fashion to empower themselves" (51). The writing tools that Storyspace provides allow the students in this class to grasp the organization of knowledge in the university and to learn an essential and universal skill about how to present that knowledge to others. What is important about Joyce's narrative is that the writing done on the computer is universalized into a fundamental quality of human intellect—something we have seen other critics like Theodor Nelson advocate, as well. While other art forms are often seen as the result of natural talent, Joyce treats writing as mundane and ubiquitous. As more and more of our everyday interaction with the world is mediated through the keyboard and screen, writing has become an increasingly natural part of everyday life. Evoking writing to think about work in general, then, depends on a mixture of its more literary and corporate uses.

## 5

We have seen that the image of the *writer* has emerged as a way to embody the actions of those working in a computing environment. We have also seen, however, that describing programmers as writers is far from a simple or neutral act, but instead invokes the whole history of the professions of journalism and novel writing. To show how these histories inform and complicate the equation of writing and programming, I would like now to shift toward an extended use of this metaphor. Specifically, I would like to turn to Neal Stephenson's 1999 manifesto *In the Beginning . . . Was the Command Line*. Despite having far less influence, Stephenson's book has some important similarities to Bush's "As We May Think" essay. Both attempt to make broad claims about the nature of computing, both are concerned with how we think and understand the world, and both use writing as the vehicle to connect these two issues. Stephenson's essay can function as a tutor text for our understanding of the literary implications of the writing metaphor for the profession of programming in the same way that Bush's essay helped to teach us about the implications for research communities of the computer.

As a fifteen-year-old prediction of the future of computing, Stephenson's book holds up poorly. Stephenson sees the PC market as one defined by a struggle between Apple and Microsoft, in which Apple's commitment to a closed system built on its own hardware will inevitably lead to its failure: "The problem, for Apple, was that most of the world's computer users ended up owning cheaper hardware. But cheap hardware couldn't run Mac OS, and so these people switched to Windows."[42] Stephenson's late 1990s view that cheaper commodity components used by Windows are an inevitable advantage against Apple seems problematic a decade or so later, but he is pursuing a much broader claim: "it is the fate of operating systems to become free" (37). That is, Stephenson sees both Windows and the Mac OS as temporary successes built on unstable business models: "the operating system market is a death trap, a tar pit, a slough of despond" (40). For him, open-source computing in which users build their own operating systems, share them with others, and incrementally improve them is the inevitable future of computing. Stephenson's predictions appear not to have been realized, since most estimates put the current market share for the open-source Linux operating system at around 2 percent, while Apple's closed system and tight control of its operating system has seen its popularity increase over the last five years as more computing has moved into mobile devices. But he articulates something in this book that remains a fundamental point of contention among those that follow computing and the future of technology: the appeal of an "open" system and the relationship between technical specialists and less savvy users of computers. The issue of specialization and professionalization is one of Bush's fundamental concerns, as well.

Stephenson's argument is built on a fairly simple premise: the GUI that has become almost synonymous with operating systems is inherently inferior to the older text-based command-line interface. "Ever since the Mac came out, our operating systems have been based on metaphors" (3), and for him this results in a fundamental vagueness in our interaction with computers. His clearest articulation of this claim occurs about halfway through the book:

> So GUIs use metaphors to make computing easier, but they are bad metaphors. Learning to use them is essentially a word game, a process of learning new defi-

nitions of words such as "window" and "document" and "save" that are different from, and in many cases almost diametrically opposed to, the old. Somewhat improbably, this has worked very well, at least from a commercial standpoint, which is to say that Apple/Microsoft have made a lot of money off of it. All of the other modern operating systems have learned that in order to be accepted by users they must conceal their underlying gutwork beneath the same sort of spackle. . . .

Most people who shop for OSes (if they bother to shop at all) are comparing not the underlying functions but the superficial look and feel. The average buyer of an OS is not really paying for, and is not especially interested in, the low-level code that allocates memory or writes bytes onto the disk. What they're really buying is a system of metaphors. And—much more important—what they're buying into is the underlying assumption that metaphors are a good way to deal with the world. (64)

My discussion of metaphors in computing throughout this chapter should suggest that I have a lot of sympathy with Stephenson's general issue here: much of our interaction with computers is highly metaphorical. In fact, he takes up many of the same terms that I have discussed, including the word *document* (63). But instead of accepting metaphors as an inherent part of our interaction with the world—the issue that Lakoff and Johnson popularized in *Metaphors We Live By*—Stephenson believes that there is a way of interacting with the world that is not metaphorical and that thinking that depends on these GUI metaphors is inherently mushy and vague.

Throughout the book, Stephenson draws a fundamental distinction between the visual and the written. For him, images mediate experience. Probably his most blunt articulation of this claim is his correlation between the GUI and Disney World, which he uses as an opportunity to describe a lazy American dependence on the visual: "Directly in front of me was a man with a camcorder. It was one of the new breed of camcorders where instead of peering through a viewfinder you gaze at a flat-panel color screen" so that "rather than go see a real small town for free, he had paid money to see a pretend one, and rather than see it with the naked eye, he was watching it on television" (47). From this he concludes, "Americans' preference for mediated experiences . . . clearly relates to the colossal success of GUIs, and so I have to talk about it some. Disney does mediated experiences better than anyone. If they understood what OSs are, and why people use them, they could crush Microsoft in a year or two" (47). Stephenson does not explain if some visual experiences could be less mediated and metaphorical (like going to see the real small town) and whether some forms of textuality can be just as metaphorical as the visual. Instead, the visual is associated with metaphor and words with the real.

I do not mean simply to criticize Stephenson's book—although as these passages suggest, his claims here are not only theoretically weak but also condescending toward the everyday user of technology. What strikes me as really important in *In the Beginning* is the very specific terms in which he articulates writing as the opposite of the metaphorical. For him, the writing of the programmer is exactly the same as the novelist: "Disney is in the business of putting out a product of seamless illusion—a magic mirror that reflects the world back better than it really is. But a writer is literally talking to his or her readers, not just creating an ambience or presenting them with something to look at. Just as the command line interface opens a much more direct and explicit channel from user to machine than the GUI, so it is with words, writer, and reader" (50). Stephenson articulates better than anyone else in this chapter the idea that the programmer is ultimately just another writer—what Knuth describes as "literature of the program genre." He goes on to apply many of our common ways of talking about the writer struggling with language to the programmer: "back in the days of the command line interface, users were all Morlocks who had to convert their thoughts into alphanumeric symbols and type them in, a grindingly tedious process that stripped away all ambiguity, laid bare all hidden assumptions, and cruelly punished laziness and impression" (61). Adopting the GUI means "abdicat[ing] the responsibility" of thinking: "Giving clear instructions, to anyone or anything, is difficult. We cannot do it without thinking, and depending on the complexity of the situation, we may have to think hard about abstract things, and consider any number of ramifications, in order to do a good job of it. For most of us, this is hard work. We want things to be easier" (ibid.). He implies that this struggle is inherent to our attempt to interact with the world, to "translate humans' vaguely expressed intentions into bits" (62). For him, "nothing is really easy and simple" (69). He makes the link between the programmer and the writer explicit. "Imagine that book reviews were written according to the same values system that we apply to user interfaces: 'The writing in this book is marvelously simply-minded and glib; the author glosses over complicated subjects and employs facile generalizations in almost every sentence. Readers rarely have to think, and are spared all of the difficulty and tedium typically involved in reading old-fashioned books'" (ibid.). Interacting with a computer—programming or simply navigating through the operating system—is not merely *like* being a writer but is instead literally the same thing: finding ways to articulate our intentions and make our ideas precise.

Stephenson's claims about writing and programming may seem quirky and individual, but the position that he articulates here is one that is frequently invoked in debates about the future of computing, and especially about the value of open-source software. In fact, in chapter 1 I noted the irony of the "My Documents" folder, which insists on ownership at the same time that it admits that most of the computer's files are not the user's in any meaningful way. Among other things, the open-source software movement expresses an anxiety about the degree to which computers remain the property of the corporations that created them. Although Linux has offered a practical open-source desktop operating system for many years, the debate about the nature and value of openness in software development has been especially strenuous recently because of Google's Android mobile operating system, which has marketed itself as fundamentally freer than the operating systems that powers Apple's iPhone. In contrast to the more straightforwardly open Linux, Google has released the source code for this OS under specific circumstances, and it has allowed individual manufacturers to adapt the OS to their particular phones and other mobile devices—even to the point where versions or "forks" of Android have been developed that bear little resemblance to the official code that Google is supplying. Google has frequently used the openness of its code and the variety of its instantiations in individual devices to argue that its corporate model is fundamentally more egalitarian than Apple's closed system. Others have extended this line of argument and asserted a fundamental right of device owners to modify their phones and tablets with whatever operating system they want.[43] This debate reflects a broader concern with the nature of the ownership of digital media, which is often encumbered with digital rights management (DRM) that restricts the use that purchasers can make of it. To take a famous example, commercial DVD players not only restrict the media they will play to certain world "zones" but they also will not allow users to skip through certain parts of the disk—such as the FBI warning against the duplication of the disk.[44]

It is this access to the code as a written artifact, which users may view and modify, that is frequently invoked in the debates about open-source software. A nice embodiment of this inclination to equate freedom and access with writing is the public dustup between Apple's Steve Jobs and Google's Andy Rubin in October of 2010. At the announcement of Apple's fourth-quarter 2010 earnings, Jobs took the opportunity to critique the equation of Android and openness:

> Google loves to characterize Android as open, and iOS and iPhone as closed. We find this a bit disingenuous and clouding the real difference between our two approaches. The first thing most of us think about when we hear the wor[d] open is Windows which is available on a variety of devices. Unlike Windows, however, where most pc's have the same user interface and run the same app, Android is very fragmented. Many Android OEMs, including the two largest, HTC and Motorola install proprietary user interfaces to differentiate themselves from the commodity Android experience. The users will have to figure it all out. Compare this with iPhone, where every handset works the same.[45]

To Jobs's critique, Rubin replied by tweet:

> the definition of open: "mkdir android; cd android; repo init -u git://android. git.kernel.org/platform/manifest.git; repo sync; make."[46]

These are the commands required to download and install Android on a device. The response is clever, but it is the style of argumentation that strikes me as especially relevant to Stephenson's book. First, this is a response that makes no sense to anyone unfamiliar with the command-line interface that Rubin in invoking. There is no attempt to broaden his claims to a nontechnical audience; instead Rubin is asserting the importance of understanding these kinds of technical details before the topic of openness can be debated. Even more important is the implicit claim that a broad topic like "openness" is too amorphous to be discussed except in these specific, precise terms. If you want to understand what it means for a device to be open, you have to know how to give it commands—to program it—so that it will install an operating system. Just as Stephenson asserts, real knowledge of the device requires writing. More broadly, at the end of the day it is this level of interaction through writing that provides a bedrock of understanding of such technical issues.

The nature of writing as a model for thinking about computing is powerfully embodied in Rubin's tweet. Writing stands for openness, for the concrete, for the root-level access to a device, in apparent contrast to Apple's willingness to control the user experience on its iPhone and iPad. But Rubin's tweet is also only possible because of a host of institutional and corporate resources—most obviously, the ability to download the source code from the Google server. Although this writing seems to be a concrete and even physical act, it is only possible because of these massive servers that exist somewhere—the user downloading the file has no idea where—that in turn support Google's corporate interests. Writing here brilliantly captures the ambiguity that we see throughout our contemporary understanding of computing, which we yearn to see as familiar and concrete while we recognize all of these abstract and corporate relationships that make it possible. Indeed, we can push this even further and note that precisely this irony is what we see in Bush's memex, which is both a physical artifact and an object that connects us to a community of others. The open software movement takes its energy from the desire to control one's own computing device, but it becomes a movement only when it links up many users and provides a library of computing resources that no one person could assemble alone—a topic to which I turn in chapter 4. Writing negotiates this complex boundary between individual and community, and the appeal to writing as our fundamental way of interacting with the computer provides a corollary that enables us to imagine the whole act of owning and using such a computing device.

We can see, then, that the ambiguity of the writing metaphor that we observed in Bush's memex essay is typical of contemporary culture rather than unique. Bush used the model of writing to talk about the way that individuals were connected to a larger community, and in the process significantly complicated the apparent promise of the writing metaphor: to make computing seem simple. The same is the case in all the texts that I have discussed throughout this chapter, from *The Social Network* to Andy Rubin's tweet. In each case writing offers a seemingly simple model for thinking about computing, while at the same time clearly invoking all of those institutional and corporate connections on which the computer depend.

# FOUR

# E-Books, Libraries, and Feelies

Over the last several years the future of reading has become a surprisingly hot topic within consumer electronic marketing. Long ignored in the rush to distribute music and film digitally, the book emerged as the next big thing in media sales with Amazon's Kindle reader. Although portable e-readers have been available for more than a decade, it is only with the launch of the Kindle that electronic book reading promised to break into the popular consciousness and move beyond the concerns of the digerati. With the release of Apple's iPad in 2010, the issue of digital distribution moved from books to magazines. Would consumers buy a digital subscription instead of receiving a package in the mail each month? What should the relationship be between these subscriptions and the information and samples available on a magazine's website? What is the best way to integrate these subscriptions into portable media devices—as information accessed through a website, as stand-alone applications, or as some element in a broader electronic newsstand? Five years later, these questions are still very much unanswered. Amazon announced in May of 2011 that it was selling more Kindle than print books,[1] but the means by which everyday consumers will buy and read periodical writing is still very much undecided.

A central component of the appeal of electronic book reading is the promise that you can carry your entire *library* with you as you travel. Products like the Kindle promise to do for books what the iPod did for music: synthesize a messy physical collection that may take up many shelves in your home and make your entire music library available on a single digital device. The energy and emotion in these debates makes clear that what is at stake is more than just the matter of the most convenient way to read a novel.

Instead, the discussion has become a reflection on the value and nature of reading, and its relationship to technology. In this sense, the concept of the digital *library* joins terms like *document* and *file* that I have discussed in other chapters as literary terms that have migrated into computing culture. As we will see in this chapter, the library has a similarly complex identity as it negotiates the promise of a concrete, physical object and the recognition of the institutional and corporate context in which digital media are used.

## 1

Debates about electronic reading have focused on several supposed weaknesses of the e-book in relation to traditional printed texts. Some have emphasized the physical relationship between reader and book that appears to be lost with an e-book. This was especially the case in the early days of electronic text, when reading meant sitting in front of a computer or, at best, holding a laptop. In 1994 Sven Birkerts complained, "As the printed book, and the ways of the book—of writing and reading—are modified, as electronic communications assert dominance, the 'feel' of the literary engagement is altered."[2] Critics complained that such environments were prone to distraction. In a 2009 *New York Times* "Room for Debate" article, Gloria Mark offers her own preference: "I'd much rather curl up in an easy chair with a paper book. It's not only an escape into the world of literature but it's an escape from my digital devices," and then suggests that digital reading will be inherently distracted reading. "I wonder about young people, who do not know of a life before the Internet, and who, growing up 'digitized,' might not prefer reading online where they are the pilots of their own information pathways. More and more, studies are showing how adept young people are at multitasking."[3]

As dedicated devices like Amazon's Kindle have increasingly come to define e-book reading, the debate has shifted. Some have complained about the lost artistry of book design and typography,[4] but most recent commentators recognize that e-book design is going through a process of refinement that will likely produce artifacts that can be just as carefully designed as printed books.[5] More recent criticism on e-books has focused on other elements of the electronic reading environment, such as the ability to carry multiple books or update the text of books. Jonathan Franzen took this approach in his recent criticism of electronic reading at the Hay Festival in Cartagena, Columbia. As the *Telegraph* reports on Franzen's talk:

I think, for serious readers, a sense of permanence has always been part of the experience. Everything else in your life is fluid, but here is this text that doesn't change.

Will there still be readers 50 years from now who feel that way? Who have that hunger for something permanent and unalterable? I don't have a crystal ball.

But I do fear that it's going to be very hard to make the world work if there's no permanence like that. That kind of radical contingency is not compatible with a system of justice or responsible self-government.[6]

The link between the individual book and larger body of texts is the inflection point at which the e-book is both defended and dismissed. For Franzen, the book's link to a network means that it can be updated at any time, and that consequently the whole text lacks permanence. However, it is precisely the link between device and library that has been the primary selling point of the Kindle for years. A Kindle or iPad is only slightly more convenient to carry than a single book; it is when we want to carry multiple books that such devices become more convenient. As the advertisements for the Kindle promise, "Carry up to 1,400 books—keep your library with you wherever you go." Amazon's emphasis on carrying a library along with you is a somewhat surprising appeal, since it seems to reflect a rather narrow habit of reading in contrast to the broader ability to buy books anywhere at any time. It may be that the Kindle has adopted the model provided by Apple's iPod, which was advertised as allowing one to carry "1,000 songs in your pocket."

As this makes clear, the concept of the *library* has a surprisingly important role in justifying the value of e-book reading. Other issues like the cost and ease of purchasing may already be a stronger appeal of this medium, but the initial framework used by Amazon and others to explain to readers why they should embrace the e-book was the personal library. The concept of the library seems like a happy point of convergence between literary and computer culture: books on a device for reading are like books in a physical library. The analogy quickly breaks down, however. One of the nagging problems in library-based electronic devices is the concept of "lending" a digital text. To a large extent, public libraries exist to lend books out, and the process of books coming and going through the library's doors is one of the surest signs of the vibrancy of the institution. There have been several attempts to extend the concept of lending to electronic libraries, with limited success. Microsoft attracted general derision in 2007 when it promised that its Zune music player would improve on the iPod because it has the ability to "squirt" a song from one player to another. This form of digital sharing was an odd mixture of old-fashioned lending (since the two Zunes between which the song moves had to be physically close) and uniquely digital qualities: the song did not leave the original Zune (the original user could still listen to it) and the squirted song was laden with DRM restrictions (it remained on the Zune for only three days or three plays). The Nook e-book reader integrates a similar lending structure for books, with similar quirks. As with traditional libraries, books that have been lent cannot be used by the lender while they are "gone." But the Nook limits lending to a single instance per book; each book may be lent only once, ever.

Probably the single best example of the problem of digital libraries is the snafu over Amazon's decision to remotely remove copies of Orwell's *1984* from Kindles when it discovered that it was inadvertently selling an unauthorized copy of the book. Annotations users had made to the book vanished, prompting threats of a lawsuit and hasty apologies from Amazon's CEO Jeff Bezos.[7] The possibility that an item, whether purchased legitimately or not, might simply disappear from a library has no equivalent in a physical collection of books, and suggests that beneath the metaphor of the Kindle holding a "library" of books is a very different relationship between device and electronic services. Similar (if less sinister) problems arise any time a music or book service with its own file format goes out of business. For example, Microsoft created and strongly advertised the (now ironically named) PlaysForSure certification for portable devices, but eventually canceled the connection to their own MSN Music store and adopted an entirely different service for its Zune Marketplace, forcing users with songs from the service to burn them to CD or adopt the products of third-party companies. Clearly, any digital library depends on devices and file formats to read this media. These electronic books are only accessible so long as the technology (and any patents that it might be encumbered by) allows that file type to be used.

These problems of bringing lending to the electronic library suggest the limitations of what seems like a natural analogy. I think, however, that there is a deeper and even more problematic tension between the understanding of the word *library* in bibli- and computer-centered environments. When we speak about a library that holds physical books, we understand that both the building and the more abstract library institution are secondary entities that serve to organize independent objects. That is to say, books exist before the library, can be moved from one library to the next, and even if every library in the world somehow disappeared, our reading life would largely be the same—if somewhat more cluttered. Henry Petroski articulates this in slightly different terms: "It may be strictly true that books can exist without bookshelves, and we can imagine the Library of Congress or even the local public library with books contained in boxes, stacked on the floor, or stored in piles like firewood or coal. The bookshelf, however, can hardly be imagined without the existence of books."[8] Books are independent of libraries.

Of course, I'm putting the matter simplistically. Most books published today include Library of Congress and Dewey Decimal categorizing information on their copyright page. Furthermore, books are written and, especially, published because they fit into recognizable and marketable categories. These are institutional conditions that preexist and shape books. Books are not like species discovered in the wild and categorized by biologists; instead, the categories themselves in part define the books that are written, published, and read. Still, we recognize in a commonsensical if somewhat naive way that books are separate from libraries: if we discarded the Library of Congress categories or dismantled the public library system, the physical book would remain and not disappear from our shelves like Amazon's Kindle version of *1984*. Alberto Manguel makes this point in his *A History of Reading*:

> Rooms, corridors, bookcases, shelves, filing cards and computerized catalogues assume that the subjects on which our thoughts dwell are actual entities, and through this assumption a certain book may be lent a particular tone and value. Filed under Fiction, Jonathan Swift's *Gulliver's Travels* is a humorous novel of adventure; under Sociology, a satirical study of England in the eighteenth century; under Children's Literature, an entertaining fable about dwarfs and giants and talking horses; under Fantasy, a precursor to Science Fiction; under Travel, an imaginary voyage; under Classics, a part of the Western literary canon. Categories are exclusive; reading is not—or should not be. Whatever classifications have been chosen, every library tyrannizes the act of reading, and forces the reader—the curious reader, the alert reader—to *rescue* the book from the category to which it has been condemned.[9]

I will return to Manguel's description of the book in the library, because we will see that the independence of the book from the library is surprisingly ambiguous. But for now we should recognize that we usually think of books as independent of their libraries, and always able to rebel against the categories that we put them into.

The use of the word *library* in a computing context is strikingly different on this point. Modern programming languages work by reusing vast chunks of standardized code; in fact, it is a principle of good programming to make any code as general and thus reusable as possible. Sometimes this is done within a single program, where one particular bit of code might be invoked multiple times to perform the same function in different contexts. Sometimes code is reused by an individual programmer or software company, where the same code might be used in different projects. The concept of code reuse is built right into modern programming languages. These languages each have what is referred to as a standard library of commands, types of data objects, and functions. This library is usually so large that all of it is not automatically included in every program; instead, programmers have to issue some command to copy the parts of the library that make the necessary objects and functions work. Here, for example, is a very simple program written in C (borrowed from an online tutorial):

```
#include <stdio.h>
int main()
{
    int this_is_a_number;
    printf( "Please enter a number: " );
    scanf( "%d", &this_is_a_number );
    printf( "You entered %d", this_is_a_number );
    getchar();
    return 0;
}10
```

All this program does is ask you to input a number and then display it back; it is a simple example of how a C program handles input and output of variables, which is why it is used at the beginning of this tutorial. But even this simple program depends on the command "include" at the beginning, which imports a file called "stdio.h." This file contains information about how to display output and receive input from the keyboard; because that is included in this file, the programmer does not have to tell the computer what commands like "printf" and "scanf" mean. The file "stdio.h" is one part of the standard C library, and there are many other files that include routines such as the handling of character strings in "string.h," time values in "time.h," and so on.

We encountered the issue of code reuse in chapter 3. There we noted that reusing a standard library of code and functions can radically streamline the creation of complex software—even though we noted that often individual programmers want simply to sit down at the computer and begin writing code. The existence of a standard library of programming code is one of the reasons why applications written for a particular operating system tend to look and work the same. Apple OS X and Microsoft Windows, for example, provide a standard library of functions that draw windows on the screen, open dialog boxes to save and load files, and so on. Most individual programmers have little firsthand experience with the code to create these visual elements; they simply know which libraries to include and which functions to use to have the elements created.

It has become common practice to refer to this resource of prewritten code as a library. It is a larger body of material on which an individual programmer may draw; like a physical library, it depends on categorization and, especially, standardization. Precisely because this code is organized into recognizable chunks it can be "included" in a program. But we should also recognize how radically different this programming library is from a physical library. As with all the electronic libraries that I have already mentioned, a central departure of this programming library from a library of books is the fact that there are infinite copies of its items. In a library of books, the individual copies can be only one place; if a library has a single copy of a book, only one patron may have it at once. The principle of the programming library is quite the opposite: anyone can include "stdio.h" who needs it. The possibility of infinite "copies" of a library item is, of course, precisely what makes the restrictions on lending books in the Nook or squirting songs on the Zune so strange. More important, I think, is the different identity of the components themselves. As I suggested before, books are generally (although not entirely) independent of the libraries in which they might be included. Programs, however, are more strongly dependent on their libraries. A program may be written to do one thing and function perfectly well; if the library on which it depends changes, the program could end up doing something quite different—or, much more likely, fail to work. The program itself—at least the part that programmers have written directly—has not changed, but the library on which it depends has. Dependence on libraries takes the operation of the program partially out of the hands of any individual programmer and makes it subject to the conditions and quirks of the library. In this sense, the computing library turns programs into multiple and contingent objects. While we might imagine books without a library, we cannot write, understand, or compile modern programs without their libraries.

## 2

I would like to offer these two models of the library as a fundamental division that organizes our understanding and use of digital media objects now and in the future. One model emphasizes the independence of the component elements; let us call this an accumulative library. The other makes those elements dependent on the larger library structure; let us call this the modular library. And when we refer to an e-book library, we are blurring these two ways of thinking about the library. This opposition echoes a tension that I noted many times in chapters 1 and 2 between solitude and connection that is typical of our networked society, and we will see here again that there is no simple distinction between these two. After all, we saw that Bush's memex was ambiguous: it was both a personal repository of individual notes built up over time and also an entree to the broader scholarly community, something passed down from parent to child and yet at the same time a vehicle of a professional organization. Bush was unable to decide what kind of library the memex implied back in 1945, and almost seventy years later our understanding of the library is split between two different models.

It is probably no surprise that the general evolution of the handling of digital media objects over the last decade has been toward the modular library and away from the accumulative library. In a general way, the model of dispersed identity and dependence of item on library emerges any time institutions and mechanisms achieve broad acceptance. This is why the Library of Congress and Dewey Decimal codes can be integrated right onto the copyright page of newer books. Digital artifacts tend to be integrated into libraries when a format for doing so achieves general acceptance. We can see these changing ideas about libraries in computer file systems. Let us consider a common digital library used by most people: iTunes. If you go to your computer and examine the folder containing iTunes music, you'll see a file structure that looks something like Figure 6.

This is actually a relatively transparent list, in which information about the library is stored in this XML file, and the individual song files appear inside the "iTunes Music" folder. We could say that the individual songs that make up your music collection remain relatively autonomous here. Although, they require specialized software to play, we could make a case that the iTunes library is more or less the sum of its parts—that is, it is relatively accumulative. But even here, the structure of the library is not exactly mirrored in the structure of the files; we have to go through the XML file to make much sense of playlists, for example. This XML file represents the point at which the iTunes library becomes something more than just a collection of individual songs.

The iTunes library remains a minimally modular library. In fact, it looks more like a collection of independent objects than most other digital libraries. In large part, this is the result of the fraught relationship between Apple, music publishers, and consumers. Apple is clearly trying to walk a

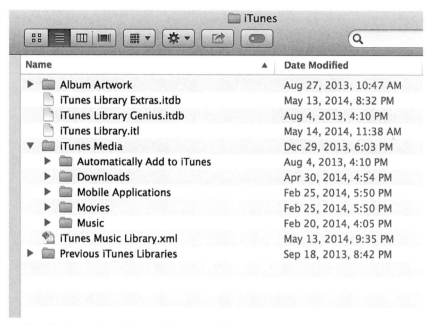

Figure 6. Screenshot of iTunes folder in Apple OS X 10.9.

very fine line between consumers' desire to own their music and publishers' desire to control its (re)distribution.[11] In fact Apple has made the library structure of iTunes relatively transparent and easily read by a variety of programs, which can use the XML data to access the iTunes library. If we stay in the Apple environment but move away from the politically charged topic of music, we can see the logic of the modular library asserting itself even more forcefully. When I go to iPhoto on my Mac and look inside the "Pictures" folder, I see that the iPhoto library is represented as a single object with no separate files for individual pictures (see Figure 7).

The visual contrast between this single iPhoto entity and the hierarchy of files that make up iTunes encapsulates the two models of the library that I have been describing. I can open this monolithic file by choosing the somewhat obscure command "Show Package Contents," and get closer to individual files (see Figure 8). Still, the organization of this data is much muddier than in iTunes, and the identity of individual pictures is much harder to pinpoint. iPhoto saves individual images in several redundant places and abstracts out part of the image to make a separate file for previews. And,

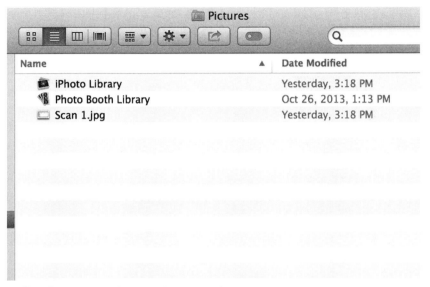

Figure 7. Screenshot of Pictures folder in Apple OS X 10.9.

of course, like iTunes, iPhoto has organizational metadata that are contained nowhere within its on-disk file structure.

Integrated library files are hardly unique to the Apple OS environment. If you look for an individual e-mail message that you received in Microsoft Outlook, for example, you will not find it as an independent entity on the hard disk; messages are not saved by that program as individual files but instead as components of a single "personal storage folder" (.pst) file type that itself is stored in an "Application Data" folder within the "My Documents" folder for that particular user. And, of course, Outlook's file structure is even more complex when connected to an Exchange server, since data files on your personal computer are a local copy of the server data.

Although it is difficult to find an e-mail program today that saves messages as individual files, it is certainly still possible to manage pictures on a computer as a system of JPEG files and folders. Of course, in doing so we give up much of the organizational power that a modern photo-management program like iPhoto brings to the task, including the automatic grouping of images and advanced features like the ability to sort by location or people who appear in the image. Most of us are willing to sacrifice the transparency of individual image file structure and identity for the convenience of

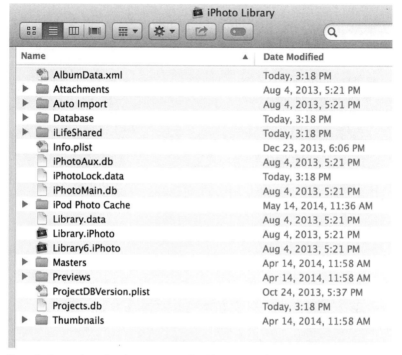

Figure 8. Screenshot of package contents for iPhoto in Apple OS X 10.9.

these features. And it seems clear that the general evolution of digital media management is away from discrete files (for an image or song) and toward programs that create libraries of these media. Libraries add organizational power, but make the individual media artifacts less and less autonomous.[12]

## 3

Where does the e-book fit in this trajectory?

As we might expect, early e-books were much like TIFF and MP3 files: treated as independent items to be placed in folders on a hard drive and interpreted using one (of many possible) programs. Even today, Project Gutenberg retains this transparent file structure, since it allows users to download books in many different file formats. Each of those books is simply saved to your hard drive, and organizing these files is left up to the user. Until the last few years, e-books have had no iTunes-like major player that has offered to integrate these individual files into vast libraries. Plenty of software for the purpose exists, of course, like Sony's eBook Library, which will seek out individual e-book files in a variety of formats and integrate them into the library. The hallmark of e-books has been the dizzying diversity of sources, and most e-book programs (and physical devices) make some effort at inclusion by reading a variety of formats. Recently Amazon's Kindle and Apple's iBook platforms have made an appeal for market dominance, and both have followed that pattern that we see in iTunes and iPhoto: making the individual book files largely invisible and inaccessible outside of specialized software. Both are pushing toward modular libraries.

For many book buyers, the degree to which e-books remain potentially or actually independent of their libraries is purely academic and only matters when they encounter some sort of restriction with which they are unwilling to live. Although many in the tech community complained for years about Apple's DRM restrictions on music, for most everyday users these limitations were either invisible or trivial. The same is true of images, as well: while the library structure of iPhoto makes individual images hard to locate at the disk level of the Finder, a simple export command and drag-and-drop control of the images makes the complexity of the library file structure usually invisible to users. It is for this reason that our interaction with the digital artifacts that we "own"—music, pictures, and, to a lesser extent, movies—has been moving steadily toward the model of the modular library. Today we are much less likely to sort our music files at the level of the OS X Finder or Windows Explorer and much more likely to depend on a specialized program like iTunes to do it for us.

There is, I think, a special reason to be wary about the model of the modular library being extended to e-books, however. Throughout its history, the book is an object whose design has been relentlessly changed and refined: from scrolls to codex pages to HTML links. Even in the relatively recent past since the rise of cheap mass printing in the eighteenth century, publishers, artists, and authors have constantly revised basic elements of book design. We might initially think of radical and one-of-a-kind book designs of the Artist Book movement, whose artifacts are frequently displayed in museum spaces. Likewise a number of avant-garde publishers come to mind like Something Else Press (1963–74), which published Robert Filliou's *Ample Food for Stupid Thought* as a box of postcards.[13] But it is a mistake to see design innovation as primarily a matter of literary high art. Janine Barchas has noted that innovative play with typography was a fundamental part of early novels like *Clarissa*.[14] More recently, the innovative design of Choose Your Own Adventure novels has brought such interface considerations to mass-produced genre fiction. Perhaps most tellingly, books written for children constantly redesign the means by which we encounter the text, from the mixture of word and image in Winnie-the-Pooh to the metafiction of the Sesame Street picture book *The Monster at the End of This Book*.[15] Design innovation is not a modernist tangent to the history of the book but rather a fundamental part of publication.

This is why no model of the e-book based on the modular library so far has proven to be satisfying—no matter what DRM restrictions or freedoms are included with it.[16] It is the nature of modular libraries to insist on uniformity of its members. Because it has long been published in multiple formats (the forty-five, eight-track, the LP, cassette) music does not seem to raise as many concerns about the uniformity imposed by the digital audio file format. Even in the case of music, however, many have felt that the contextless purchase of single tracks has lost some of the experience provided by the whole album, on which artists could impose more creative control. Apple's attempt to recreate the experience of the LP (including album art and lyrics) in iTunes LP several years ago suggests an awareness of this problem, although that format has had very little impact. The problem is even greater when extended to e-books, since books routinely challenge and redefine their interface with the reader.

### 4

I might seem naive in suggesting that books be allowed to retain their ability to redefine the experience of reading in a digital environment. After all, the benefits of creating a uniform library of e-books seem to outweigh the occasional limitation on authors to create unusual designs. There is, however, a kind of digital artifact that accomplishes exactly this resistance to library integration: computer games. Game designers—especially those working at high-profile, big-budget development studios—pride themselves on pushing the limits of available computer hardware and redefining the user's interaction with the system. It is not uncommon for gamers to upgrade hardware to take advantage of a new high-profile game, and even games with more modest hardware demands frequently require players to download video-card drivers and updated graphics software like Microsoft's DirectX. Games like this frequently do not play well with each other, requiring settings that might have to be tweaked differently for each game. (Some games, for example, may benefit from running two graphics cards, while others may require that one be disabled to avoid crashes or slowdowns.) Graphics-intensive computer games are demanding, prickly digital objects that frequently only function smoothly on a wide variety of systems after multiple patches and tinkering by individual game owners.

In this regard, computer games are the antithesis of the unifying logic of the modular library: they demand to be treated like wildly individual objects and pay the user back for this effort by (sometimes) reshaping the experience of the screen and its represented spaces. Games are the truest embodiment of Alan Kay's well-known remark, "People who are really serious about software should make their own hardware."[17] Of course, things were not always this way—especially in 1982 when Kay made this comment. Indeed, the dominance of the text-based adventure game in the early 1980s represents a path ultimately not taken by PC computer gaming. The text adventure game embraces the modular library. The descendant of these games, interactive fiction, shows all the hallmarks of such a library organization. This fiction is written using one of several formats (Inform, TADS, ADRIFT) and depends on another piece of software to interpret the story code for the reader. The text adventure game or interactive fiction story is made up of multiple files, some of which are shared between individual works. For example, LucasArts produced some of the most influential and popular early (graphic) adventure games like the Monkey Island series. Many of these games depended on a scripting language called SCUMM (Script Creation Utility for Maniac Mansion) through which the games were written. Because these games depend on this utility to organize the presentation of the basic locations and objects of the game world, programmers have been able to port these old games to newer platforms by creating a virtual SCUMM environment. It is precisely because these early adventure games are modular and depend on shared library structures that they can be ported to operating system environments for which they were never intended. Behind the SCUMM model is a fundamentally different attitude toward game design, one that emphasizes the relatively simple development of story content over the innovative redesign of UI. This is even more the case with classic text adventures from Infocom, which depend on a uniform language and user-client. In fact, in 1996 Infocom gathered together thirty-three works to make a cross-platform CD-ROM *Classic Text Adventure Masterpieces of Infocom;* such a compilation captures the library-like quality of these games and marks a striking contrast from subsequent game design.[18]

Today, then, digital media objects seem to fall into two categories. In one category are objects like music and pictures, which have largely been integrated into modular libraries. We can expect that, increasingly, we will encounter these sorts of objects through specialized software that organizes and controls the way we interact with them. In the second category are games, which remain messy individuals. To the extent that an avid gamer might have a "library" of games, this is clearly an accumulative library: a collection of objects that fail to conform to any systematic ordering. In fact, such a game library is likely to make incompatible hardware demands—some games requiring cutting-edge video settings, others needing to be run in an emulation mode or even using a virtual OS like DOSBox. Serious gamers often own multiple gaming systems—a PS3, Xbox, PC, Nintendo DS, and so on. In contrast to the way that the modular library smoothly organizes the experience of digital media like music and pictures, such a game library is a messy affair in which the user of the library must organize the objects and define the conditions by which they are encountered. The overwhelming momentum within consumer electronics today is toward the integration of more and more of our digital media into libraries. Games remain the exception to this rule, the wild objects that defy larger wholes.

There are, however, signs that the modular library is moving even into game space. The success of Apple's App Store has set a new model for cheap, causal games that are distributed through online without a physical medium. These games are clearly part of a modular library, since your purchase history can be accessed from any of Apple's iOS devices, and most such games can be run on any such device, creating a unified body of items. Apple's success has prompted other game manufactures like Sony and Microsoft to integrate digital downloads and game libraries. Even on the PC, where developers have been the most willing to push the boundaries of hardware, there are signs of modular libraries. The Steam system, developed by the game studio Valve, provides a unified library and DRM framework for games that are downloaded directly from the Steam servers. As with the SCUMM model, many Steam games currently are back-catalog products that were released first on traditional DVD- or CD-ROM. However, it is likely that in coming years more and more games will be downloaded directly onto devices, and will be integrated into game library systems. Already Microsoft's Xbox Live and Apple's Game Center allow players to track their in-game achievements, and so unify disparate games into a single set of trophies. This trend toward the integration of games is likely to continue.

## 5

I want to return to the uniqueness of books and their relationship to the library that Manguel asserts, since without recognizing the way that books are dependent on the library, we cannot really understand why the library metaphor in computing is so powerful. For all that the avant-garde has tried to create books that are unique objects that resist our normal ways of reading,[19] we can all recognize that the urge to integrate books into libraries is nearly universal. It was once common practice, for example, for owners of large private libraries to have their books bound or rebound to create uniformity and to show good taste.[20] For every time that an author has tried to reinvent the form in one way or another, there is a publisher bringing out another uniform Little Leather Library of the "Thirty World's Greatest Masterpieces."[21] Literary critics have pointed out that readers obey conventional rules and sort works by genre even before they begin reading. As Peter Rabinowitz notes, "'reading'—even the reading of a first paragraph—is always 'reading as.'"[22] Despite our love of individually quirky books, there seems to be an equally powerful urge for uniformity. Indeed, this is the basis for the library, which depends on a constrained variation of size and content. Too much variation in the objects contained within a library and it begins to seem closer to a museum, whose objects can be displayed in various ways. Indeed, among the various types of collections, the library insists on the most consistency of its objects—much more so than the museum or gallery.

I want to move away from the general reading conventions that Rabinowitz is describing to focus more narrowly on the way that we think about the library itself as a unified collection that has its own identity that transcends its constituent members. In *The Gutenberg Elegies,* Sven Birkerts tells the story about when he worked at a used and rare bookshop, and was "often asked to appraise and purchase libraries—by retiring academics, widows, and disgruntled graduate students."[23] He meets a professor "only a year or two older" who was selling everything because he became convinced that computers were the future. "The room was wall-to-wall books and neat as a chapel," Birkerts explains, before describing it as "a remarkable collection. It reflected not only the needs of his vocation—he taught nineteenth- and twentieth-century literature—but a book lover's sensibility as well. The shelves were strictly arranged, and the books themselves were in superb condition."[24] This story is part of Birkerts's characterization of contemporary life, which he sees as neglectful of books in general; he spends some time critiquing television a few pages later. But the description of the library here seems to me to capture important rhetorical connotations of the term that I have neglected thus far. The library is a reflection of the person who owns it, and moving on to another phase of one's life means jettisoning the library that one has collected. More importantly, the library is a whole whose qualities describe the person. The books are not merely professional but also carefully tended in a way that identifies their owner. We saw the same thing in Bush's memex, which was both an individual possession and the link between an individual and a larger professional community. The library and the memex are the meeting point of the personal and the professional.

The term *library* here performs an essential function for Birkerts, since it defines the balancing point between the individual object and the whole collection. Birkerts does not identify any particularly valuable book, nor does he suggest that the collection as a whole is full of rare or special texts. For him, what is important about the collection are the qualities of the whole— its neatness, care, and organization. The library here is defined not so much by its individual members, but by its total quality and organization. And yet, at the same time, it is clear that what makes this library well tended is precisely this concern for each individual book. This peculiar balance between the collective and the individual is something insisted on by Manguel, as well. Despite his focus on the individuality of books, he opens his history of reading by describing their organization into a library:

> I first kept my books in a straight alphabetical order, by author. Then I began dividing them by genre: novels, essays, plays, poems. Later on I tried grouping them by language, and when, during the course of my travels, I was obliged to keep only a few, I separated them into those I hardly ever read, those I read all the time, and those I was hoping to read. Sometimes my library obeyed secret rules, born from idiosyncratic associations. . . . It seemed to me that the literature taught at school . . . was as arbitrary or as permissible a selection as the literature I could construct myself, based on my findings along the crooked road of my own readings and the size of my own bookshelves.[25]

Here the library becomes a reflection of his own life and memory; he notes later that the collection of books was necessary "in the way of memoranda."[26] The library becomes an embodiment of its owner's memory and life experiences.

Viewed from this perspective, the library of the computer and book are not that different. Both promise to organize individual items but in the end make those items dependent on the collective for their identity. This is a common theme in much of the writing about collections. In their introduction to *Cultures of Collecting,* John Elsner and Roger Cardinal assert, "Classification precedes collection. . . . In effect, the plenitude of taxonomy opens up the space for collectables to be identified, but at the same time the plenitude of that which is to be collected hastens the need to classify."[27] In fact, the concept of a library of electronic books (or, for that matter, programming functions) may get much of its power from our implicit awareness of this ambiguity—the fact that the library really is more than the sum of its parts. This helps to explain, I think, why these libraries are so consistently embodied in particular devices: these sexy and shiny new electronic gadgets come to represent the music or reading library just as surely as "the size of my own bookshelves" do with print books. In fact, the ambiguity of the word *library,* which means both the collection of books and the room in which they are stored, nicely captures this complicated relationship between the individual and the collective. The same ambiguity is true of the book-reading gadget, which is both the individual device and a link to the larger system of books owned by its user.

The link between the library and its owner also helps to make sense out of the importance of ownership in this relationship.[28] In fact, we already noted that Bush's treatment of the memex reveals a similar fascination with the physical device that is owned personally and passed down generationally. I noted that one of the fundamental complexities of digital media is their dependence on corporations, which must continue to produce the devices and supporting file formats without which we are unable to use them. This issue of ownership has been central to debates about digital media since the introduction of the DVD, with its built-in restrictions on the way that content there can be viewed. It makes some sense, then, to think about our access to digital media as more akin to a subscription than a traditional library. Subscribe to Netflix and you instantly have access to a huge library of streaming films. And yet access to this type of collection rarely has the same connotations as the ownership of a library. Steve Jobs remarked in 2007, when asked about supporting a music subscription plan in iTunes, "People want to own their music."[29] Given the success of video rental, it seems that ownership is less important in film. In contrast, books are anchored in traditions of both private ownership and public lending libraries. Nonetheless, Jobs recognized an essential element of our relationship to libraries: today at least, the collective is meaningful primarily when it can be linked to personal ownership, because only then do the qualities of the library say something about that person. In this regard, our ideas about the ownership of digital media within a library are very much in flux. Someday will the collections and services to which individuals subscribe have the same cultural value as the collections owned? Will the history of one's use and recommendations—such as the Netflix queue—come to take the place of the library built up through ownership, or will ownership become increasingly culturally marginal, more equivalent to the trade in antiquities than everyday music collections? This uncertainty is embodied in that alternate model described by Bush—the trail. In contrast to the individually owned memex, the trail implied that the individual merely occupies the scholarly archive for a brief time, "owning" it only to the extent that he or she found a unique way through material that belongs to others. In fact, part of the incoherence of the memex may reflect Bush's inability to decide on a single model for his scholarly library—to decide, in other words, on the difference between the iTunes model of ownership and the Netflix model of subscription. The changes and tensions swirling around the digital library shifts attention to what it means to personally inhabit this shared collection. In both cases, however, the relationship between the individual and the collective body of digital material is very much still to be decided.

## 6

Before concluding this chapter, I would like to focus on one final issue in our relationship to book libraries: the role of the physical object. This might seem to be a strange note on which to end, since one of the promises of the electronic book is to remove these physical objects from the equation. And, given the popularity of the Kindle, it is clear that for the vast majority of our everyday reading, our physical interaction with the text is not all that important. Apparently, most readers would gladly trade the pleasures of fine paper or interesting typography for the convenience of being able to carry around every book they own in a device that weighs less than a pound. Once we have gotten used to being able to quickly search a PDF or Word file for a particular phrase, being unable to do the same thing for a printed book begins to feel cumbersome. As more of our books become electronic, the limitations of printed texts without search-copy-paste will rankle more and more. It is unlikely and probably undesirable that books should become the equivalent of computer games—finicky objects that demand attention and care before we can use them.

In the near future books probably will be seen primarily as hybrid objects, quite literally half content and half form and used in different ways in different contexts. Our urge to integrate the objects into libraries is a natural embrace of the content that makes up the vast majority of our reading pleasure. But we need to keep alive the ability for books—even in an electronic environment—to break the design rules that the library might impose on them. Could the Choose Your Own Adventure novel have been invented in the age of the Kindle? We also need to recognize that readers use books in several different ways: sometimes enjoying design, sometimes quickly skimming for argument, fact, or plot. Academics concerned about the future of the book have, to a large extent, rightly focused on the issue of a shared and open format. Calls for the widespread adoption of the EPub standard fight against publishers like Amazon, which sells its e-books in the proprietary AZW format, locking purchases to the Kindle or Amazon-controlled environments for reading. Likewise, Apple's recent introduction of a modified EPub format for its iBooks Author software (IBA) has been criticized by advocates for such standards. Although many users may prefer the simplicity of using a single client and format for their reading—just as they might stay within the iTunes ecosystem for music—it is important that content purchases be transferrable between devices. But focusing the debate over the future of e-books entirely on the issue of open standards concedes that the book will simply become one more item in a modular library, and this is something we should not accept once we recognize the importance of book design throughout the history of reading. We need to find a way to allow books to be integrated into libraries, while at the same time preserving authors' and publishers' ability to produce design innovations.

Fortunately modular libraries provide many opportunities for accessing the text in individual ways. Indeed, the modular nature of modern digital objects—made up, as they are, of multiple files that represent different parts of the song, movie, or book—provide precisely the format for balancing the dual role as uniform object in the library and unique item that challenges conventional design. Consider the model provided by the SCUMM emulator. What this emulator does is separate the original program from its data files, disregarding the requirements of the original program (which frequently will no longer run on modern operating systems) in order to present the content of the story. This split, between original presentation to the player and data files that might be interpreted in convenient ways by a variety of clients, is one that publishers would do well to emulate. In this model, an e-book would actually be a combination of two different elements: a general data file (say, in the EPub or some other open format) and a designed interface for reading that data file. The data file might be integrated into some portable library structure, but we would recognize that such a library is merely an emulation of the original book. For many books, there might be little or no difference between the content as it appears on a Kindle and the designed interface provided by publisher and author; in other cases, this designed interface might provide a significant depth to the content.

Although there are no technical limitations for designing e-books of this sort, many practical and cultural hurtles remain. If a book's content files can be accessed by a Kindle or other e-book reader, what technical device will be used to access the author-designed interface for that file? Web-based HTML files provide a simple standard, but other authors may wish to present their books as executable files to be read directly on a computer desktop. Still others might insist on a physical component to their works. In the golden age of text adventure games, Infocom packaged some of its stories with physical "feelies"—story props that ranged from the merely collectable, such as the paper ordering the destruction of the Earth in *The Hitchhiker's Guide to the Galaxy,* to a scratch-and-sniff card that provided players of *Leather Goddesses of Phobos* with clues about how to solve some of the game's puzzles.[30] Henri-Jean Martin argues in *The History and the Power of Writing* that "writing is nothing by itself." That is, writing does not have the same effect on each society, and its introduction does not involve some inherent meaning: "It serves little purpose to introduce writing techniques into closed societies; at best they will just use them to immobilize and set down sacred words as secrets that give an oligarchy its power. The use of writing cannot develop spontaneously until small groups fuse and organize into a society."[31] We can apply the same logic to the nature of the book today: books do not mean anything to the culture by themselves but instead take their place among a whole series of cultural definitions about ownership, creativity, the sharing of ideas, and technology. David Pearson articulates it this way: "The changes on the horizon are likely to affect not only the ways in which we transmit and read the kind of information which was traditionally contained in books, but also our whole framework of values around them. They will affect our relationships with books individually, and collectively in libraries."[32]

We may come to see physical books as something of the same sort of feelie: a physical prop that is a supplement to the electronic data file that might be integrated into an e-book library. Pearson argues for "books beyond texts"—that is, we should separate the physical object of the book and the text that it contains.[33] Such physical and digital elements that go beyond the simple core data file of the book need not be a component of all books but could supplement a small number of works whose authors want to challenge or extend our reading experience. While standardization is essential for the data component of these books—since readers will want to integrate them into libraries—I see no reason to insist on standardization for the designed elements of reader experience. Some authors may choose to supplement their e-books physically, others with stand-alone executable files, still others with HTML documents. We should hope that such supplementary elements that challenge and redefine the reader's interaction with the text become part of the culture of book buying and reading as it moves into a digital age. The problems of implementing this model are not technical (based, as they are, on the twenty-year-old technology used in Maniac Mansion), but involve a fundamental cultural struggle over how we think about the creation, selling, buying, reading, and storing of books in the future. If everyday readers think about every book as having these two components (even if they may really only attend to one of them for most of the books they read), we retain a space within our culture for the kinds of publishing innovations that have been a part of the history of reading.

There are, however, fundamental questions about how such physical objects will function in a future where digital libraries are increasingly ubiquitous. Most of us see the feelies in *Hitchhiker's Guide* as quirky marketing gimmicks—toys more than objects of serious aesthetic concern. Although physical books may have a role for the collector in a future where every book is available electronically, it is not clear that gathering up these kinds of physical objects will have the same cultural significance. Walter Benjamin remarks, in his notes on collecting in the *Arcades Project,* "The true collector detaches the object from its functional relations."[34] The feelie seems to be an example of the kind of object collected, which Benjamin describes as "allied with the tactile, and stand in a certain opposition to the optical."[35] But it is not clear that such "useless" objects encompass what Manguel and others see as the essence of building a library—which, after all, takes its power to represent the individual from the fact that these books were actually read. In the future, will we see the collectors of books as we see people who collect teapots or toy soldiers today—individuals with quirky obsessions that may cost or earn them money but without larger meaning within their spiritual or intellectual life? Once libraries lose their connection to these physical objects and the accidental life history that Manguel describes, it may be that the idea of the library itself may cease to have its same cultural meaning.

# FIVE

# Invention, Patents, and the Technological System

It is common to refer to software as a "tool" for different professional and recreational activities. The choice of a page-layout program by a publishing house or photo-editing software by an amateur photographer initially seems to be much the same as the choice of a particular tile saw by a construction company or lawn mower by a suburban homeowner. But this comparison is problematic, and the complexity of treating software as a tool tells us a lot about how computers depend on supporting technology. Back in 1997 Steven Johnson remarked in a seemingly offhand way about the difference between traditional tools and "the tools offered by the computer itself": "in fact, 'tool' wouldn't seem to be the word for it anymore, since what is now emerging is really more like an environment, or a space."[1] Software generally imposes stronger pressure to adopt complementary technologies. While any tool may require accessory purchases—additional saw blades, rechargeable batteries, camera lenses—software is much more strongly integrated into a larger ecosystem. The choice of a photo-editing suite depends not only on the computing hardware to be used (the speed of the processor and RAM) but also on the cameras that it must support, the third-party plug-ins that the company's workflow has come to depend on, and so on. This interconnection is even more obvious at the level of the computer's operating system itself. We frequently refer to the combination of a computer and its supported software as a "platform," and this metaphor captures an essential complexity: an operating system is not simply a tool but rather a whole environment that allows other tools to be used. Although there are some parallels to physical tools, software seems to create a much stronger overall environment in which the user operates.

We have already seen the same ambiguity in Bush's memex. This device in some ways seems simply to be a tool for recording thoughts and finding past research. However, Bush also makes it clear that the memex eventually becomes the repository of a lifetime of thinking, and suggests that a father could hand down a memex to his son. In this sense, the memex is no longer one tool among many but instead fuses with the results of thought. The memex, in other words, is less a physical device than a platform, a much broader network of thought that transcends the individual's work. From the very outset of this book I suggested that Bush's memex poses problems for how we think about our most fundamental ideas of knowledge, writing, and research. It is clear that both the imagined memex and real computers likewise challenge our ideas about tools and invention. Where the traditional (physical) tool is used to make some other thing that is ultimately independent of it—the house generally does not look like the hammer that built it—computer technologies often remain connected to the objects that they produce. Create a file in Microsoft Word and you continue to need that program to access that document; create a movie using Adobe Premier and you need, at the very least, hardware that is able to decode the file type that you have saved your work into—MPEG-2, H.264, QuickTime, and so on.

Ultimately I argue that writing plays a key role in the ambiguities of software as a tool. We have already seen that writing provides an essential metaphor for the way that software uses preexisting code and standardized libraries of functions. As a result, software is itself already a dispersed form of invention that both depends on these larger systems and integrates the resulting work into the structures provided by those systems. All computers are made up of components manufactured by other companies—sometimes the very companies that the computer is competing with. A Dell computer might use a Toshiba hard drive and a Samsung LCD screen, for example, even as it competes against laptops branded by those component manufactures. The challenge, then, is understanding invention in the context of this kind of network of existing components and related processes—what I call, following Neil Postman, the technological system. I raised this issue in chapter 1 by invoking Steiner's distinction between invention and creativity. Having unpacked the writing metaphor over the last four chapters and explored not only the tensions between the individual and corporate models of writing but also the dependency of computing on related ideas like the library, we are now in a position to understand a crucial but thus far overlooked quality of Bush's memex: the relationship between our computing activity and the physical device that we use. The memex is a tool, but it is a tool in a very specific sense: networked and thus linked to a host of distant information, but at the same time small, personal, and even intimate. We will see that this focus on the personal tool is an important part of the writing metaphor in computing.

1

Back in chapter 1, I noted the rise of small, intimate computing devices imagined in William Gibson's *Neuromancer* as a cyberspace "deck" and realized in actual products as a notebook or tablet computer. Gibson's image of the cyberspace deck seems much more modern than the SF images that we see just a few years earlier because he transforms the computer from an institutional abstraction into a physical gadget. The term *gadget* is a loaded one, and it invokes consumer culture. A gadget is a relatively inexpensive and trivial object to be purchased and (usually) carried, an object of relatively transient industrial production. It is certainly the case that today computers have moved from being large corporate purchases to objects owned by individuals, and that shift from mainframe to desktop to smartphone has made these objects increasingly personal and even intimate possessions. In chapter 1 I noted the tendency to see the computer as a tool for thought— what Jobs calls a "bicycle for the mind." One of the fundamental components of this way of thinking about the computer is the personal ownership and connection involved. We have seen the same thing in Bush's memex, which is an object to be owned and even passed down to others. This issue of the ownership of such gadgets is part of the general shift towards modern computing that we see throughout the 1970s and 1980s. This is the heart of Nelson's 1974 *Computer Lib/Dream Machines:* "There is a new world called the world of 'personal computers'—except that computers have always been personal. And there is really no personal computer world, distinct from the rest. There is only one computer world; all parts of it interconnect."[2]

In using the term *gadget,* I am also invoking psychoanalytic work on the relationship between technology and desire. Joshua Gunn and Mirko Hall provide a nice summary of this work in an article on the iPod as a gadget: "As an indefinite name for 'a comparatively small fitting, contrivance, or piece of mechanism,' a gadget is usually a tool or mechanism that is fetishized because of its novelty. From a psychoanalytic perspective, however, gadgets are devices fabricated expressly for stimulating various human desires or 'drives,' sometimes by direct insertion into an orifice, but also by inviting the attention of one (e.g., as television does the eyes and ears)."[3] It is easy to see the marketing of small, personal technological devices like the iPod as depending on this relationship between pleasure, bodily intimacy, and ownership. But we should recognize that these technologies invoke an older tradition of prosthetic devices. Laurence Rickels describes the novel this way, as a kind of proto-gadget that works to "keep the recorded voice, the life-sized double, from coming back as the uncanny, and in the place where it was to be kept hidden and forgotten. The novel is the place where all doubling between the media-technological sensurround and vampirism gets introduced."[4] This is certainly the case in *Neuromancer,* which uses this gadget not only to extend physical abilities but also as a form of remembering the dead. For example, our hero, Case, navigates cyberspace in part with the help of the memory of Dixie Flatline, a famous programmer whose personality has been transformed into a kind of artificial intelligence: "It was disturbing to think of the Flatline as a construct, a hardwired ROM cassette replicating a dead man's skills, obsessions, knee-jerk responses."[5] The computer in *Neuromancer* is just the kind of intimate gadget for negotiating the uncanny memory that Rickels describes.

Although the psychoanalytic reading of the intimate technological gadget seems to be a long way from Bush's serious scholarly tool, it is clear that Bush, too, sees the memex as a physical prosthesis. We might recall his description of a wearable camera (see Figure 9) that will allow the user to record documents: "Let us project this trend ahead to a logical, if not inevitable, outcome. The camera hound of the future wears on his forehead a lump a little larger than a walnut. It takes pictures 3 millimeters square, later to be projected or enlarged, which after all involves only a factor of 10 beyond present practice."[6]

Such a camera becomes a straightforward prosthesis recording everything that the scientist sees:

> The cord which trips its shutter may reach down a man's sleeve within easy reach of his fingers. A quick squeeze, and the picture is taken. On a pair of ordinary glasses is a square of fine lines near the top of one lens, where it is out of the way of ordinary vision. When an object appears in that square, it is lined up for its picture. As the scientist of the future moves about the laboratory or the field, every time he looks at something worthy of the record, he trips the shutter and in it goes, without even an audible click.[7]

Although this jump from research to prosthesis might at first seem strange, Bush's example makes clear that any inquiry into note taking is a way of providing external records for internal experience. In writing about the archive, Derrida notes this urge "to *represent on the outside* memory" and describes the issue of the "prosthetic experience of the technical substrate" of the archive.[8]

Figure 9. Drawing on head-mounted camera produced for *Life* 19, no. 11 (1945).

As this example suggests, the definition of the computer as a tool is especially vexed and complex, and there is an inherent tension between gadget and platform that writing captures. I want to build my analysis in this chapter around the way that Heidegger describes physical tools as "equipment" in *Being and Time*, because that concept emphasizes precisely this network of related technologies. Heidegger has long been recognized as an influential theorist of the tool, and the concept of equipment arises more specifically out of his analysis of our interaction with things in the world.[9] Heidegger describes "the kind of Being which equipment possesses" as *readiness-to-hand*. Such an object that is ready-to-hand "is not grasped theoretically."[10] Heidegger's understanding of our tools is especially important for thinking about the computer, since these user-interface metaphors seem to contradict his theory. For Heidegger, our interaction with the hammer is not "theoretical"; it is clear that before we can identify our use of an iPad as a form of writing, we must do a certain kind of conceptual work that seems to be absent in the physical motion of the hammer. Over the last two decades cognitive theory has explored the nature of embodied thought, prompted in part of Lakoff and Johnson's work on metaphor. In particular, *Philosophy in the Flesh* (1999) argues that the seemingly cognitive nature of metaphor is fundamentally based on bodily experience: "Our understanding of what mental acts are is fashioned metaphorically in terms of physical acts like moving, seeing, manipulating objects, and eating, as well as other kinds of activities like adding, speaking or writing, and making objects. We cannot comprehend or reason about the mind without such metaphors."[11] From this perspective, metaphors are already based on embodied experience, which in turn depends on conceptually "blending" established frames. Manuel Imaz and David Benyon summarize the concept of the frame in cognitive theory as "a data structure for representing a stereotyped situation"; they give the example of a "commerce frame," which has elements like buyer and seller, goods and payment. Other related concepts are the script (a frequent event sequence) and the scenario (which "has an initial state, a sequence of events, and a final state").[12] These frames, scripts, and scenarios depend on physical experience even though they are ultimately abstract. These kinds of prepackaged cognitive structures are, like language, building blocks that support invention—the creation of new things out of familiar elements.

This work on cognitive theory has been especially important to human–computer interface (HCI) design. I already touched on interface design in chapter 2 when I discussed writing metaphors in operating systems and instruction manuals. HCI has long recognized the importance of metaphor as the means by which users can understand how to use a computer.[13] This was especially the case in the 1980s, when computers were emerging into mainstream use and users were confronted by the need to rethink the workplace.[14] The attempt to connect computer interface design to physical experience can be traced back to Ben Shneiderman's concept of the "direct manipulation" of elements on the computer embodied in the graphical UI most broadly, and in particular input devices like the mouse or light pen more specifically. In 1963 Ivan Sutherland designed the proto-CAD program Sketchpad, which he describes as "mak[ing] it possible for a man and a computer to converse rapidly through the medium of line drawings."[15] By introducing an alternate form of interaction based on directly touching screen with pen, Sutherland broke fundamentally with the tradition of using the keyboard as the primary form of computer input: "the Sketchpad system, by eliminating typed statements (except for legends) in favor of line drawings, opens up a new area of man–machine communication."[16] Sketchpad raised the issue of our physical interaction with the computer, and suggested the need to reconsider fundamentally the role of the body in human–computer interaction. Imaz and Benyon describe Tim Rohrer's work on "the felt sense of embodied interactions" in computing, and cite one of his examples of "zooming windows": "when a person double clicks on a file icon on a computer, the image zooms out toward the person much in the same way as a page gets larger if you move the book toward your face."[17]

In other words, the metaphors at the heart of HCI arise out of corporeal experience.

Heidegger's theory of equipment is an especially important supplement to these physical metaphors because it links the tool with larger institutional and conceptual networks. The term he uses for the tool is *equipment* (*Zeug*), which is a collective noun. John Macquarrie and Edward Robinson, the English translators of *Being and Time*, explain the implications of this word choice: "while it may mean any implement, instrument, or tool, Heidegger uses it for the most part as a collective noun which is analogous to our relatively specific 'gear' (as in 'gear for fishing'). . . . For the most part Heidegger uses the term as a collective noun, so that he can say that there is no such thing as '*an* equipment.'"[18] The collective nature of the term *equipment* is important because it asserts the link between one tool and the set of other objects connected to the same task: "Equipment—in accordance with its equipmentality—always is *in terms of* its belonging to other equipment: ink-stand, pen, ink, paper, blotting pad, table, lamp, furniture, windows, doors, room."[19] Heidegger reminds us that tools are not simple objects but instead connected to a whole structure of activities and supporting "equipment." Byron Hawk and David Rieder likewise invoke Heidegger's concept of equipment in their discussion of contemporary digital devices, what they call "small tech": "Technologies, especially in the case of small tech, are never distinct objects: they are only experienced in relation to other entities arranged in complex constellations to form particular environments."[20] The nature of the connections between various pieces of equipment is somewhat obscure in Heidegger's discussion, but I suggest we might think of these links as a material condition with institutional and conventional sources. In his explication of *Being and Time,* Hubert Dreyfus interprets equipment this way:

> It is important to note, however, that Heidegger is not defining equipment merely in terms of its in-order-to. A chimp using a stick in order to reach a banana is not using equipment. Equipment always refers to other equipment. "In the 'in-order-to' as a structure there lies an *assignment* or *reference* of something to something." An "item" of equipment is what it is only insofar as it refers to other equipment and so fits in a certain way into an "equipmental whole."[21]

A stick cannot function as equipment for the chimp, Dreyfus implies, because it is improvised and has no defined place within an "equipmental whole." Such a whole implies well-established categories of human activity—such as "gear for fishing." Fishing, after all, is different from simply acquiring a fish so that you have something to eat; it is a hobby with its own commercial and social meaning.

The connections between components of an "equipmental whole" dovetail with the emphasis that I already noted on broad conceptual frames for metaphorical actions; in both cases, individual objects are located within a whole network of human activities and concepts. When we call a computer file a *document* or refer to the space in which the user interacts with files as a *desktop,* we are invoking a whole set of activities—filing, sorting, transmitting—that have an elaborate professional and commercial context. Heidegger identifies this essential and often overlooked element of the UI metaphor of writing. Writing implies not a single action but rather a network of objects and relationships with which we interact. Thinking about the nature of creativity in the context of these material and institutional connections obviously takes us a long way from our traditional understanding of creation as an act that begins from nothing. These kinds of institutions are part of traditional, concrete activities (like writing at a desk), but it is clear that in digital media individual tools and devices are even more dependent on their broader commercial and technological context. After all, my starting point for this chapter was the observation that the software tools that we use today depend on components, file formats, and supporting technologies in a way that earlier tools did not.

In 1992 Neil Postman offered a suggestive if broad critique of the contemporary embrace of technology in *Technopoly* that helps to explain the implications of this shift. Postman contrasts three types of culture. In tool-using cultures, "tools were largely invented to do two things: to solve specific and urgent problems of physical life . . . or to serve the symbolic world of art, politics, myth, ritual, and religion."[22] In contrast, technocracies subordinate culture to its tools, making technology and science the basis on which decisions are made. For him, technocracies are characterized by a healthy tension between technology and pretechnological values: traditions in nineteenth-century America "are a troublesome residue of a tool-using period, a source of criticism of technocracy. They represent a thought-world that stands apart from technocracy and rebukes it" (46). Technopoly is simply a state of culture in which this transition from tools to technocracy is complete:

> Technopoly eliminates alternatives to itself. . . . It does not make them illegal. It does not make them immoral. It does not even make them unpopular. It makes them invisible and therefore irrelevant. And it does so by redefining what we mean by religion, by art, by family, by politics, by history, by truth, by privacy,

by intelligence, so that our definitions fit its new requirements. Technopoly, in other words, is totalitarian technocracy. (48)

Here *technopoly* defines not just the means by which industry and science operate, but the nature of human society as a whole. We see the world through technology: "To a man with a pencil, everything looks like a list. To a man with a camera, everything looks like an image. To a man with a computer, everything looks like data" (14). Although Postman's theory is very general and explicitly alarmist, he usefully raises the issue of our changing relationship with tools in an age when technological systems are everywhere. As he suggests, frequently our engagement with technology—the purchase of a new computer, for example, or a new contract with a wireless telephone carrier—is disconnected from any specific problem that this purchase is designed to solve and instead becomes simply part of the fabric of our lives.

Heidegger's concept of equipment offers a philosophical articulation of the state of industrial culture that Postman is describing. Our tools are not simply individual things, but rather parts of a larger system of material and social relations. Technology supplies the writing desk, the paper, the ink, and so on. A visit to any office supply store shows these systems on display, since they explicitly guide purchasers about the kinds of objects that are necessary for a well-supplied office and impose standards for everything from the size of paper to the number of holes (usually three in the United States, often two or four elsewhere) in a ring binder. Vilém Flusser makes this point: "In addition to typewriters and pens, besides printer paper and other writing paper, stationery stores carry other writing implements: clamps, folders, glue. Overall, they offer an insight into the universe of literature."[23] Postman makes clear that as we move beyond the office supply store that technology continues to provide a system that organizes our activities. When we use a computer to edit photos taken on a family vacation, we depend on desktop software's ability to link to the camera hardware. We may store these images locally on our computer and also export them in some format to be shared to an online site or to a photo-printing service—as long as both are able to read the format of the image files that we send them. In turn, our photo-sharing site may collect metadata about the images that we are uploading and report (for example) on the most popular cameras in use today—which we might then use when we buy our next camera. In all of these cases, the software that we use to manage these photos is far from a simple tool and is instead one contact point in a much larger system of digital content creation, distribution, and consumption.

2

In no other part of contemporary culture is the intersection between invention and the "equipmental whole" made possible by technology clearer than in U.S. debates about the scope of patent protection. Initially this may seem like a tangent from the way that I have been discussing the computing-as-writing metaphor, since I have focused on design and metaphors rather than on the material and legal conditions under which this work is done. But the issue of software patents is profoundly connected to this discussion because it reflects a changing way of thinking about individual creativity and invention that we have already seen to be a fundamental concern of the computer from Bush's initial description of the memex. Even more important, as I show, patents have become a *written* genre over the last two centuries, and many of the problems of today's patent system reflect the tension between a system designed to protect physical tools and a process of approval that increasingly depends on the conceptual possibilities provided by writing.

Although a detailed analysis of the legal basis for software patents is beyond the scope of this book, it is possible to introduce the broad issues and to highlight some places where this debate touches on the themes of invention and technology that I have been analyzing. In contrast to copyright, which usually has a narrow application but a long time frame for rights, patents provide the awardee with a much broader and more powerful right but do so for a much shorter time period. The U.S. Constitution gave Congress the power to make laws "to promote the Progress of Science and useful Arts, by securing for limited Times to Authors and Inventors the exclusive Right to their respective Writings and Discoveries."[24] Title 35 of the U.S. Code concerns patents, and Section 101 has been the center of many recent court cases because it is here that the scope of what can be patented is articulated: "Whoever invents or discovers any new and useful process, machine, manufacture, or composition of matter, or any new and useful improvement thereof, may obtain a patent therefor, subject to the conditions and requirements of this title."

Traditionally, patents applied primarily to the invention of physical machines. A classic example is Eli Whitney's 1794 patent for the cotton gin used for separating cotton fibers from seeds. The test for a patentable object most often focuses on issues such as nonobviousness, novelty, and utility. More recent forms of technological development have made an emphasis on physical devices seem limiting. Writing in the 2010 case *Bilski v. Kappos,* Justice Kennedy emphasized this range of work: "Patents for inventions that did not satisfy the machine-or-transformation test were rarely granted in earlier eras, especially in the Industrial Age. . . . But times change. Technology and other innovations progress in unexpected ways. . . . As numerous amicus briefs argue, the machine-or-transformation test would create uncertainty as to the patentability of software, advanced diagnostic medicine techniques, and inventions based on linear programming, data compression, and the manipulation of digital signals."[25] The *Bilski v. Kappos* decision is the most recent in a series of cases over the last forty years that have worked through the complex issues of patents applied to the conditions of modern technology and business.

Two conventional exemptions to patent law have particularly been the focus of these court cases: business practices and abstract scientific and mathematical discoveries. The ban on business practices is the primary focus of *Bilski v. Kappos,* in which the applicant requested a patent for "a procedure for instructing buyers and sellers how to protect against the risk of price fluctuations in a discrete section of the economy." Traditionally the patent office has assumed that business methods were unpatentable, based in part on the 1908 circuit court decision in *Hotel Security Checking Co. v. Lorraine Co* that a "system of transacting business disconnected from the means for carrying out the system is not, within the most liberal interpretation of the term, an 'art.'"[26] The ban on awards for scientific discoveries likewise tries to avoid abstract ideas. An influential case in this regard is *O'Reilly v. Morse* in 1853, in which Samuel Morse applied for a patent related to technology for the telegraph. Of particular interest is Morse's eighth claim, which requested a patent for a very broad scientific discovery:

> I do not propose to limit myself to the specific machinery or parts of machinery described in the foregoing specification and claims; the essence of my invention being the use of the motive power of the electric or galvanic current, which I call electro-magnetism, however developed for marking or printing intelligible characters, signs, or letters, at any distances, being a new application of that power of which I claim to be the first inventor or discoverer.[27]

The court decided that this was too broad: "He claims the exclusive right to every improvement where the motive power is the electric or galvanic current, and the result is the marking or printing intelligible characters, signs, or letters at a distance. If this claim can be maintained, it matters not by what process or machinery the result is accomplished." In the 1972 case *Gottschalk v. Benson,* the court cited *O'Reilly v. Morse* to address the issue of a mathematical algorithm used by a computer:

It is conceded that one may not patent an idea. But in practical effect that would be the result if the formula for converting BCD numerals to pure binary numerals were patented in this case. The mathematical formula involved here has no substantial practical application except in connection with a digital computer, which means that if the judgment below is affirmed, the patent would wholly pre-empt the mathematical formula and in practical effect would be a patent on the algorithm itself.[28]

This ban on patenting algorithms seems out of keeping with the court's later decision in *Bilski*.

It is easy to see why computers problematize the distinction between an abstract idea and a particular machine. In fact, the 1972 case that is often seen as fundamental to current patent debates, *Gottschalk v. Benson,* starts from the challenge of patenting technologies in "general-purpose digital computers." More recently in *Bilski* Justice Kennedy noted that the precedent tended to favor "processes similar to those in the Industrial Age—for example, inventions grounded in a physical or other tangible form." The invention of a method of "data compression" will be based in software rather than a tangible form and may not result in any physical transformation. To say, for example, that software has transformed a film from a MPEG-2 file into a H.264 file depends on a fundamentally abstract distinction. Physically, both files exist as binary data stored on a magnetic disk or held in computer memory. More importantly, the difference between the two files is circular and self-fulfilling. In the case of *Diamond v. Diehr,* at issue was a "process for molding raw, uncured synthetic rubber into cured precision products"—a transformation that is evident even if we know nothing about the utility of the product that results.[29] In the case of data compression, however, it is possible to recognize the transformation only if we have the technical context to be able to interpret the file format itself already.

This shift toward more abstract patents goes hand in hand with the increasing centrality of writing in the process. In fact, the Patent Act of 1790 specifically suggested that patent applications include models, clearly placing an emphasis on physical devices: "That the grantee or grantees of each patent shall, at the time of granting the same, deliver to the Secretary of State a specification in writing, containing a description, accompanied with drafts or models, and explanations and models (if the nature of the invention or discovery will admit of a model) of the thing or things, by him or them invented or discovered, and described as aforesaid, in the said patents."[30] The Patent Act of 1952 simplifies this to emphasize writing: "Written application—an application for patent shall be made, or authorized to be made, by the inventor, except as otherwise provided in this title, in writing to the Director."[31]

The transition is, of course, inevitable given the increasingly abstract nature of the inventions receiving patent protection. This emphasis on writing makes possible what have been described as "speculative" patents—those that describe possible devices that have not and may never actually be built.[32] Writing is, of course, especially good at describing such a broad range of possibilities, and it has always been the goal of the patent applicant to describe the invention in broad terms that will cover a wide variety of possible applications; we might recall Morse's (ultimately rejected) claim to a broad understanding of the telegraph: "I do not propose to limit myself to the specific machinery or parts of machinery described in the foregoing specification and claims."[33] By describing an invention as potentially embodied in a wide range of possible machines, writing is one of the central means by which patents have expanded into abstract territory. The contemporary speculative patent is very much a written genre.

The circularity that I have just noted in many patentable technologies is the heart of debates about software protection. Traditionally patent law is based on a relatively concrete model of the physical tool as the invention. Such tools can be described and reconstructed by others; their effects can be observed and their utility can be evaluated.[34] As we move into software patents, however, this traditional grounding becomes increasingly problematized. This is the basis for Justice Stevens's dissenting opinion in *Diamond v. Diehr*. He begins by noting that patenting software undermines a fundamental assumption of earlier patent law: "Prior to 1968, well-established principles of patent law probably would have prevented the issuance of a valid patent on almost any conceivable computer program. Under the 'mental steps' doctrine, processes involving mental operations were considered unpatentable. . . . The mental-steps doctrine was based upon the familiar principle that a scientific concept or mere idea cannot be the subject of a valid patent."[35] In an earlier time, it is easy to see why purely mental operations would have been considered unpatentable, since the core of the patent application was the description of a physical invention. However, software increasingly performs purely mathematical operations; although bits of information may be moved through memory, that movement is not itself the basis for the patent application. As Justice Stevens suggests, once we have shifted invention into the realm of the abstract manipulation of symbols, very little of our understanding of the traditional patent applies any longer.

Stevens's dissenting opinions in *Diamond* and especially in *Bilski* seem to me the articulation of a desire to return to a machine-based model of the invention. In particular, in the later dissent he focuses much more rigorously on the original definition of the patent as intended "to promote the

Progress of Science and useful Arts."[36] While Justice Kennedy is generally happy to challenge conventional definitions of the patent law as excluding business practices without providing a clear explanation of the resulting expanded scope of patent law, Justice Stevens's opinion is much more concerned with providing concrete guidance and limits to this potential patent material. As he explains, "Rather than making any broad statements about how to define the term 'process' in §101 or tinkering with the bounds of the category of unpatentable, abstract ideas, I would restore patent law to its historical and constitutional moorings." Noting that "for centuries, it was considered well established that a series of steps for conducting business was not, in itself, patentable" (613), Stevens turns to the historical record of court cases involving patent law. In particular, Stevens objects to Kennedy's argument that "the Patent Act must be read as lay speakers use those terms, and not as they have traditionally been understood in the context of patent law" (618). Stevens argues that the seemingly broad and vague language of the 1952 act ("any new and useful process, machine, manufacture, or composition of matter, or any new and useful improvement thereof") in fact depends on a whole legislative and court history that gives these terms, especially *process,* a much more specific meaning.[37] To provide this context, he quotes Justice Holmes's observation that "a page of history is worth a volume of logic" and returns to the English and early American backdrop for the original Patent Act. Stevens notes that seventeenth- and eighteenth-century innovations in business organization were not patented under the English system, and then turns to the particularly crucial line from the U.S. Constitution, "the Progress of . . . useful Arts." He discusses the term's definition in early American dictionaries to conclude that "Webster's definition likely conveyed a message similar to the meaning of the word 'manufactures' in the earlier English statute. And we know that the term 'useful arts' was used in the founding era to refer to manufacturing and similar applied trades" (633). Stevens mines the context of the Constitutional Convention, noting the kinds of examples given of useful arts ("all of which involved the creation or transformation of physical substances" [633]) and concludes, "Numerous scholars have suggested that the term 'useful arts' was widely understood to encompass the fields that we would now describe as relating to technology or 'technological arts'" (634).

This emphasis on the technological arts in the original conception of patent law is crucial for Stevens, because it is the ground on which he rejects the majority opinion's expansion of patents to business practices. The lesson for our attempt to understand invention in the age of computing is, however, that the movement away from concrete devices toward more abstract conceptual systems—which are central to contemporary technology like data compression—raises fundamental problems for our traditional models of creativity. The physical devices that Stevens emphasizes provide a reassuring and familiar model for how we create and work, while these more abstract conditions of contemporary work unmoor us from concrete tools.

### 3

Computer technology, then, makes invention—with its basis in predefined elements and integration with larger business and technological systems—the center of contemporary creative activity. Such systems bring the objects (such as file formats) into existence, and then regulate and organize them. This strange and paradoxical kind of creativity is the reef on which current patent law seems to have beached itself, as justices have struggled to explain what it means to create something in the age of Postman's technological systems. I would like to return to Heidegger because he provides a broader philosophical perspective on this process. Specifically, I would like to examine Heidegger's "The Question Concerning Technology" in the light of Stevens's critique of the expansion of patentable technology. Heidegger's understanding of technology suggests how new inventions can cause the natural material on which those inventions operate to come into being.

Heidegger approaches "the essence of technology" as instrumental: "The instrumental definition of technology is indeed so uncannily correct that it even holds for modern technology. . . . Even the power plant with its turbines and generators is a man-made means to an end established by man."[38] Especially relevant to Stevens's opinion is Heidegger's focus on how technology acts on the material world. This is evident in the way that he reframes the traditional definition of the four causes (the material, the form, the end, and the *causa efficiens*, "which brings about the effect that is the finished" object [290]). He notes that Greek thought treated causality not as "bring[ing] about and effecting" but instead as "that to which something else is indebted": "the four causes are the ways, all belonging at once to each, of being responsible for something else" (290). His example is the silver chalice: "The chalice is indebted to, i.e., owes thanks to, the silver for that of which it consists" (290–91). It is also indebted to the form of the chalice, "the aspect (*eidos*) of chaliceness" (291), to the silversmith that makes it, and so on. Although these other forms of indebtedness are a part of technology, his focus is clearly on what would normally have been called the material cause—the physical nature on which the silversmith acts. This material cause is important because it raises the issue of the relationship between technology and nature, which, as he notes, appears very different from the past: the windmill and the coal mine do not act on nature in the same way. Precisely this material is what is at issue in computer technology. What does it mean to "act on" an MP3 file?

The differences between these two forms of the technological transformation of nature are explained by focusing on the relationship between technology and knowledge. Heidegger sees all making as a form of poesis, of "bringing-forth." He quotes Plato: "Every occasion for whatever passes beyond the nonpresent and goes forward into presencing is *poiēsis,* bringing-forth" (293). For him, making is a way of knowing or what he calls "unconcealment": "Bringing-forth brings out of concealment into unconcealment. . . . The Greeks have the word *alētheia* for revealing. The Romans translate this with *veritas.* We say 'truth' and usually understand it as correctness of representation" (293–94). Of course, there is a traditional debate about the equation between truth and art—it is possible for the beautiful artwork to be in some way dishonest or fundamentally wrong? I think that Heidegger means something narrower here, however. For him, this truth means revelation:

> Not only in handicraft manufacture, not only artistic and poetic bringing into appearance and concrete imagery, is a bringing-forth, *poiēsis. Physis* also, the arising of something from out of itself, is a bringing forth, *poiēsis. Physis* is indeed *poiēsis* in the highest sense. For what presences by means of *physis* has the bursting open belonging to bringing-forth, e.g., the bursting of a blossom into bloom, in itself. In contrast, what is brought forth by the artisan or the artist, e.g., the silver chalice, has the bursting open belonging to bringing-forth, not in itself, but in another, in the craftsman or artist. (293)

Here *poiēsis* and *physis* both describe how the material world comes to be seen—either as it reveals itself (in the case of the flower) or is revealed through the manipulation of the artist. Through this theory of creativity Heidegger joins a long tradition of aestheticians who have argued for a continuity between scientific and artistic forms of representation.[39]

Heidegger's attempt to redefine making is particularly relevant to Stevens's minority opinion, since the latter attempts to ground our understanding of the patentable invention in the transformation of physical materials. The key that Heidegger emphasizes is how making leads us to see new things in nature. This revisioning of the natural world begins to address the problem with which I began this section—how to think about creativity when the objects on which creativity operates are themselves the products of human activity. Heidegger is quite straightforward in equating technology and revelation: "What has the essence of technology to do with revealing? The answer: everything. For every bringing-forth is grounded in revealing" (294). He describes technology as "a mode of revealing" (295) before then turning to consider how modern technology differs from the older handcraft models that clearly where the basis of the U.S. founders' conception of invention and the "useful arts." For Heidegger, modern technology changes the relation between this revealing and the natural world on which it acts:

> the revealing that holds sway throughout modern technology does not unfold into a bringing-forth in the sense of *poiēsis*. The revealing that rules in modern technology is a challenging, which puts to nature the unreasonable demand that it supply energy which can be extracted and stored as such. But does this not hold true for the old windmill as well? No. Its sails do indeed turn in the wind; they are left entirely to the wind's blowing. But the windmill does not unlock energy from the air currents in order to store it. (296)

Heidegger's concept of nature being *challenged* is somewhat obscure; it reflects his belief that modern technology leaves nature changed once it acts on it: "A tract of land is challenged in the hauling out of coal and ore. The earth now reveals itself as a coal mining district, the soil as a mineral deposit. The field that the peasant formerly cultivated and set in order appears different from how it did when to set in order still meant to take care and to maintain" (296). Challenging nature in this regard changes the relationship between technology and revealing. In the past, when a craftsperson used a material to make an object, it could be said that this material became visible—that this making was a way of revealing qualities of the raw material. In modern technology, however, this material remains merely the condition for other work. The coal extracted from the ground does not become an object to be seen but merely a source of power that will be used for some other purpose. Heidegger makes this clear when he discusses the way that the Rhine becomes the source for power through a hydroelectric plant: "let us ponder for a moment the contrast that is spoken by the two titles: 'The Rhine,' as dammed up into the *power* works, and 'The Rhine' as uttered by the *art* work, in Hölderlin's hymn by that name" (297). The Rhine in this sense is no longer an object to be looked at as "a river in the landscape" that might be represented in a poem but instead an abstract source of power. As he explains, "Whatever stands by in the sense of a standing-reserve no longer stands over against us as an object" (298).

Heidegger's observations about the way that modern technology *challeng-es* nature seems to me an insightful description of our changed relation-ship to the natural world today, and they explain why Stevens's admirable effort to push back against the problematic expansion of the scope of pat-ent law is ultimately unsatisfying. I noted that it is the nature of the con-temporary software patent to create the entities that seem to be undergoing transformation—for example, in data compression. Heidegger's understand-ing of unconcealment emphasizes the way that technology remakes the basic objects of the world. In explaining how this unconcealment happens, Heidegger focuses on the sort of interrelated systems Postman describes when he discusses the Rhine plant:

> The hydroelectric plant is set into the current of the Rhine. It sets the Rhine to supplying its hydraulic pressure, which then sets the turbines turning. This turning sets those machines in motion whose thrust sets going the electric cur-rent for which the long-distance power station and its network of cables are set up to dispatch electricity. In the context of the interlocking processes pertain-ing to the orderly disposition of electrical energy, even the Rhine itself appears to be something at our command. (297)

It is these "interlocking processes" that are at the heart of current patent law debates. They are a mixture of technological innovation and business prac-tices, a method of attaining power but also a way of integrating it into a sys-tem of storage and distribution.

Heidegger's description of technology as unconcealment captures the most problematic aspect of software technology, in which the objects to be created and acted on themselves depend on the technology to bring them into being. These objects fit uncomfortably in the traditional model of the physical device that is the basis for the patent, and to which Stevens appeals in the *Bilski* opinion. Bruno Latour would call these "quasi-objects" because they exist between physical and social entities. Latour comes to the need for this term by noticing modern culture's separation of objective and sub-jective. He notes in Boyle's scientific writing a dependence on nonhuman actors as the basis for scientific knowledge: "these nonhumans, lacking souls but endowed with meaning, are even more reliable than ordinary mortals, to whom will is attributed but who lack the capacity to indicate phenomena in a reliable way."[40] Science seems to separate the objective world from moral and political values: "the suffocating bird, the marble cylinders, the descending mercury are not our own creations, they are not made out of thin air, not of social relations, not of human categories."[41] Latour is interested in this separation between the social and the natural primarily because this line seems so problematic today. He begins by listing natural phenomena that he will characterize as hybrids: the hole in the ozone layer, the AIDS epidemic, the merging of human and science in frozen embryos, the mixing of computer and animal in "whales wearing collars fitted with radio tracking devices": "once again, heads of state, chemists, biologists, desperate patients and industrialists find themselves caught up in a single uncertain story mixing biology and society."[42] He proposes an "anthropological analysis of the modern world" and to explore the "sociotechnologial networks."[43]

At the core of Latour's analysis is a recognition that the objects of science are inherently woven with the political, institutional, social, and moral networks in which they will be studied, discussed, and used. This is precisely the situation in which we find ourselves with software patents: the object of invention depends on a whole set of social, technological, and institutional networks that not only make this entity meaningful but even allow it to become visible in the first place. It is in this context that Postman's critique of technopoly is especially relevant. As I have already noted, in a technopoly our ability to recognize the basic components of the world are defined by technology instead of other moral or social systems. In fact, both Postman and Latour insist that technological objects become part of our social imaginary. Foucault's *Archeology of Knowledge* reminds us that "the formation of objects" begins with what he calls "the first *surfaces* of their *emergence*." Focusing on the emergence of madness, he writes, "In these fields of initial differentiation, in the distances, the discontinuities, and the thresholds that appear within it, psychiatric discourse finds a way of limiting its domain, of defining what it is talking about, of giving it the status of an object—and therefore of making it manifest, nameable, and describable."[44] This is certainly the case with software patents, where the object itself emerges only through complex systems of discourse and technical knowledge. Early industrial patents described processes that were usually visible and obviously technological; today we depend on specialized knowledge to make these objects visible. In turn, those technological objects are naturally integrated into business systems. It is no surprise that computing emerged as a discipline only when large mainframe computers found their home in corporations and such calculations became part of everyday business practices. Already we can see this in the case of patents for data compression, which satisfy both technical and business needs. After all, data compression is the basis for streaming and downloadable media of all sorts; it is what makes iTunes convenient and Netflix's Watch Instantly features possible.

An especially good example of our dependence on technology to define the objects of knowledge is provided by John Bender and Michael Marrinan's recent book, *The Culture of the Diagram*. They open with the example of computer-assisted eye surgery. The surgeon does not hold a scalpel or see the eye that is being operated on directly. Instead, the doctor wears a helmet with a head-mounted display: "What the doctor 'sees' is a real-time, stereoscopic image of the movement and position of his microsurgical tools."[45] A few pages later Bender and Marrinan ponder whether the computer is providing the doctor with a description of the patient's eye, and answer in the negative: "The digital data-stream is not a description of the eye but a *diagram*. A diagram is a proliferation of manifestly selective packets of dissimilar data correlated in an explicitly process-oriented array that has some of the attributes of a representation but is situated in the world like an object. Diagrams are closer in kind to a Jackson Pollock than to a Rembrandt."[46] This description of the instrument as providing a diagram is especially striking because it is so explicitly based on a specific technical use. The patient's eye has no connection to traditional social or personal meanings ("the surgeon cares little if the patient has green or blue eyes") but is instead defined entirely by its role within the surgery being performed.[47] Twenty years ago postmodernist critics might have offered the sort of Baudrillardian critique we see from Stephenson in chapter 3 and argued that our sense of reality today is being lost in a haze of simulation. But Bender and Marrinan make a convincing case that this kind of diagrammatic representation is essential to being able to *do* things with certain forms of data. In this sense, diagrammatic representation is essential to the physical and technical activity itself. The elements of the eye are stripped down to the components essential for the operation. We can see in this diagram the ability of computer technology to create objects that reflect technological systems of knowledge. Flusser makes this observation: "Now that numbers are beginning to liberate themselves from the pressure of letters and computing is being mechanized, their visionary power can unfold. Having undergone centuries of purification through the discipline and clarity of distinctness, numbers can now serve creative vision as they have never and nowhere been able to do before."[48]

## 4

As Heidegger and Latour both explain in their separate ways, the increasingly abstract nature of "invention" in modern technology blurs what has traditionally been a sharp line between the patentable machine and the unpatentable business practice. As we have seen, it is in the nature of contemporary technology that these systems create the objects that they seem to manipulate and transform.

This observation helps to explain the importance of some current patent debates focused on the *appearance* of the computer interface. Let us take the example of Apple's 1994 suit against Microsoft for its use of the GUI in Windows 2.0 as an early example of what will become a common form of patent dispute in computing.[49] In many ways, this case is a poor match for the patent cases that I have been discussing. Apple sued Microsoft on the basis of copyright rather than patent violation, and the case itself ultimately turned on a rather narrow reading of the terms of Apple's licensing of its UI to Microsoft for Windows 1.0 in 1985. However, the expansion of patent law in the subsequent two decades means that Apple has pursued patent violation suits against companies like Samsung when it feels that competitors are borrowing too liberally from its designs. Even in this earlier case, the problematic nature of the intellectual property that is under debate is clear. Apple famously charged Microsoft with stealing the "look and feel" of the Macintosh interface—something that cannot be equated with a single device that performs a function. This has especially been the case with recent Apple patents for abstract UI elements like the "pinch to zoom" and "slide to unlock" gestures pioneered on the iPhone.[50] Such patents are often held up as examples of the unworkable nature of current patent law, and yet it is clear that Apple *did* invent (or at least synthesize and popularize) a gestural language for interacting with mobile devices that many competing manufactures have imitated, just as it created a commercially viable windows-based GUI with the original Macintosh. The question, of course, is whether that kind of invention deserves patent protection. As is clear from the Microsoft case, just twenty years ago Apple felt that such an invention was best protected under copyright law.

Such UI designs seem to represent a particularly clear intersection between two principles for rejecting a patent application: the mathematical algorithm and the business practice. Perhaps the best example of this kind of patent is Amazon's notorious "one-click buying" patent: "In response to the selection of the order button, the client system sends to the server system a request to purchase the identified item. The server system receives the request and combines the purchaser information associated with the client identifier of the client system to generate an order to purchase the item in accordance with the billing and shipment information whereby the purchaser effects the ordering of the product by selection of the order button."[51]

This patent is often used as an example to show the absurdity of modern patent law, since having a single button that allows a customer to purchase something at an online store seems obvious. Although the patent has been narrowed considerably by later court rulings, it reveals some of the unique challenges to thinking about creativity in the design of computing. Here business practice and UI design have merged into a single abstract system that appears across many websites and computer devices. The processing of a request links to a server, and the option to make that request in turn is represented in the UI of the website in a certain way. Although I have discussed Stephenson's dismissal of the GUI in chapter 3, these visual user elements actually reflect the complex position of the software patent much better than a command-line interface would. Here the GUI works to represent to the user a business process. Although Amazon's "invention" of the one-click purchase seems much less original than Apple's slide-to-unlock or pinch-to-zoom language, all of these are ways of representing complex computing requests made by the user.

Stephenson's insistence that the GUI is merely an illusion hiding a fundamentally material command-line level that is the *real* nature of the computer, which I discussed in detail in chapter 3, misses what is most important about the role of the UI in the function of the computer as a tool. As the example of the Amazon patent suggests, the UI reminds us that it is the nature of the computer almost since its invention to create a network of distributed tasks. It is a detail in the history of computing frequently overlooked that Xerox PARC invented both the GUI and Ethernet more or less at the same time. Michael Hiltzik explains in his history of the influential research laboratory:

> [Gary] Starkweather's [laser printer] and [Ron] Rider's character generator were two of the four legs of the complete interactive office environment PARC was creating on the fly. In the same period Thacker, McCreight, and Lampson were building the Alto; Alan Kay and his Learning Research Group were designing a graphical user interface aimed at making computers intuitively simple to use; and Bob Metcalfe and David Boggs were designing a network—the Ethernet—to tie all the other components together.[52]

The fact that the GUI and the Ethernet were created at the same place at the same time is usually regarded as a quirk of industrial history, or perhaps as a testament to the intellectual foresight of the PARC research. In the context of this analysis of tools and networked systems, however, it is easy to see that they are natural complements. The design of the UI brings to the

Figure 10. Xerox Star 8010 interface (1981). Polaroid photograph courtesy of DigiBarn Computer Museum.

surface the issue of how we depend on and imagine our tools, and those tools in turn depend on a network of other relationships as equipment. To design tools is to insert them within a network of relations. This is very much the heart of Xerox's Star OS, which mixed documents, folders, e-mail programs, and networked devices like printers. The visual design of the GUI, in other words, was a way of representing not just documents, but the relationship between documents and a networked environment for printing and distribution (see Figure 10).

Although similar to the modern desktop in Windows or Mac OS X, this space mixes many heterogeneous kinds of objects: documents, windows, applications, and physical devices connected to the computer network. Nothing could be more natural, in other words, than to search for a method of networking computers once you have begun to design a GUI for representing their actions, because the creation of abstract entities like the in-box is inherently linked to the network that makes them possible. Alan Liu goes further and suggests that this emphasis on design is fundamental to the way that knowledge workers locate themselves within their corporate environment and reconcile the relationship between their personal and work lives: "design is precisely the discipline that promises to fuse the production and consumption of culture so as to integrate undecidably the lives of work and nonwork."[53]

Many critics have associated contemporary network culture with such abstract, immaterial entities. When Michael Hardt and Antonio Negri describe the contemporary information economy, it is specifically by the way that computing and networked relationships transform work: "One face of immaterial labor can be recognized in analogy to the functioning of a computer. . . . Today we increasingly think like computers, while communication technologies and their model of interaction are becoming more and more central to laboring activities."[54] Eugene Thacker makes this point in his foreword to Alexander Galloway's influential book on networks and control, *Protocol:* "Networks are not tropes for notions of 'interconnection.' They are material technologies, sites of variable practices, actions, and movements."[55] Networks, as Thacker puts it, "Are Real but Abstract."[56] Galloway captures this material complexity when he refers to the network as a "diagram": "Throughout the years new diagrams (also called graphs or organizational designs) have appeared as solutions or threats to existing ones. Bureaucracy is a diagram. Hierarchy is one too, as is peer-to-peer. Designs come and go, serving as useful asset managers at one historical moment, then disappearing, or perhaps fading only to reemerge later as useful again."[57] Latour makes this same point about the ambiguous realness of "networks my colleagues in science studies and I have traced": "Is it our fault if the networks are *simultaneously real, like nature, narrated, like discourse, and collective, like society?*"[58] Galloway invokes Deleuze for his model of space,[59] and it is helpful to recall the way that the latter describes the "Body without Organs":

> A BwO is made in such a way that it can be occupied, populated only by intensities. Only intensities pass and circulate. Still, the BwO is not a scene, a place, or even a support upon which something comes to pass. It has nothing to do with phantasy, there is nothing to interpret. The BwO causes intensities to pass; it produces and distributes them in a *spatium* that is itself intensive, lacking extension. It is not space, nor is it in space; it is matter that occupies space to a given degree—to the degree corresponding to the intensities produced.[60]

Like Galloway, Deleuze emphasizes the material effects of what initially might seem merely a representation of space: "It is not at all a notion or a concept but a practice, a set of practices."[61]

Diagrams, networks, GUIs—these are not secondary to some more fundamental reality but instead a condition of that reality. This is why Apple's extremely general patent for touchscreen gestures has seemed patentable: it describes a system for operating the computer, and that system is as fundamental a part of the experience as the physical components that make up the machine. As we think about the computer as a kind of tool, it is essential that we recognize that these networked links are part of the effectiveness of those UI designs. This whole set of technologies is what Apple and Amazon are seeking patent or copyright protection for, but obviously such technologies move problematically away from the concrete machines that have been the basis for traditional patent law. And seeing computing as a form of writing is essential to this abstraction, since it is through such writing that, as Brooks remarks, we can build "castles in the air, from air, creating by exertion of the imagination."[62] Seeing computing through writing makes these abstract, speculative inventions the center of contemporary technology.

## 5

We have seen, then, that the contemporary information economy depends on tools that can be troublingly abstract. The much-maligned one-click purchasing button that Amazon "invented" is no button at all—it is merely a region of screen space treated as if it were a physical button. This is true of all the devices that are characteristic of our interface with computers; the windows that are central to the modern GUI are not windows at all but rather regions of a screen designed to behave in a certain way. This is one of the central characteristics of the memex: it is a tool only because it connects up and accesses databases of information. Bush's loving description of the physical details of the memex is similar to Apple's meticulous attention to the details of its UI. Both are attempts to create a sense of the physical device, a gadget, in an age of networked abstraction. And this, in turn, helps to explain why the writing metaphor is so important to our particular cultural moment, since writing evokes the physical device. When we think of writing, we imagine a physical act—from the student writing out an essay longhand in the library to Faulkner hunched over his typewriter. Seeing computing as a form of writing, in other words, is a way of emphasizing the physical tool in an age of abstract resources.

This understanding of writing as helping us to negotiate the toolishness of work in an age of virtual processes and devices can help to explain the tendency of GUIs to adopt machine-line, "skeuomorphic" designs. *Skeuomorphism* refers to designs that make decorative use of elements that are no longer necessary for the functioning or manufacture of an object. Well-known examples include ornamental "stitching" in vinyl seats, flame-shaped lightbulbs, and the nonfunctional shutters often attached to modern single-family homes. Skeuomorphism can often function as a way to make unfamiliar objects or processes meaningful and accessible, and as a result it has had an especially significant role in the design of UIs in computing environments. Skeuomorphism has been an explicit element since the arrival of graphical interfaces; a classic example is the tendency for programs that play audio files to imitate the look of physical devices, including on-screen "buttons" for pausing and playing the audio that mimic those on older tape decks. On some level, of course, we could argue that even the fundamental metaphors of the GUI environment are skeuomorphic, but traditionally we distinguish between those features that serve a functional purpose (like the ability to "scroll" through a document) and those that are decorative, such as the layout of buttons on the music program. Skeuomorphism has emerged as a particularly heated issue with Apple's recent UI design. A particularly egregious example is the appearance of leather materials in Apple's recent calendar on the Macintosh OS X and the Find My Friends App on the iPhone (see Figure 11).

Critics have noted the irony of Apple's embrace of such decorative elements in its software but its fondness for minimalism in physical design.[63] A great deal of attention has been given to this recent design shift at Apple, and it is certainly possible that it can be explained simply by Apple's desire to reach an audience that is not comfortable with technology; it may be that technological neophytes genuinely find these design elements reassuring. More broadly, however, the tendency to design software based on such skeuomorphic elements may reflect an anxiety about the creativity implicit in software design. To make a program look like a machine is to make an indirect claim that it deserves the protections and respect awarded to traditional, physical inventions. Is it any surprise that Apple, the technology company most eager to defend its inventions in court and most likely to believe that the rest of the industry has stolen its ideas,[64] would gravitate towards skeuomorphism and the equation of software and the physical devices traditionally protected by patents?

Katherine Hayles argues that skeuomorphism is characteristic of "threshold devices" that mark the transition from one conceptual model to another.[65]

Figure 11. Skeuomorphic design in Apple's Find My Friends App, version 1.1.

For her, skeuomorphism today is particularly a response to the immateriality of contemporary life. She cites Alvin Toffler: "the central event of the 20th century is the overthrow of matter."[66] We have seen this to be a central feature of the writing-as-computing metaphor, most obviously in the way that the individual item depends on the library for its meaning. Is the Kindle book a distinct thing, or merely an item within a library? Is the individual program separated from its "include" command a distinct thing? This broad technological system has been in tension with the small hand-held gadget since the rise of the personal computer at the end of the 1970s. The writing metaphor emerges into a system for thinking about computing most powerfully just as two seemingly opposed things happen: computers become smaller, physical, and almost personal devices, and the immaterial network relationships become a part of the everyday work of using a computer. The skeuomorphism of so much software design in the last several years reflects these central tensions in computing today. There should be little surprise that when companies want to emphasize values such as individuality, creativity, and physical ownership that appear to be in tension with "immaterial" corporate servers and shared library resources, they most often appeal to skeuomorphism and the writing metaphor in the form of iPads and notebook computers. Ultimately, this is central to Bush's memex, as well—an object that connects to a network, a physical device that can be carried as a tool while accessing all the abstract resources of the modern computing age.

# SIX

# Audience Today

*Between Literature and Performance*

Thus far, I have discussed the computing-as-writing metaphor primarily as a feature of computing. We have seen how this metaphor changes our thinking about the work of programming, the place of computers in our everyday lives, the "libraries" of electronic texts, and even the invention at the heart of the patent system. I have, however, thus far ignored the issue of how this prevalent metaphor influences the way that we think about the work of being a writer outside of computing. If we have begun to think about computing as a form of writing, does that in turn mean that computing has become important to our ways of imagining the task and vocation of the novelist, the journalist, the scholar, the critic? At the beginning of this book I quoted Kenneth Goldsmith's assertion that the writer today resembles a programmer, but how common is this understanding of creative writing outside of the avant-garde context in which he works? In other words, I am interested in the nature of creative writing in the age of computing.

As I argue in this chapter, this inquiry naturally takes us back to questions about the relationship between the writer and audience. We have already seen this in very general terms in Bush's memex, where the "trails" created by the scholar moving through the archive of previous research appear to become part of the archive. Such trails are created incidentally, without being directed at or created for others; their communicational function is tangential. The same is true of the result of a Google search, which is generated for the user without any actual human being typing the information. Writing code likewise appears to transform the nature of the audience since the code is directed at a machine rather than at the humans who use the resulting programs. Obviously, these changes in computing need not have an effect on the image of the audience in the mind of the novelist when he or she sits down at a desk to begin a story. To understand that broader but less technical shift, we need a more general inquiry into the nature of audience today. This will ultimately lead us back to the issue of profession that we examined in chapter 2, and help us to understand the writing metaphor's ability to straddle contradictions in contemporary culture's thinking about the work of being a writer.

1

Many critics have noted that the computer assumes a fundamentally different relationship between author, text, and reader. Espen Aarseth offers an influential formulation of this relationship in *Cybertext* (1997), where he asks, "So, what is a text?" and offers as part of the answer the distinction between textons and scriptons:

> It is useful to distinguish between strings as they appear to readers and strings as they exist in the text, since these may not always be the same. For want of better terms, I call the former *scriptons* and the latter *textons* . . . . In a book such as Raymond Queneau's sonnet machine *Cent mille milliards de poèmes,* where the user folds lines in the book to "compose" sonnets, there are only 140 textons, but these combine into 100,000,000,000,000 possible scriptons.[1]

A text created on the computer is what Lev Manovich calls "variable": "a new media object is not something fixed once and for all, but something that can exist in different, potentially infinite versions."[2] Aarseth is eager to show that such variability is not impossible in print texts, but clearly it is a much more common feature of texts produced and encountered on the computer. More broadly, Aarseth identifies the fact that texts created in this environment involve more extensive design work, and that the writing that an author does in constructing it is not intended to be read directly or as a whole by the reader. Many critics have noted that even the diligent reader of hypertext narratives may never encounter and thus never read many of the textons because they are hidden along pathways that the reader has not pursued.

Other writers have emphasized the nature of written code, which is rarely seen by a human audience. In his 1991 novel *The Gold Bug Variations* Richard Powers toys with the narrative use of code by offering summaries of the characters' relationships as code: "sea_change(ressler,koss,X) if in_love( ressler,koss) and not(knows( X ))."[3] The poetic and narrative uses of this kind of computer language suggested by Powers has been subsequently developed in what is called "codework" poetry, which John Cayley describes this way: "Potentially *codework* is a term for literature which uses, addresses, and incorporates code: as underlying language-animating or language-generating programming, as a special type of language in itself, or as an intrinsic part of the new surface language or 'interface text,' as I call it, of writing in networked and programmable media."[4] The resulting text often creates "a multiplicity of reference" according to Rita Raley, with individual words and phrases meaningful both as code and as a poetic statement.[5] One example is Talan Memmott's use of the term "exe.termination" in *Lexia to Perplexia* to invoke ideas of death, communication through terminals, and the computer program as a file with the .exe file type.[6] Another good example is the work of Australian codework artist Mez, whose "ev.o[h!]lution::Pre Alphanumeric//Mezangelleing Daze::" opens this way:

> if:
>      pre alphanumeric//pre network n-cluded use ov com.put[ty/fillah]ers offline
>      then:
>      n-turr-rest in network system[ic]z stemmed fromme a more organic base, collaborationz were via real-time fleshmeat N n-stallation based[7]

Mez draws on command structures for programming, including the simple if/then protocol as well as the more sophisticated use of "com.put" syntax. The double slash, hyphens, and brackets work to break up common words and introduce an ambiguity of reference, such as in "n-turr-rest." McKenzie Wark notes that codework poetry departs from the better-known form of literary writing for the computer, hypertext, which retains a more traditional model of authorship and audience: "it doesn't really rethink who the writer is, in the new network of statements that the expansion of the Internet makes possible. For all the talk of the death of the author, the hypertext author assumes much the same persona as his or her avant-garde literary predecessors."[8]

Codework poetry reminds us that there are at least two audiences in all programming language, and that there is no simple line between what is written for the computer and what is written for the human. As Cayley remarks, "Reading codework as code-in-language and language-in-code also risks stunning the resultant literary object, leaving it reduced to simple text-to-be-read, whereas there are real questions of how such work is to be grasped as an object: is it text, process, performance, instrument?"[9] Although the esoteric and often dense nature of codework poetry might seem far away from our everyday use of language and writing—in fact, it is common to frame codework in the tradition of modernist typographical experimentation[10]—codework is powerful because it connects to our everyday interactions with computers. Most of us are aware that even the simplest writing that we do on a computer involves coding: the "hidden characters" that mark spaces and paragraphs on a word processor, the HTML code that renders websites, the @ addresses that we use to send e-mail. I noted the prevalence of this kind of code in chapter 2, and I think that our awareness of this programming language behind even simple textual documents helps explain the relevance of codework. It is because this mixed language is all around us that Wark's contrast between codework and the avant-garde orientation of hypertext rings true: codework writing reveals through exaggeration the ways that we deal with language addressed both to people and to computers all the time. Back in graduate school my e-mail address at Penn State was *djp5,* and friends with whom I shared this address understood that the *5* in this address was not for them—it was not some kind of subtle hint about my identity—but instead a way for the university servers to distinguish between the various *djp*s that worked and studied there. Even such an innocuous and commonplace act of naming has elements that are addressed to the computer rather than to the people using them.

Although codes like this seem to reveal themselves disruptively—after all, we usually only see the block of code when a file fails to load properly or when an e-mail is returned to us as undeliverable—we should recognize that code frequently *does* have a human audience. Of course, many critics have treated code as a kind of *other* to natural language, a form of writing without a real audience. Katherine Hayles quotes Ellen Ullman approvingly: "Finally, a computer program has only one meaning: what it does. It isn't a text for an academic to read. Its entire meaning is its function."[11] Theodor Nelson makes a similar point in a (characteristically) more dramatic way in *Computer Lib/Dream Machines:* "A computer language is a system for casting spells. This is not a metaphor but an exactly true statement."[12] As we noted in chapter 3, however, code is written not just for the computer but also for programmers to keep track of the design of the software for debugging, updates, and so on. In fact, the difference between good and bad coding has as much do to with its intelligibility to other programmers as with purely technical efficiency. As Donald Knuth says, "There are many senses in which a program can be 'good,' of course. In the first place, a program is especially good when it works correctly. Secondly, a program is often good if it is easy to change, when the time for adaptation arises. Both of these goals are achieved when the program is easily readable and understandable to a person who knows the appropriate language."[13] The literate programming movement fundamentally arises from this insight that code is written for people and not solely for computers.

It is clear from these examples that writing in this programming environment is characterized by multiple forms of address and that coding is not simply a matter of two distinct levels of language in the way that Aarseth implies. Codework poetry makes this explicit—as when Memmott uses the term *exe.termination* to invoke a variety of literary and computing contexts—but this complexity is quite clear even in mundane programming, where variable names (for example) are addressed not just to the compiler but also to human programmers, who can use well-chosen names to reveal the purpose of these elements of the program. An important part of this multiple address is the way that it connects the text to larger corporate and institutional structures. We saw this at the outset of this book in Bush's memex, which was an archive that linked scholars together, and it reappeared in the concept of the library. In all of these cases, what initially seems like an isolated and independent thing—the book, the program, the research database—ends up being connected to and dependent on these networked systems. Code emphasizes this duality.

## 2

It is clear, then, that an interest in the nature of writing on the computer as a form of textuality naturally leads us back to a question of the audience to which this code is addressed. So far, I have focused entirely on the specific technical context in which code is written and read. But changing notions of audience become more important when they transcend the narrow context of programming and reshape our notions of writing and authorship in the culture as a whole—what Katherine Hayles refers to as "work that remains in print but nevertheless bears within its body marks of its electronic composition."[14]

Hayles's analysis in *My Mother Was a Computer* of these issues focuses in part on Neal Stephenson's writing, whose anti-GUI manifesto I discussed at length in chapter 3. I find Hayles's reading of Stephenson somewhat limited for my uses because she largely handles his work thematically—treating *Cryptonomicon* primarily as having something to say about the nature of code and figurative language, rather than asking how the novel enacts these insights in its style or structure. But the central opposition that she finds here is, I think, far-reaching and important: "the tension between performative code and figurative language runs through many of Stephenson's books; indeed, it is no exaggeration to say that it is central to his creation of fictive worlds."[15] Hayles identifies a broad model for writing based in code that certainly has the potential to transcend the specific context of programming. What would it mean for writers in general to begin to think of their work as performative? Immediately we recognize that this model of writing departs from our traditional ways of talking about literary representation, like the mimetic and romantic expressive theories. In his classic work, *Mimesis*, Erich Auerbach offers us "an investigation into the literary representation of reality" and opens with the opposition between *The Odyssey* and the Book of Job:

> The two styles, in their opposition, represent basic types: on the one hand fully externalized description, uniform illumination, uninterrupted connection, free expression, all events in the foreground, displaying unmistakable meanings, few elements of historical development and of psychological perspective; on the other hand, certain parts brought into high relief, others left obscure, abruptness, suggestive influence of the unexpressed, "background" quality, multiplicity of meanings and the need for interpretation, universal-historical claims, development of the concept of the historically becoming, and preoccupation with the problematic.[16]

From this point of view, writing styles can be understood according to how they represent reality. Conversely, the expressive theory of writing emphasizes the author as the source of the text. M. H. Abrams summarizes this theory in *The Mirror and the Lamp*: "Almost all the major critics of the English romantic generation phrased definitions or key statements showing a parallel alignment from work to poet. Poetry is the overflow, utterance, or projection of the thought and feelings of the poet; or else (in the chief variant formulation) poetry is defined in terms of the imaginative process which modifies and synthesizes the images, thoughts, and feelings of the poet."[17] The mimetic and expressive theories are two of the fundamental models for literary writing.

Hayles suggests a different way of evaluating writing—by what it does. This sounds like a return to an even older rhetorical model of language use, one based in its effects on the audience.[18] Although the world of classical rhetoric seems very far from contemporary computer code, this is the way that programming is universally represented in film—when it is represented at all. In chapter 3 I described the opening of *The Social Network*, whose description of the Facesmash site culminates in crashing the Harvard university servers. The same is true of programming in films from *Tron* to

*The Matrix,* where programmers are inevitably shown typing (although we rarely see *what* they are typing) in order to bypass some security system *(Tron: Legacy),* to load a virus *(Office Space),* or to access restricted information *(The Social Network, The Matrix).*[19] Within such narratives, programming is represented only by what it accomplishes, and it is rare that we are shown any code itself on the screen.[20]

The idea that contemporary writing provides more license for the reader to act in various ways has been a common claim about print as well as electronic reading. Back in 1988, Linda Hutcheon saw computer-based narrative as a particularly extreme instance of the general postmodern emphasis on reader performance: "Simultaneous with a general dethroning of suspect authority and of centered and totalized thought, we are witnessing a renewed aesthetic and theoretical interest in the interactive powers involved in the production and reception of texts. The most extreme example I can think of in art is, perhaps, 'interactive fiction' or computerized, participatory 'compunovels.' Here process is all; there is no fixed product or text, just as the reader's activity as producer as well as receiver."[21] Although frequently criticized,[22] this equation of performance in postmodernism remains common; for example, in a recent book on hypertext literature, Jaishree Odin finds a similar focus on reader performance in Calvino's print novel *Invisible Cities,* which she says "creates a performative space that the reader can enter and explore in multiple ways."[23] The idea that the contemporary novel places more emphasis on authorial or readerly performance often remains theoretically vague, however.

Raoul Eshelman has recently reinterpreted this common association by offering the narrower concept of *performatism* as a response to textuality *after* postmodernism. According to Eshelman, postmodernism is defined by undecidability and a resistance to unity and closure: "author, work, and reader all tumble into an endless regress of referral that has no particular fix point, goal, or center."[24] Performatist works respond to this suspicion with an entirely different kind of aesthetics:

> The answer lies in a new, radical empowerment of the frame using a blend of aesthetic and archaic, forcible devices. Performatist works are set up in such a way that the reader or writer at first has no choice but to opt for a single, compulsory solution to the problems raised within the work at hand. The author, in other words, imposes a certain solution on us using dogmatic, ritual, or some other coercive means. (2)

Specifically, Eshelman argues that works like this impose a frame whose values must be accepted. Using the example of the problematic voice-over narration at the end of the film *American Beauty,* he claims that the viewer cannot indulge suspicion toward this happy ending: "if you are at all serious about analyzing the movie as it stands, you have little choice but to accept this authorially certified argument as an indispensable part of the film as a whole" (3). The contrast to postmodernist aesthetics seems quite clear in this case, since instead of indeterminacy and incoherence the viewer of this film is forced to accept a point of view on the film that does provide closure—even though we may suspect that that closure is not wholeheartedly embraced by the author. Eshelman sees this as an aesthetic mode that appears in literature, film, and architecture.

This focus on performance is one that is evident in codework poetry, as well. Wark associates codework with an interest in what language can *do*: "What codework draws attention to is the pragmatic side of language. Language is not an abstract and homogenous plane, it is one element in a heterogeneous series of elements linked together in the act of communication. Writing is not a matter of the text, but of the assemblage of the writer, reader, text, the text's material support, the laws of property and exchange within which all of the above circulate, and so on."[25] Rita Raley makes a similar claim about the fundamental importance of different modes of performance in hypertext: "Put more directly, both operator and machinic processor are crucial components of the performance of the system. The performance that encompasses user and the machinic system is an interactive one and to some degree collaborative. Further, the performance collapses processing and product, ends and means, input and output, within a system of 'making' that is both complex and emergent."[26] According to her, a shift to digital poetics draws our attention to the performance of author, reader, and system: "hypertext must be conceived in terms of performance and that approaching the problem of a difference between the analog and the digital must be done in a mode through which digital textuality can emerge on its own terms" (ibid.).

Eshelman's theory of performatism in literature and art clearly has its inspiration in the broader theoretical embrace of performance as a model for meaning. Much of this theoretical work has its roots in Foucault's late writings, which turn from an interest in institutions and sign systems to a concern for the way that selves are created by their actions. In *The Use of Pleasure,* Foucault describes his intention to "investigate how individuals were led to practice, on themselves and on others, a hermeneutics of desire, a hermeneutics of which their sexual behavior was doubtless the occasion, but certainly not the exclusive domain."[27] This is, of course, not a complete break from the emphasis on the production of knowledge and power in Foucault's middle period,[28] but the increased emphasis on the productive nature of institutions and power has been adopted by many other critics. Judith Butler embraces the performative nature of gender, both as a matter of broad discursive and philosophical systems and in individual, everyday behaviors.[29] For many critics, the language of performance marks a break from poststructuralist emphasis on systems and texts and emphasizes the tenuous nature of power and language. As Michael Hardt and Antonio Negri explain in *Multitude,* "Performance, like habit, involves neither fixed immutable nature nor spontaneous individual freedom, residing instead between the two, a kind of acting in common based on collaboration and communication."[30]

We can see the same appeal to performatism in Eshelman's theory, which is offered explicitly as a post-postmodernist artistic style. Faced with widespread suspicion toward meaning and unity, writers might naturally be attracted to an emphasis on what a text does rather than what it is or says. If we see performance as a compelling alternative to postmodernist uncertainty, where does that leave the individual writer? As I noted above, it is clear that attention to performance returns us to a tradition of thinking about the relationship between author and audience in rhetorical terms. James Porter has recently argued that the emergence of networked communication and digital media has fundamentally changed the writer–audience relationship: "developments in network-based technology—particularly the emergence and success of 'the networked information economy' and of Web 2.0 social networking—will dramatically change rhetorical theory and the practice of writing."[31] Porter frames his topic as a broader inquiry into the ways that these technologies have changed our understanding of rhetoric: "When rhetoric asks questions about audience and purpose—What is my purpose for writing? Who is my audience?—it is also implicitly asking questions about the economics of delivery. What motivates someone to produce and distribute a piece of writing? What motivates someone else to access it, read it, interact with it?"[32]

Collin Gifford Brooke has argued that the issues raised by Porter are in fact an element of the long-neglected rhetorical canon of delivery. Although the other canons (invention, arrangement, style, and memory) have gotten much more attention since the shift away from oral presentation, Brooke argues that "recent developments in information technology, and the Web in particular, have resuscitated the question of delivery" and argues for a broad interpretation of delivery: not merely "delivery as a procedural or practical matter" but also as "decidedly political, ethical, and economic."[33] I interpret Porter's approach to the changing relationship between writer and audience as just this sort of attention to the changing nature of digital distribution. Especially well known is Cass Sunstein's articulation of the political and social implications of this transformation. He has argued that audience and author are mutually self-selecting. He opens *Republic.com* with a portrait of the future of online reading that turns out not to be so futuristic at all:

> It is some time in the future. Technology has greatly increased people's ability to "filter" what they want to read, see, and hear. With the aid of the Internet, you are able to design your own newspapers and magazines. You can choose your own programming, with movies, game shows, sports, shopping, and the news of your choice. You mix and match.
>
> You need not come across topics and views that you have not sought out. Without any difficulty, you are able to see exactly what you want to see, no more and no less. You can easily find out what "people like you" tend to like and dislike. You avoid what they dislike. You take a close look at what they like.[34]

Sunstein's central example of this kind of filtering is the personalized electronic edition of newspapers, and more generally the personalized home page that most ISPs help their users to create. But his observation extends well beyond such explicit forms of self-selection. Time-shifting technologies like the DVR, which allows users to watch only what they want when they want it, are another way in which consumers take greater control over the media they consume. And with the changing economics of publication on the Web, it is possible to create sites with increasingly specific readerships. The rise of news aggregation sites like *Huffington Post* likewise pull stories out of their original publication context and allow readers to surf between the particular content that they are interested in.

This author–audience self-selection is a central way that the rhetorical model of the writer manifests itself in contemporary computing culture, and it is a sharp break from the way that we learned to view writing during modernism. In his 1964 essay "After Joyce," Donald Barthelme summarizes the modernist aesthetic: "with Stein and Joyce the literary work becomes an object in the world rather than a text or commentary on the world—a crucial change in status which was also taking place in painting."[35] He goes on to contrast modernism to an oral storytelling model: "the reader is not listening to an authoritative account of the world delivered by an expert (Faulkner on Mississippi, Hemingway on the corrida) but bumping into something that is *there*, like a rock or a refrigerator."[36] In chapter 3 I noted that our idea of the contemporary writer can be helpfully contrasted with the model provided by the modernists—who clearly cast a long shadow over twentieth-century writing. Whether or not postmodernism represented a welcome return to an interest in audience and the human scale of creativity or an extension of modernist alienation into increased self-reflexivity is an open question.[37] It is, however, clear that an interest in audience and its immediate relationship with the author made possible by social media represents a break from the dominant model of the first part of the twentieth century.

It is nothing new to complain that the American public space is being transformed by media. Jill Walker Rettberg notes that this trend is not unique to the Internet: "the decline of the public sphere has regularly been lamented," going back to media like television and radio.[38] But Sunstein sees this individuation of our media consumption as having deeply problematic implications for political debate, which he argues depends on encountering ideas that you do not already agree with: "Unplanned, unanticipated encounters are central to democracy itself. Such encounters often involve topics and points of view that people have not sought out and perhaps find quite irritating."[39] He notes that our ideas of free speech depend on the existence of a public forum in which that speech can be heard: "hence, governments are obligated to allow speech to occur freely on public streets and in public parks—even if many citizens would prefer to have peace and quiet, and even if it seems irritating to come across protesters and dissidents when you are simply walking home or to the local grocery store."[40] In the Internet, conversely, Sunstein sees a kind of ad hoc community that develops in these special-interest sites, and as such they depart strikingly from the institutionally defined and authorized communities that we associate with the religious, civic, or academic spaces. These latter, more traditional spaces preexist the political uses to which they are put; only in these spaces can individuals encounter points of view that they have not explicitly sought out. For all that the era of three broadcast networks in the United States seems like a period of hegemony and political uniformity, this predefined media space had the advantage of creating encounters with political ideas that individuals found disagreeable. The ad hoc spaces that Sunstein sees in online communication, conversely, lack the permanence and ability to challenge audiences to engage with foreign ideas.

The change that Sunstein identifies in Internet publishing and communication is clearly part of a larger trend in contemporary marketing and economics. In 2006 Chris Anderson coined the term *the long tail* to identify what he saw as a fundamental change in the economics of the contemporary marketplace; this idea is part of Porter's attempt to rethink rhetoric in a digital age. Anderson defines "the world the blockbuster built" as one that emerged in "the postwar broadcast era of radio and television" based on a small number of hit songs, films, and television shows.[41] In this environment, the media landscape is relatively homogeneous. He reflects on his own adolescence in the 1970s and 1980s, "We all saw the same summer blockbusters in the theater and got our news from the same papers and broadcasts" (2). However, this model of relative media scarcity and uniformity is "starting to tatter around the edges" (2):

> With unlimited supply, our assumptions about the relative roles of hits and niches were all wrong. Scarcity requires hits—if there are only a few slots on the shelves or the airwaves, it's only sensible to fill them with the titles that will sell best. And if that's all that's available, that's all people will buy.
>
> But what if there are infinite slots? Maybe hits are the wrong way to look at the business. There are, after all, a lot more non-hits than hits, and now both are equally available. What if the non-hits—from healthy niche product to outright misses—all together added up to a market as big as, if not bigger than, the hits themselves? (8)

The result is an economic model where the tail of the curve of sales—"very long relative to the head" (10)—is the focus, the "millions of niches" rather than mass markets.

This fragmentation of audience has become even more pronounced in the last decade as advertising in online media has become more sophisticated. The ads that Google places on the pages that display your search results are tuned precisely to the search that you have just done, using demographic information culled from millions of other searches and subsequent activities. The pages that you see, in other words, are precisely calibrated to your interests and history. The model of audience and public sphere that emerges from these changes in technology seems to me to break from that based on mass media from the previous century. In *The Culture Industry* Theodor Adorno rails against a repressive system that not only commodifies music but compels individuals to listen. "Regressive listening appears as soon as advertising turns into terror, as soon as nothing is left for the consciousness but to capitulate before the superior power of the advertised stuff and purchase spiritual peace by making the imposed goods literally its own thing. In regressive listening, advertising takes on a compulsory character."[42] Adorno sees little nuance in this link between advertising and "light music," equating the consumer with "the prisoner who loves his cell because he has been left nothing else to love."[43] Media here are essentially imposed from the top down by corporations, and individuals are locked within a commercialized and uniform public sphere. The contrast to the fragmented contemporary public space that Sunstein describes could not be starker. Ultimately, of course, we may say that this individuality is limited and defined by a larger corporate structure: we get our individualized ads on Google, but we cannot opt to do without ads. This individualization of on-line spaces is certainly relevant to the situation of the writer, whose address to an audience is defined by this relationship of selection.

It is this changing relationship between author and audience that Porter identifies as a feature of digital media distribution and, especially, of social media. Consider what might initially seem like a trivial example: the author–audience relationship in Twitter, in which a group of people "follows" someone, receiving the brief 140-character messages as a kind of instantaneous publication anytime that person has something to say. Although there have been experiments with Twitter as a basis for storytelling, I have in mind much more mundane and mainstream ways that authors have used this new form of communication. Writers routinely create Twitter identities in part as a form of advertising and outreach to their audiences, with one's number of followers a peculiar gage of popularity and influence. In this sense, Twitter can function as the equivalent of a reading tour. Novelist Tayari Jones makes this point in an article in *Poets and Writers:* "Twitter, for me, is a place to chat, a way to connect with my readers. Because of Twitter, people come to my readings when they realize I am in their area."[44] In this sense, Twitter is very much about a self-selecting group establishing a relationship with the author. This is a point made recently by Anne Trubek in a *New York Times* article, "Why Authors Tweet." In contrast to the traditional image of the author ("A young man, in his garret, writes furiously, crumpling up papers and throwing them on the floor, losing track of time, heedless of the public, obsessed with his own imagination. He is aloof, elusive, a man whom you know only by his writing and the portrait in his book"), Trubek describes "new conceptions of authorship" that have come with the digital age.[45] Some writers interviewed here claim to use Twitter to try out personae, to collaborate, and, most tellingly, to evaluate the effects of their writing; one author "finds hearing from readers helps her understand the influence her novels have on them." Although tweeting is far from universal among authors, it clearly represents one element of the increasingly rhetorical and performative understanding of contemporary writing.

3

It should be clear by now that I am trying to develop a notion of authorship that recognizes the way that economics and technology have changed our understanding of writing. The need to consider audience as an immediate presence throughout the writing and publishing process has become more pronounced. This broad model of authorship is reinforced by our everyday experience with computing: if we want to visit a website, we type a URL into our browser to perform a Google search and something *happens.* But I want to be careful not to suggest that the notion of authorship has disappeared entirely, or that the audience has somehow replaced the role of the writer. In fact, I would like to suggest that the tension between the performatist and the more traditional literary models for authorship are roughly parallel to the two versions of writing that I discussed in chapters 2 and 3: the pragmatic, inventive, corporate model of the researcher connected to a vast network of resources, and the more personal understanding of the writer as a creative individual working with everyday tools. The tension between these two models of writing animates our understanding of authorship and audience today.

It is helpful to pause for a moment on Henry Jenkins's influential theory of participatory culture because it represents a celebration of the power of communities of readers to transform the conditions of texts that serves as a useful contrast to my account here. Jenkins's original work on fan cultures focused on how they challenged traditional hierarchies of taste and value. Fans are "readers who appropriate popular texts and reread them in a fashion that serves different interests, as spectators who transform the experience of watching television into a rich and complex participatory culture."[46] The fans apply techniques of close reading that are normally considered only appropriate to serious literary works, and dedicate time to works that are usually considered only worthy of transitory consumption.[47] As a result, these fans become more active in the process: "Far from sycophantic, fans actively assert their mastery over the mass-produced texts which provide the raw materials for their own cultural productions and the basis for their social interactions. In the process, fans cease to be simply an audience for popular texts; instead they become active participants in the construction and circulation of textual meanings."[48]

Jenkins is no doubt right that fan cultures challenge and transform our ways of thinking about what it means to be an audience, and these cultures have certainly become more important as they have moved online. In recent work Jenkins has embraced Pierre Levy's notion of "collective intelligence" rooted in online communities, which "explores how the 'deterritorialization' of knowledge, brought about by the ability of the net and the Web to facilitate rapid many-to-many communication, might enable broader participation in decision making, new modes of citizenship and community, and the reciprocal exchange of information."[49] With the instantaneous speed of communication online, fans are a much more direct and active presence even to the producers of the show. Jenkins notes, "As the community enlarges and reaction time shortens, fandom becomes much more effective as a platform for consumer activism,"[50] and the producers of television shows in turn have learned to appeal to their fan communities directly, "often soliciting their support through networked computing."[51] Jenkins even notes that the producers of television shows like *Survivor,* which depend on audience surprise, monitored online forums trying to guess the outcome of the show, both to help market the show and to shape its reception.[52] Above I suggested that online social networking helps fracture audiences into small pockets of very specific reading predispositions. But Jenkins reminds us that this fracturing of audience is merely the flip side of the growing importance of community in reception:

> the age of media convergence enable communal, rather than individualistic, models of reception. Not every media consumer interacts within a virtual community yet; some simply discuss what they see with their friends, family members, and workmates. But few watch television in total silence and isolation. For most of us, television produces fodder for so-called water cooler conversations. And, for a growing number of people, the water cooler has gone digital.[53]

This duality is nicely exemplified by the concept of Twitter followers: authors depend on individuals to opt into this system of messages, but in turn they can gauge their popularity by the collective measure of the number of people following them.

In recognizing the growing importance of these more active online audiences, we should be careful, however, not to suggest that the notion of the author is becoming irrelevant. There are certainly times when Jenkins implies this, as in *Textual Poachers* when he observes that "fandom does not preserve a radical separation between readers and writers. Fans do not simply consume preproduced stories; they manufacture their own fanzine stories and novels, art prints, songs, videos, performances, etc."[54] While this is true of some forms of fan culture, the deference to an author is also well established even in very active online communities. Jenkins's most extensive examples of these fan communities focus on *Twin Peaks* and *Survivor,* and both of these instances retain a fundamental role for the author. In the former, Jenkins notes that David Lynch remained a constant presence whose cleverness and trickery were the basis of the community's investigation: "The fans' pleasure lay simultaneously in their mastery over the text (their ability to successfully predict the next turn of its convoluted plot) and their vulnerability to Lynch's trickery (their inability to guess what is likely to happen next). Matching wits against Lynch became the ideal test of their own intellectual rigor and creative impulses."[55] The same is certainly the case with *Survivor;* one community nicknamed executive producer Mark Burnett "Evil Pecker Mark" because of his "active role in shaping the flow of information around the series."[56] In both of these cases, the concept of an author as the figure around which the community is organized continues to exist—and in fact appears to be mythologized into a trickster figure. In other words, even in these fan communities the name of the author continues to play a key role; just as Foucault argues, it is a "function of discourse" around which study and commentary are organized.[57]

The same crucial role of the author is evident in other forms of participatory culture that initially might seem to have moved away from these traditional relationships. In a recent book on YouTube, Jean Burgess and Joshua Green observe this tension. While it is tempting to see YouTube as a kind of electronic folk culture independent of commercial interests, in fact the situation is considerably more complex: "YouTube is experienced in a range of different ways by consumer-citizens via a hybrid model of engagement with popular culture—part amateur production, part creative consumption."[58] They note the curious case of YouTube celebrity, those unlikely homemade videos that go viral and propel some everyday person into temporary fame. Although this seems revolutionary, the structure of celebrity is much the same in YouTube and traditional media. "Even when ordinary people become celebrities through their own creative efforts, there is no necessary transfer of media power: they remain within the *system* of celebrity native to, and controlled by, the mass media" (23). A good example of the continued power of authorship even in YouTube is the Lonelygirl15 hoax. Initially posted to YouTube as what appeared to be an amateur video blog by a young woman, Bree, at odds with her religious parents, the series became immensely popular (with around 300,000 views for each episode) and prompted many to speculate that the blog might in fact be the work of a professional company. It turns out that these speculations were correct, and that Bree was an actress and the blog a "filmmaking experiment by independent producers Mesh Flinders and Miles Beckett" (28).

The case of Lonelygirl15 is probably the most famous example of YouTube celebrity, and the ironies of this project nicely encapsulate the complex model of authorship and audience that I have been analyzing in this chapter. Here is a series that appeals to participatory culture outside traditional media forms, but ultimately the blog becomes more engaging and powerful once fans begin to question the authenticity of the work: "users began openly to query the authenticity of the videos in comments on YouTube, in online discussion, and in replies to blog posts" (28). The activity is much the same as what Jenkins describes surrounding *Survivor* or *Twin Peaks:* an online community energized by the need to analyze and investigate an author (Bree or, eventually, her producers) to discover the truth that is being hidden by these tricksters. Here is an audience constructed independently of traditional media structures (there is no traditional prime-time television slot that was awarded to Lonelygirl15), and yet the relationship between audience and author depends on an inequity, with the audience challenged to interpret the identity and meaning of the author's work.

### 4

This uncertain and changing relationship between artist and audience can also be seen even in writers who are thoroughly and traditionally literary in their aspirations. Let us consider two novelists who have recently gotten into very public conflicts with their fans and readers in the United States: Jonathan Franzen and J. K. Rowling. Although a well-known and critically praised novelist, Franzen is probably most famous for his very public fight with Oprah Winfrey over his novel *The Corrections.* Winfrey had scheduled the novel to be discussed on her television program as part of the Oprah Book Club in the fall of 2001. Franzen participated in some preliminary interviews with Winfrey in preparation for the show, but he expressed misgivings about his appearance—first to the *Oregonian* and then on NPR's *Fresh Air.* In the latter interview, he explains his concerns by noting that traditionally the book club chose female authors:

> So much of reading is sustained in this country, I think, by the fact that women read while men are off golfing or watching football on TV or playing with their flight simulator . . . I continue to believe that, and now, I'm actually at the point with this book that I worry . . . I had some hope of actually reaching a male audience, and I've heard more than one reader in signing lines now in book stores that said, "If I hadn't heard you, I would have been put off by the fact that it is an Oprah pick. I figure those books are for women and I would never touch it." Those are male readers speaking. So, I'm a little confused about the whole thing now.[59]

In response to these comments, Winfrey famously rescinded her invitation to appear on the show; the "feud" between them was only ended when Franzen appeared on the show in 2010 to discuss his novel *Freedom.* What is striking about the way that Franzen handles this matter is the way that he vacillates between different definitions of the vocation of the writer. In the NPR interview, he invokes the traditional idea that the novelist is disconnected from the immediate needs of the audience, that the novel demands that the reader step outside his or her immediate moment to approach it. Speaking of "the fiction writer's responsibilities," he defines them as to "remind people of darkness; remind yourself of darkness; remind yourself that there's a world out there that is unhappy; remind yourself that death exists. And then, in dark times, try to remember the comedy and the ridiculousness of things." Franzen is perhaps some distance from the classic modernist distain for the audience,[60] but this passage seems to hold the audience's immediate desires at a distance. But his views about his appearance on Oprah's Book Club also reflect quite the opposite—a concern for how his readers will respond. In particular, Franzen expresses a somewhat surprising sense of responsibility for shaping the context for reading in the United States. He feels an obligation to create a space in which men feel comfortable engaging in an activity that is seen primarily as a female hobby. Franzen, then, incompletely embraces the rhetorical, performative model of author–audience relationship that we see in contemporary U.S. culture.

This tension between a traditional model of authorship and the performative one—which I have suggested is typical of digital culture—is even more clear in the essays that make up Franzen's essay collection *How to Be Alone*. Paul Dawson has argued that Franzen's writing in this collection and in his fiction, like *The Corrections*, form "a broader project to reassert the authority of the novel in contemporary culture."[61] Franzen's 2002 introduction to this essay collection, which includes writing going back to 1996, argues for a narrative arc that can be seen across the various attitudes toward writing: "I intend this book, in part, as a record of a movement away from an angry and frightened isolation toward an acceptance—even a celebration—of being a reader and a writer."[62] Franzen is clearly torn here between two models of writing. In one model, writer and reader are isolated, and integrating any concern for social issues remains fundamentally difficult (58). Franzen is quite explicit is describing this isolation: "the essence of fiction is solitary work: the work of writing, the work of reading" (66). In other places, however, Franzen reflects a rhetorical approach to writing. He embraces an academic study showing that the concept of a "general audience" is a myth, even though he notes that "to the extent that novelists think about audience at all, we like to imagine a 'general audience'" (75). In this regard, Franzen accepts the changing models of audience that have been implied by Porter, Sunstein, and Anderson. In fact, his late essay

"Mr. Difficult" addresses the Oprah controversy and offers two competing models of authorship:

> It turns out that I subscribe to two wildly different models of how fiction relates to its audience. In one model, which was championed by Flaubert, the best novels are great works of art, the people who manage to write them deserve extraordinary credit, and if the average reader rejects the work it's because the average reader is a philistine. . . . We can call this the Status model. It invites a discourse of genius and art-historical importance.
>
> In the opposing model, a novel represents a compact between the writer and the reader, with the writer providing words out of which the reader creates a pleasurable experience. Writing thus entails a balancing of self-expression and communication within a group. (239–40)

We saw exactly this conflict in the controversy over Franzen's appearance on Oprah. He is torn between a traditional image of the distant modernist author and a rhetorical understanding of the writer speaking directly to an audience.

A parallel example is J. K. Rowling, whose place within British and U.S. culture is likewise curiously split between a traditional and performative model of the writer. News coverage of the Harry Potter book series vacillates just as wildly as Franzen does in his NPR interview. Typical is a 2007 article in the *Christian Science Monitor,* which reports on a 2006 study of how the book series has affected kids' attitudes toward reading. The study suggested positive changes not only in reading habits but in the quality of schoolwork in general. Here we see much the same concern for audience that Franzen expressed. In fact, the article includes an inset, "Harry Potter by the Numbers," which lists publication facts showing the popularity of the series. It is easy to imagine the distain with which a modernist like Faulkner would view this fetishized interest in the number of books sold. But, like Franzen, the *Christian Science Monitor* frames these issues of audience by appealing to traditional literary values at the outset of the story: "The seventh and last Harry Potter book will be released in July. Millions of Potter fans won't have another book to look forward to after that. But Harry's effect on many young people—and their love of reading—may be magical enough to last a lifetime."[63] Here a concern for sales and popularity is balanced against a traditional and reassuring interest in the power of reading. News stories move between asserting the intellectual and cultural value of the series as a spark in children's reading to analyzing the commercial implications for the publishing industry. This is an explicit if somewhat simple model of performatism in writing: Rowling is evaluated as a writer in large part by the effects that she has on her readers, and those effects are measured by the easily consumable facts about the number of books sold and the amount of money she has earned.

And, like Franzen, Rowling has faced her own conflicts with the larger media environment because of this ambiguous relationship to her audience. In 2007 Warner Brothers and Rowling brought a suit against RDR Books, who intended to publish a print version of *The Harry Potter Lexicon,* which originally had been developed as a free online guide to the Harry Potter world.[64] Rowling herself had spoken positively about the guide (saying that she had used it herself to check some details from the previous books while writing), and online resources like this formed part of the connection to the audience that made the series so popular. In turn, that sort of online popularity was one of the ways that critics would demonstrate Rowling's influence as an author. The basis for Warner Brothers/Rowling's complaint was twofold: that the publication of the book would hurt the proceeds of the official encyclopedia that Rowling herself intended to write, and that the lexicon drew too much material wholesale from the books themselves. The September 2008 ruling in the U.S. district court was in favor of Warner Brothers and Rowling, although the decision was far from unequivocal. The ruling notes that "the Lexicon . . . contains at least a troubling amount of direct quotation or close paraphrasing of Rowling's original language," but it also asserted that the book fit within "the narrow genre of non-fiction reference guides to fictional works." In the end, the tendency for the lexicon to follow Rowling's style too closely was the basis for the infringement decision. But Warner Brothers and Rowling had their stronger claim to "their right to control the production of derivative works" rejected because the lexicon gave those facts a new purpose and is thus transformative. Especially problematic is Rowling's emotional appeal during the trial to the reference work's "theft" of her efforts. Such comments appear to support RDR's claim that Rowling's understanding of her ownership of these books "would dramatically extend the reach of copyright protection, and eliminate an entire genre of literary supplements."[65]

Rowling's ambivalent relationship to the fan community that she profited from becomes more coherent when read against Franzen's conflicted relationship to Oprah's Book Club. Both seem to be keenly aware of their influence on an audience, and to see themselves in part as performing to bring that audience into existence. Both, however, also hold to traditional literary values at odds with these performative effects: the distance of book and audience in Franzen's case, and the ownership of character by author in Rowling's. Both writers have taken on very public roles in negotiating the emergence of this performative model. Their evident discomfort and conflict with their audiences is a testament to its liminal nature.


## 5

The examples of Franzen and Rowling suggest that writing occupies a conflicted place within contemporary U.S. culture, which seems dependent on the performative model of the author creating an audience and at the same time hesitant to relinquish older models of the novelist as creating an aesthetic object that users must find their way to. As we have seen over and over again, writing itself supplies a crucial metaphor for contemporary culture, so it is no surprise that the novelist feels these changes and pressures with particular sensitivity. We saw this tension in chapters 2 and 3: writing is both a quality of the contemporary corporate workplace and a form of individual creative activity. It is clear that writing not only can mean both but carries both connotations in all cultural forms—everything from the "My Documents" folder on your desktop to the way that we think about Franzen's argument with Oprah. Writing is able to bridge literary and computing uses without resolving the differences between these contexts. In many ways Apple's decision to name its new device an iPad is very much like the *Christian Science Monitor*'s praise of Rowling's novels—an invocation of writing and its traditional virtues that also contains elements undercutting this literary context.

Let us briefly turn to two instances where writing appears as a quite literal bridge between the worlds of literature and computing. Consider for a moment the representation of writing in Rowling's books. Ironically, very few characters *read* in the Harry Potter novels in the sense that I have been discussing in the previous section. Rowling's heroine Hermione Granger is certainly a bookworm, but she appears to read exclusively textbooks and works of history; the running joke about her studiousness is that her spare time is spent reading *Hogwarts: A History,* a book about the school she is attending. The only writing in the series that is intended to be entertaining is the yellow journalism of the unethical journalist Rita Skeeter, and even here the writing is fundamentally historical and political in nature. There are no writers or readers of "useless" fictional literature in the Harry Potter series, except for those stories produced explicitly for children, such as fairy tales. We suspect that Harry Potter would never spend his time reading *Harry Potter.*

That does not, however, mean that no one writes imaginatively in the novels. A key example of writing in the series is a diary produced by Rowling's villain Voldemort as a teenager. Initially the book appears to be blank, but once the characters write in it they discover that the book is quite literally interactive:

> Harry sat on his four-poster and flicked through the blank pages, not one of which had a trace of scarlet ink on it. Then he pulled a new bottle out of his bedside cabinet, dipped his quill into it, and dropped a blot onto the first page of the diary
>
> The ink shone brightly on the paper for a second and then, as though it was being sucked into the page, vanished. Excited, Harry loaded up his quill a second time and wrote, "My name is Harry Potter."
>
> The words shone momentarily on the page and they, too, sank without a trace. Then, at last, something happened.
>
> Oozing back out of the page, in his very own ink, came words Harry had never written.
>
> *"Hello Harry Potter. My name is Tom Riddle. How did you come by my diary?"*[66]

This is a great example of the kind of performative writing that produces an ad hoc space for the audience that I have been demonstrating throughout this chapter. The Riddle diary is not a vehicle for self-expression but rather a stage constructed by its author through which the audience is manipulated. In turn, that space is made powerful by being addressed to a willing audience. Riddle victimizes and controls the young girl Ginny Weasley through this diary precisely because she is willing to become his audience: "I suppose the real reason Ginny Weasley's like this is because she opened her heart and spilled all her secrets to an invisible stranger" (309). In the end, Riddle was "patient. I wrote back. I was sympathetic, I was kind. Ginny simply *loved* me" (309). It is difficult to imagine a more concise example of the kind of performative writing that defines contemporary culture.

The links between this image of writing and the performative nature of the computer are obvious. Harry's interaction with the book is essentially a command-line interface: he writes a sentence, and the book writes back a response. It is telling that this image of the book as computer is coupled to a visionary space; the book literally creates a virtual reality that Harry experiences as the words of the diary fall away. We can see this as a way of articulating the logic of programming in a nontechnical way. We know that computing is a kind of writing, but we also know that computing creates a new virtual environment for us—either metaphorically in the operating system desktop or more literally in the three-dimensional space we occupy in a video game. Rowling's diarist Riddle is essentially the programmer-as-writer

that I have been describing throughout this book. If this seems like an unlikely connection between writing and programming, we see exactly this
same tenuous use of the literary-computing link in the influential video
game series *Myst*. This series of games focuses on the central character,
Atrus, who has a magical power to create new worlds. Exactly how he does
this is not clear in the games, but visually the action seems to be much the
same thing that Harry Potter does—writing longhand in a paper book. In
the games players use these books to travel between worlds, and access to
the books is a central gating mechanism that controls progression through
the game. We access these books in the game much like Harry accesses the
visionary space of Riddle's diary: by touching the page of the book and being
swept into its world. As the series develops, the tensions in this kind of invented world and their creator increasingly come to dominate the story line.
The third game in the series, *Myst: Exile,* concerns the resentment of one of
these created worlds' inhabitants, whose home has been destroyed by Atrus's
sons.[67]

Initially this parallel might seem unlikely—a weird coincidence of two
unrelated narratives—but *Myst* and the Harry Potter series actually occupy similar cultural spaces. Rowling's books are held up as a kind of literary
bulwark against other encroaching media—especially video games and
television—even though the books have spawned a cross-media empire. The
same is the case with *Myst,* whose CD-ROM storage format allowed the
game to present much more realistic (albeit static) images of its fictional
worlds. The creators of the game, Rand and Robyn Miller, describe themselves as authors rather than programmers or directors, and describe the
game in its accompanying manual using literary terms: "You are about to
be drawn into an amazing alternative reality. The entire game was designed
from the ground up to draw you in with little or no extraneous distractions
on the screen to interfere with the feeling of being there. Myst is not linear,
it's not flat, it's not shallow. This is the most depth, detail and reality you've
ever experienced in a game."[68] It is clear in this passage that playing *Myst* is
supposed to be a literary experience. Both series, then, ruminate on the place
of writing in contemporary computing culture, and both offer remarkably
similar answers: writing is the means by which an author creates a virtual
space for a receptive (and specific) audience and steers that audience through
a series of experiences. Just as important, writing accomplishes this in a
schizophrenic way by appealing both to the performative work in an institutional context (the game is a space produced commercially and based
on at the time cutting-edge photorealistic technology) and literary self-
reflection and immersion.

These two unlikely examples of performative writing are interestingly anachronistic in treating writing as a matter of hand penmanship. Writing in both of the texts is an example of what Charles Acland calls *residual media,* forms of communication that are explicitly nostalgic and obsolete.[69] Rowling's series adopts this kind of anachronism routinely as part of its charm; the characters of the magical world of the book can do amazing things impossible in the nonmagical world but depend on technologies—like handwriting, parchment, and quills—based in the England of hundreds of years earlier. Is there a reason that Harry Potter cannot take notes with a ballpoint pen? The same is certainly true of the *Myst* series, whose gameplay has been frequently described as "steampunk" for its use of Victorian-era mechanical details and design. For all that the world appears to come into existence through magic in these games, navigating the space means pushing levers, toying with devices, and riding on cable cars that could have easily been manufactured in the 1920s. The exaggeratedly traditional image of writing here does much the same work as the skeuomorphism that I noted at the end of chapter 5: it offers a model that suppresses the anxiety and tensions in the changing landscape for contemporary creative activity. Harry's quill is like Gibson's cyberspace deck or Bush's memex: a familiar physical device that nonetheless allows him to connect to an abstract, immaterial, and networked space.

# Conclusion

*Invention, Creativity, and the*
*Teaching of Writing*

I hope that I have shown in this book that writing is a crucial model for our thinking about computing culture broadly, and especially for helping us understand the nature of our individual and creative activities in relationship to a larger professional and corporate context. I have shown that appeals to writing depend on two very different models: the professional work of the researcher drawing on shared materials for pragmatic purposes and the literary writer creating individually using mundane tools located within everyday life. It is this mundane quality of writing that makes it a particularly powerful model for thinking about our relationship to computers and the activities that they support. At the outset of this book I argued that the tensions within our understanding of writing were particularly relevant and visible in the way that we teach writing. In chapter 2 we saw that the way that students struggle with online resources and the patchwriting strategies that they adopt in response could both be seen as reflecting the problems of thinking about their own work in the archive. Is the work of writing a paper creative or inventive? Is their "trail" through the archive merely an experience of information already there, or have they created something new when they collect, summarize, and respond to these research materials? The common model of writing as a conversation, I argued, provides student writers with little guidance on these crucial topics.

By way of conclusion, I would like to push this observation further and argue that the teaching of writing must be in part about the investigation of our understanding of writing as a cultural act intimately connected, but not reducible, to work and profession. When writing teachers talk about "becoming a writer" it is often with an evangelical air of helping students see themselves as capable of an activity that may intimidate them. The ubiquitous focus on writing as a process that emerged in the U.S. academy in the late 1960s emphasizes the need to see writing as an ongoing activity, and to adopt personal strategies that will help the writer be effective. Viewed in this context, the writing classroom must help the student to see him- or herself as a writer capable of responding to a wide variety of rhetorical situations, with habits that are flexible and effective both in the university and in life after school.[1] Becoming a writer, in this regard, means becoming capable of using writing in a wide variety of professional, personal, and civic contexts.[2] As a 2007 CCCC position statement asserts, "To restrict students' engagement with writing to only academic contexts and forms is to risk narrowing what we as a nation can remember, understand, and create. As the world grows smaller, we will live by words as never before, and it will take many words framed in many ways to transform that closeness into the mutuality needed to pursue peace and prosperity for our generation and those to come."[3]

In this book I have shown, however, that writing carries with it much broader and often contradictory implications that we must begin to address in the composition classroom. To be a writer is in part to become a knowledge worker. When we talk about writing in the classroom, we often exhort our students to think about their real-world usage: the letter to the editor, the professional memo sent out to coworkers, the report hoping to win a business contract. We rarely ask students to imagine themselves sitting in a cubicle all day, interacting with coworkers though e-mail. Nor do we usually talk with students about the blurring of the line between work and leisure that Liu describes—even though the ubiquity of writing (especially through e-mail and social media) is one of the ways in which our work and private lives mix. Normally when we talk about the ubiquity of writing it is a way to emphasize its importance, and to help students care about what might seem like a boring academic subject. Liu's cultural critique and the way that it informs my analysis of computing culture suggest that writing can become a site where we talk about what it means to work today.

Likewise, the composition classroom rarely investigates the difference between invention and creativity, or helps students to develop a nuanced understanding of how work is owned beyond exhortations against plagiarism. Kenneth Goldsmith describes a class that he teaches at the University of Pennsylvania called "uncreative writing": "In it, students are penalized for showing any shred of originality and creativity. Instead, they are rewarded for plagiarism, identity theft, repurposing papers, patchwriting, sampling, plundering, and stealing. Not surprisingly, they thrive. Suddenly, what they have surreptitiously become expert at is brought out into the open and explored in a safe environment, reframed in terms of responsibility instead of recklessness."[4] Although Goldsmith's method is designed to be intentionally provocative, the issue that he raises is central to writing in the age of computing: how can we develop a more nuanced understanding of the new amid so much material available for use? Is *new* even the best term for what students are expected to produce?

Finally, we should recognize that writing is not merely at skill in itself, or only a part of other professions in a broader "writing across the curriculum" initiative—as valuable as such programs can be. In addition, writing is a component of how we think about a host of professions themselves. If programmers think of themselves as writers, how can we begin to address those models when we teach first-year composition? Can we begin to frame the nature of work and creativity, as well as the tools for creating something, in terms sufficiently broad that those lessons carry over from the writing to the programming class? Can we begin to model traditional rhetorical techniques like "invention" in a way that transcends the writing situation and becomes a framework for making new things more broadly, or to conceptualize process and revision in a way that applies beyond traditional composition? Can we provide students with tools for thinking about the ownership of ideas and writing—be it a letter, a report, or a snippet of code? As writing becomes the model for a host of activities that are central to the culture of information, the writing classroom can become a place where we think about the nature of work, tools, habits, and creativity.

# Acknowledgments

Many people have helped me to think through this project, and have provided advice and feedback. The earliest section on e-book libraries was presented at the first ASAP conference, and a conversation with Nick Montfort there was very helpful. Later the *Electronic Book Review*'s editors and readers further helped me refine the discussion. Many thanks as well to Edward Maloney and Kelly Marsh for their feedback on a talk about narrative and patents at the 2012 International Narrative Conference, which provided some of the material for chapter 4.

At Purdue Calumet discussions with Lizbeth Bryant and Karen Bishop-Morris have been invaluable in thinking through the implications of this project for the teaching of composition. In particular, they brought Rebecca Moore Howard's work on patchwriting to my attention, which is essential to chapter 2, and provided some background on theories of professional writing that informs the project as a whole. Thanks as well to the philosophy faculty who allowed me to try out some of these ideas at one of their Philosophy Club events. As always, the Interlibrary Loan office staff have been invaluable, especially Eloise Gonzalez, Tammy Guerrero, and Dorothy Starks.

My thanks as well to the readers at the University of Minnesota Press, whose careful reading of this manuscript prompted a reorganization that significantly sharpened the argument. Doug Armato was essential in helping me work through that reorganization, and in particular to reshape the preface and initial framing.

This project was initially composed between 2009 and 2013, and my experience of that time was defined in part by a series of technology podcasts that I listened to alongside my son, Sam. In particular a series of podcasts on technology and software development produced by the 5 by 5 Network (especially John Gruber, Dan Benjamin, John Siracusa, and Marco Arment) provided the background dialogue that helped shape my thinking about our day-to-day experiences of computers and programming. Although all of those podcasts have now ended and their hosts have gone on to other projects, the general context provided was essential for my thinking about the work of programming and how it relates to broader cultural conditions and debates. My thanks to Sam for sharing these with me.

Special thanks to my father, Tom, who attended his first academic conference to hear my talk on *The Social Network*.

# Notes

*Preface*

1. Vannevar Bush, "As We May Think," in *From Memex to Hypertext: Vannevar Bush and the Mind's Machine,* ed. James M. Nyce and Paul Kahn (Boston: Academic Press, 1991), 85–107; J. C. R. Licklider, *Libraries of the Future* (Cambridge, Mass.: MIT Press, 1965); Alan C. Kay, "A Personal Computer for Children of All Ages" (paper presented at the ACM National Conference, Boston, 1972), http://www.mprove.de/diplom/gui/Kay 72a.pdf; Theodor Nelson, *Computer Lib/Dream Machines* (Redmond, Wash.: Tempus Books, 1987).

2. Jay David Bolter, *Writing Space: The Computer, Hypertext, and the History of Writing* (Hinsdale, N.J.: Lawrence Erlbaum Associates, 1991); Michael Joyce, *Of Two Minds: Hypertext Pedagogy and Poetics* (Ann Arbor: University of Michigan Press, 1995); Janet H. Murray, *Hamlet on the Holodeck: The Future of Narrative in Cyberspace* (Cambridge, Mass.: MIT Press, 1997).

3. Sherry Turkle, *Life on the Screen: Identity in the Age of the Internet* (New York: Simon and Schuster, 1995).

4. Espen J. Aarseth, *Cybertext: Perspectives on Ergodic Literature* (Baltimore, Md.: Johns Hopkins University Press, 1997), 13–14.

5. Markku Eskelinen, "Towards Computer Game Studies," in *First Person: New Media as Story, Performance, and Game,* ed. Noah Wardrip-Fruin and Pat Harrigan (Cambridge, Mass.: MIT Press, 2004), 36.

6. Lev Manovich, *The Language of New Media* (Cambridge, Mass.: MIT Press, 2001), 49.

7. Nick Montfort and Ian Bogost, *Racing the Beam: The Atari Video Computer System* (Cambridge, Mass.: MIT Press, 2009), viii.

8. Lev Manovich, *Software Takes Command* (New York: Bloomsbury, 2013).

9. Matthew G. Kirschenbaum, *Mechanisms: New Media and the Forensic Imagination* (Cambridge, Mass.: MIT Press, 2008), xiii.

10. See Kevin Nguyen's discussion of the recently released applications Hemingway and Writer Pro: "Basically, Hemingway is a writing tool with a syntax highlighter, which identifies word types and sets them in different colors. This is a long-standing feature in

text editors built for coding; it makes programming languages more readable and errors easier to identify" ("Death and Syntaxes," *Bygone Bureau,* February 17, 2014, http://bygonebureau.com/2014/02/17/death-and-syntaxes/).

11. For a good overview, see Patrik Svensson's "Beyond the Big Tent," in *Debates in the Digital Humanities,* ed. Matthew K. Gold (Minneapolis: University of Minnesota Press, 2012), 36–49.

*1. My Documents*

1. Vannevar Bush, "As We May Think," in *From Memex to Hypertext: Vannevar Bush and the Mind's Machine,* ed. James M. Nyce and Paul Kahn (Boston: Academic Press, 1991), 102.

2. Michael Joyce, *Of Two Minds: Hypertext Pedagogy and Poetics* (Ann Arbor: University of Michigan Press, 1995), 22.

3. Bush, "As We May Think," 88–89.

4. G. Pascal Zachary, *Endless Frontier: Vannevar Bush and the American Century* (Cambridge, Mass.: MIT Press, 1999), 224.

5. Paul E. Ceruzzi, *A History of Modern Computing,* 2nd ed. (Cambridge, Mass.: MIT Press, 2003), 15.

6. David Golumbia, *The Cultural Logic of Computation* (Cambridge, Mass.: Harvard University Press, 2009).

7. Doreen Starke-Meyerring, Anthony Paré, Natasha Artemeva, Miriam Horne, and Larissa Yousoubova, eds., *Writing in Knowledge Societies* (Anderson, S.C.: Parlor Press, 2011).

8. Patrick Dias et al., "Preface," in *Worlds Apart: Acting and Writing in Academic and Workplace Contexts,* ed. Patrick Dias, Aviva Freedman, Peter Medway, and Anthony Paré (Mahwah, N.J.: Lawrence Erlbaum Associates, 1999), xi.

9. Bruno Latour, *Science in Action: How to Follow Scientists and Engineers through Society* (Cambridge, Mass.: Harvard University Press, 1987), 59.

10. Alan C. Kay, "A Personal Computer for Children of All Ages" (paper presented at the ACM National Conference, Boston, 1972), http://www.mprove.de/diplom/gui/Kay 72a.pdf.

11. Ibid.

12. Theodor Nelson, *Computer Lib/Dream Machines* (Redmond, Wash.: Tempus Books, 1987), 50.

13. For a good discussion of this quotation and its place within the development of the Macintosh, see Andy Hertzfeld's book of Apple folklore, *Revolution in the Valley: The Insanely Great Story of How the Mac Was Made* (Sebastopol, Calif.: O'Reilly, 2005), 36–37.

14. J. C. R. Licklider, *Libraries of the Future* (Cambridge, Mass.: MIT Press, 1965), xii.

15. This difference between data and documents is one much up for debate today. Until the last few years, there has been a general belief that more and more of our knowledge was moving onto the Web, and that eventually our default form of information would be the web page. The idea that eventually all our computing would merely involve accessing websites is the basis for Google's Chrome operating system, which is little more than a mechanism for launching a web browser. The popularity of stand-alone applications in Apple's iOS has offered a competing model, in which data reside in individual applications. Google's founder Sergey Brin recently called these data "lost" because they are not available to web-based search engines like Google: "There's a lot to be lost. . . . For example, all the information in apps—that data is not crawlable by web crawlers. You can't search it" ("Web Freedom Faces Greatest Threat Ever, Warns Google's Sergey

Brin," *Guardian,* April 15, 2012, http://www.guardian.co.uk/technology/2012/apr/15/web-freedom-threat-google-brin.).

16. Bush, "As We May Think," 104.

17. Paul Kahn and James M. Nyce, "The Idea of a Machine: The Later Memex Essays," in *From Memex to Hypertext: Vannevar Bush and the Mind's Machine,* ed. James M. Nyce and Paul Kahn (Boston: Academic Press, 1991), 137.

18. Tim Oren, "Memex: Getting Back on the Trail," in *From Memex to Hypertext: Vannevar Bush and the Mind's Machine,* ed. James M. Nyce and Paul Kahn (Boston: Academic Press, 1991), 319.

19. Vannevar Bush, "Memex II," in *From Memex to Hypertext: Vannevar Bush and the Mind's Machine,* ed. James M. Nyce and Paul Kahn (Boston: Academic Press, 1991), 171.

20. Ibid., 183.

21. Theodor H. Nelson, "As We Will Think," in *From Memex to Hypertext: Vannevar Bush and the Mind's Machine,* ed. James M. Nyce and Paul Kahn (Boston: Academic Press, 1991), 257.

22. Bush, "Memex II," 172–73.

23. George Steiner, *Grammars of Creation: Originating in the Gifford Lectures for 1990* (New Haven, Conn.: Yale University Press, 2001), 17, 35.

24. Vilém Flusser, *Does Writing Have a Future?,* trans. Nancy Ann Roth (Minneapolis: University of Minnesota Press, 2011), 6.

25. Marjorie Perloff, *Unoriginal Genius: Poetry by Other Means in the New Century* (Chicago: University of Chicago Press, 2010), 17.

26. Kahn and Nyce, "Idea of a Machine," 120.

27. Bush, "As We May Think," 94.

28. Michael Heim, *Electric Language: A Philosophical Study of Word Processing* (New Haven, Conn.: Yale University Press, 1987), 192, 208.

29. Bush, "As We May Think," 94–95.

30. Jonathan Franzen, *How to Be Alone: Essays* (New York: Picador, 2002), 66.

31. Flo Conway and Jim Siegelman, *Dark Hero of the Information Age: In Search of Norbert Wiener, the Father of Cybernetics* (New York: Basic Books, 2005), 108.

32. *Dr. Strangelove or: How I Learned to Stop Worrying and Love the Bomb,* directed by Stanley Kubrick (1964; Culver City, Calif.: Sony Pictures, 2001), DVD.

33. Matthew G. Kirschenbaum, *Mechanisms: New Media and the Forensic Imagination* (Cambridge, Mass.: MIT Press, 2008), 4–5.

34. Georges Ifrah, *The Universal History of Computing: From the Abacus to the Quantum Computer,* trans. E. F. Harding (New York: Wiley, 2001), 180.

35. Ceruzzi, *History of Modern Computing,* 16.

36. Ibid., 30.

37. Edmund Callis Berkeley, *Giant Brains or Machines That Think* (New York: Science Editions, 1961).

38. Remington Rand, "Introduction to Computers," Bitsavers.org, http://www.bitsavers.org/pdf/univac/univacl/IntroToComputers_ECD-13.pdf.

39. Eckert-Mauchly Computer Corp., "Preliminary Description of the UNIVAC," February 1956, http://archive.org/details/bitsavers_univacuniviptionoftheUNIVAC_3051262.

40. For a more general introduction to the theory of metaphor based on "conceptual blending," see Gilles Fauconnier and Mark Turner, *The Way We Think: Conceptual Blending and the Mind's Hidden Complexities* (New York: Basic, 2002). See especially page 18 for a general definition and pages 22–24 for the application specifically to the computer.

41. Manuel Imaz and David Benyon, *Designing with Blends: Conceptual Foundations of Human-Computer Interaction and Software Engineering* (Cambridge, Mass.: MIT Press, 2007), 62–63.

42. Jacob Rabinow, "Magnetic Memory Device," U.S. Patent 2,690,913, filed March 14, 1951, issued October 5, 1954.

43. Kirschenbaum, *Mechanisms*, 80–81.

44. Robert S. Casey and James W. Perry, *Punched Cards and Their Applications to Science and Industry* (New York: Reinhold, 1951), 128.

45. This is not to say that the metaphorical use of *document* and *page* hadn't appeared before. See, for example, the use of the term *document* to refer to a "section of input information" in the Atlas operating system discussed by Tom Kilburn, R. Bruce Payne, and David J. Howarth, "The Atlas Supervisor," in *Classic Operating Systems: From Batch Processing to Distributed Systems,* ed. Per Brinch Hansen (New York: Springer, 2001), 71.

46. David C. Smith, Charles Irby, Ralph Kimball, and Eric Harslem, "The Star User Interface: An Overview," in *Classic Operating Systems: From Batch Processing to Distributed Systems,* ed. Per Brinch Hansen (New York: Springer, 2001), 468.

47. Ibid., 469.

48. Michael K. Buckland, "What Is a 'Document'?" *Journal of the American Society for Information Science* 48, no. 9 (1997): 804.

49. Ibid., 805.

50. Kirschenbaum, *Mechanisms,* 93.

51. In *Software Takes Command* (New York: Bloomsbury, 2013), Lev Manovich notes an additional complexity, that most messages and recordings encountered on the computer are shaped by the particular software and environment in which they are rendered: "Instead of fixed documents that could be analyzed by examining their structure and content . . . we now interact with dynamic 'software performances'" (33).

52. Thomas Haigh, "Technology's Other Storytellers: Science Fiction as History of Technology," in *Science Fiction and Computing: Essays on Interlinked Domains,* ed. David L. Ferro and Eric G. Swedin (Jefferson, N.C.: McFarland, 2011), 20.

53. Patricia S. Warrick, *The Cybernetic Imagination in Science Fiction* (Cambridge, Mass.: MIT Press, 1980), xvi.

54. Ibid., 10, 62.

55. Ibid., 18.

56. Minsoo Kang, *Sublime Dreams of Living Machine: The Automaton in the European Imagination* (Cambridge, Mass.: Harvard University Press, 2011), 36.

57. Isaac Asimov, "Introduction: Robots, Computers, and Fear," in *Machines That Think: The Best Science Fiction Stories about Robots and Computers,* ed. Isaac Asimov, Patricia S. Warrick, and Martin H. Greenberg (New York: Holt, Rinehart, and Winston, 1984), 4.

58. Murray Leinster, "A Logic Named Joe," in *The Best of Murray Leinster,* ed. J. J. Pierce (New York: Ballantine, 1978), 220.

59. Ibid., 221.

60. Jef Raskin is usually credited with the idea of the computer as an appliance. He was the creator of the Macintosh project at Apple before being forced out by Steve Jobs, and he went on to found Information Appliance Inc. For an account of Raskin's role in the Macintosh, see Hertzfeld, *Revolution in the Valley,* 272–74, and Walter Isaacson, *Steve Jobs* (New York: Simon and Schuster, 2011), 108–13. The argument for seeing the computer as an appliance is articulated in Raskin's 1979 essay "Computers by the Millions,"

*SIGPC Newsletter* 5, no. 2 (1982), http://www.digibarn.com/friends/jef-raskin/writings/millions.html.

61. In an interview with Larry McCaffery in the *Mississippi Review*, Gibson remarks, "When I'm writing about technology, I'm writing about how technology has *already* affected our lives. I don't see myself as extrapolating in the way I was taught an SF writer should" (Larry McCaffery, "An Interview with William Gibson," *Mississippi Review* 47, no. 48 [1988]: 228). George Slusser generalizes: "cyberpunks claim to be the first generation of SF writers to live in an SF world" ("Introduction: Fiction as Information," in *Fiction 2000: Cyberpunk and the Future of Narrative*, ed. George Slusser and Tom Shippey [Athens: University of Georgia Press, 1992], 3).

62. William Gibson, *Neuromancer* (New York: Ace, 1984), 52.

63. Ibid., 46.

64. Kay, "A Personal Computer," 6.

65. Ibid., 2.

66. Manovich, *Software Takes Command,* 101.

67. The name "Canvas" was suggested in the run-up to the iPad launch by Cabel Sasser and discussed briefly by Apple commentator John Gruber ("Canvas?" *Daring Fireball,* January 22, 2010, http://daringfireball.net/linked/2010/01/22/canvas).

68. Matthew Kirschenbaum, "What Is Digital Humanities and What's It Doing in English Departments?," in *Debates in the Digital Humanities,* ed. Matthew K. Gold (Minneapolis: University of Minnesota Press, 2012), 8–9.

*2. Writing, Work, and Profession*

1. Christina Haas, *Writing Technology: Studies on the Materiality of Literacy* (Mahwah, N.J.: Lawrence Erlbaum Associates, 1996), 3.

2. Kenneth Goldsmith, *Uncreative Writing: Managing Language in the Digital Age* (New York: Columbia University Press, 2011), 3.

3. Jacques Derrida, *Of Grammatology,* trans. Gayatri Chakravorty Spivak (Baltimore, Md.: Johns Hopkins University Press, 1976), 24.

4. Ibid., 65.

5. Roland Barthes, *S/Z,* trans. Richard Miller (New York: Hill and Wang, 1970), 20.

6. John M. Ellis, *Against Deconstruction* (Princeton, N.J.: Princeton University Press, 1989), 115. Such dismissals of the role of the reader in interpretation are at least somewhat ironic, since New Criticism often used a similar language of movement. In *The Verbal Icon: Studies in the Meaning of Poetry* (Lexington: University Press of Kentucky, 1954), W. K. Wimsatt invokes the metaphor of interpretation as a path when he responds to the question "Wohin der Weg?" with "Kein Weg! Ins Unbetretene" (12). In *The Well Wrought Urn: Studies in the Structure of Poetry* (New York: Harcourt Brace Jovanovich, 1947), Cleanth Brooks likewise embraces the metaphor of the poet as explorer (74) and often describes the reader as traveling the same path as the poet, and being "prepared" for poetic elements (165).

7. Jacques Derrida, *Edmund Husserl's Origin of Geometry: An Introduction,* trans. John P. Leavey Jr. (Lincoln: University of Nebraska Press, 1989); Jacques Derrida, "*Ousia* and *Grammē:* A Note on a Note from *Being and Time,*" in *Margins of Philosophy,* trans. Alan Bass (Chicago: University of Chicago Press, 1982), 29–67.

8. Theodor H. Nelson, "As We Will Think," in *From Memex to Hypertext: Vannevar Bush and the Mind's Machine,* ed. James M. Nyce and Paul Kahn (Boston: Academic Press, 1991), 252.

9. Ibid., 254.

10. George P. Landow, *Hypertext 2.0: The Convergence of Contemporary Critical Theory and Technology* (Baltimore, Md.: Johns Hopkins University Press, 1997).

11. G. Pascal Zachary, *Endless Frontier: Vannevar Bush and the American Century* (Cambridge, Mass.: MIT Press, 1999), 40.

12. Ibid., 95.

13. Norbert Wiener, *The Human Use of Human Beings: Cybernetics and Society* (Garden City, N.Y.: Doubleday Anchor, [1950] 1954), 16.

14. Ibid., 17.

15. Ibid., 51–52.

16. Flo Conway and Jim Siegelman, *Dark Hero of the Information Age: In Search of Norbert Wiener, the Father of Cybernetics* (New York: Basic Books, 2005), 75.

17. Quoted in ibid., 240.

18. Herbert Marcuse, *One-Dimensional Man: Studies in the Ideology of Advanced Industrial Society* (Boston: Beacon Press, 1964), x.

19. Harold Perkin, *The Rise of Professional Society: England since 1880* (London: Routledge, 1989), 2.

20. Ibid., 3, 4.

21. Elliott A. Krause, *Death of Guilds: Professions, States, and the Advance of Capitalism, 1930 to the Present* (New Haven, Conn.: Yale University Press, 1996), 32.

22. Michael Hardt and Antonio Negri, *Empire* (Cambridge, Mass.: Harvard University Press, 2000), 280.

23. Richard Florida, *The Rise of the Creative Class: And How It's Transforming Work, Leisure, Community and Everyday Life* (New York: Basic Books, 2002), 41.

24. Ibid., 135.

25. Ibid., 218. A nice example of this shift in workplace environment is provided by programmer Ellen Ulman in *Close to the Machine: Technophilia and Its Discontents* (San Francisco: City Lights, 1997) in her discussion of having a virtual company (125–26). One of the reasons why programmers feel that they have jobs that are closer to those of writers is because of this freelance model. See in particular Ulman's discussion of the differences between her job and the more traditional company her father ran (127).

26. Robert B. Reich, *The Work of Nations: Preparing Ourselves for 21st-Century Capitalism* (New York: Knopf, 1991), 177.

27. Michael Heim, *Electric Language: A Philosophical Study of Word Processing* (New Haven, Conn.: Yale University Press, 1987), 199–200.

28. John Blossom, *Content Nation: Surviving and Thriving as Social Media Changes Our Work, Our Lives, and Our Future* (Indianapolis, Ind.: Wiley, 2009), 1.

29. Andréa Suzanne Webb Davis, Dundee Lackey, and Dànielle Nichole DeVoss, "Remix, Play, and Remediation: Undertheorized Composing Practices," in *Writing and the Digital Generation: Essays on New Media Rhetoric*, ed. Heather Urbanski (Jefferson, N.C.: McFarland, 2010), 187.

30. Dennis Baron, *A Better Pencil: Readers, Writers, and the Digital Revolution* (Oxford: Oxford University Press, 2009), 157.

31. Alan Liu, *The Laws of Cool: Knowledge Work and the Culture of Information* (Chicago: University of Chicago Press, 2004), 77.

32. William Paulson, *Literary Culture in a World Transformed: A Future for the Humanities* (Ithaca, N.Y.: Cornell University Press, 2001), 30.

33. Ibid.

34. Quoted in Jennifer Ruth, *Novel Professions: Interested Disinterest and the Making of the Professional in the Victorian Novel* (Columbus: Ohio State University Press, 2006), 3.

35. Magali Sarfatti Larson, *The Rise of Professionalism: A Sociological Analysis* (Berkeley: University of California Press, 1977), x.

36. Mary Poovey, *Uneven Developments: The Ideological Work of Gender in Mid-Victorian England* (Chicago: University of Chicago Press, 1988), 102.

37. Ruth, *Novel Professions,* 5.

38. Mark McGurl, *The Program Era: Postwar Fiction and the Rise of Creative Writing* (Cambridge, Mass.: Harvard University Press, 2009), 26.

39. Larson, *Rise of Professionalism,* xvi.

40. Poovey, *Uneven Developments,* 101.

41. Ibid., 102–3.

42. Perkin, *Rise of Professional Society,* 23.

43. Poovey, *Uneven Developments,* 108.

44. Although it is tangential to my topic in this chapter, it is worth noting that writers in particular are defined by their individuality in contrast to many of the communal ways in which professions function. In *The Imaginary Puritan: Literature, Intellectual Labor, and the Origins of Personal Life* (Berkeley: University of California Press, 1992), Nancy Armstrong and Leonard Tennenhouse note, "By the appearance of 'the author' we mean the emergence of the group who first gave the term its modern meaning, the class of people on whom writing conferred authority by placing them in a new and distinctive relationship with themselves, with other people, and with a world of objects" (1).

45. Paul Auster, *The New York Trilogy* (New York: Penguin, 1987), 10.

46. Ibid., 8.

47. Jeffrey T. Nealon, "Work of the Detective, Work of the Writer: Paul Auster's *City of Glass,*" *Modern Fiction Studies* 42, no. 1 (1996): 96.

48. Ibid., 98.

49. Clifford Siskin, *The Work of Writing: Literature and Social Change in Britain, 1700–1830* (Baltimore, Md.: Johns Hopkins University Press, 1998), 5.

50. Darren Wershler-Henry, *The Iron Whim: A Fragmented History of Typewriting* (Ithaca, N.Y.: Cornell University Press, 2005), 2.

51. Charles Bazerman, *The Informed Writer: Using Sources in the Disciplines,* 5th ed. (Boston: Houghton Mifflin, 1995), 3.

52. Sue Dinitz, "Writing and Responding as Conversation in First-Year Composition," in *The Letter Book: Ideas for Teaching College English,* ed. Sue Dinitz and Toby Fulwiler (Portsmouth, N.H.: Boynton/Cook, 2000), 15.

53. Mark Gaipa, "Breaking into the Conversation: How Students Can Acquire Authority for Their Writing," *Pedagogy* 4, no. 3 (Fall 2004): 422. Voice is a common critical concept used to discuss writing throughout the postwar period. Mark McGurl notes the importance of the concept of writerly "voice" in the rise of creative writing programs in *The Program Era,* which he notes works to link creative and scientific writing: "Note the rapport the pedagogical rhetoric of voice sought to sustain between fiction and nonfiction, creative writing and composition, and the authority it sought as a literary concept relevant even to scientists" (234–35).

54. George Steiner, *Language and Silence: Essays on Language, Literature, and the Inhuman* (New York: Atheneum, 1967), 16. Cited by Gregory L. Ulmer, *Applied Grammatology: Post(e)-Pedagogy from Jacques Derrida to Joseph Beuys* (Baltimore, Md.: Johns Hopkins University Press, 1985).

55. Steiner, *Language and Silence,* 20.

56. Joseph J. Comprone, "Textual Perspectives on Collaborative Learning: Dialogic Literacy and Written Texts in Composition Classrooms," *Writing Instructor* 8 (Spring 1989): 119.

57. Rebecca Moore Howard, "A Plagiarism Pentimento," *Journal of Teaching Writing* 11, no. 3 (Summer 1993): 236.

58. Rebecca Moore Howard, "Plagiarisms, Authorships, and the Academic Death Penalty," *College English* 57 (1995): 791.

59. Ibid.

60. Kay Halasek, *A Pedagogy of Possibility: Bakhtinian Perspectives on Composition Studies* (Carbondale: Southern Illinois University Press, 1999), 122.

61. Bruno Latour, *Science in Action: How to Follow Scientists and Engineers through Society* (Cambridge, Mass.: Harvard University Press, 1987), 40.

62. Ibid., 22.

## 3. Programmer as Writer

1. Geoff Cox and Alex McLean, *Speaking Code: Coding as Aesthetic and Political Expression* (Cambridge, Mass.: MIT Press, 2013), 6.

2. Ibid., 17.

3. *War Games*, directed by John Badham (1983; Beverly Hills, Calif.: MGM, 1998), DVD. *Office Space*, directed by Mike Judge (1999; Beverly Hills, Calif.: Twentieth Century Fox Home Entertainment, 2002), DVD. *Tron: Legacy*, directed by Joseph Kosinski (2010; Burbank, Calif.: Buena Vista Home Entertainment, 2011), DVD.

4. *The Social Network*, directed by David Fincher (2010; Culver City, Calif.: Sony Pictures, 2011), DVD. *The Matrix*, directed by Andy and Larry Wachowski (1999; Burbank, Calif.: Warner Home Video, 2001), DVD.

5. *Desk Set*, directed by Walter Lang (1957; Beverly Hills, Calif.: Twentieth Century Fox Home Entertainment, 2004), DVD.

6. *Tron*, directed by Steven Lisberger (1982; Burbank, Calif.: Buena Vista Home Entertainment, 1998), DVD.

7. This same approach is carried over into the recent *Tron* sequel. The work of repairing the code for the digital character Quorra (Olivia Wilde) is represented as the removal of a kind of DNA that is simply plucked out of the air by Kevin Flynn. The only representation of the interaction with code is Sam Flynn's (Garrett Hedlund) attempt to bypass the security on his father's computer, which requires him to access the system by guessing passwords. Even Neal Stephenson's novel *Cryptonomicon* (New York: Avon, 2002), which represents computer programming in a much more sophisticated and detailed way, equates programming with the hacking of a code—specifically by tracing the origins of computer design to World War II work on military code breaking.

8. *Amadeus*, directed by Milos Forman (1984; Burbank, Calif.: Warner Home Video, 2002), DVD.

9. Hugh Kenner, "Inventing Literary Lives: The Biographical Fallacy," *Harper's Magazine* (October 1978): 99.

10. Steve McConnell, *Code Complete*, 2nd ed. (Redmond, Wash.: Microsoft, 2004), 13.

11. Frederick P. Brooks Jr., *The Mythical Man-Month: Essays on Software Engineering*, anniversary ed. (Boston: Addison Wesley Longman, 1995), 7.

12. Scott Rosenberg, *Dreaming in Code: Two Dozen Programmers, Three Years, 4,732 Bugs, and One Quest for Transcendent Software* (New York: Crown, 2007), 18.

13. Ibid., 24.

14. Ibid., 98.

15. We should recognize, however, that equating programming with writing can emphasize both the positive and negative aspects of the profession of writing. In "Don't Call Yourself a Programmer, and Other Career Advice" (*Kalzumeus*, October 28, 2011, http://www.kalzumeus.com/2011/10/28/dont-call-yourself-a-programmer/), Patrick

McKenzie argues that the term *programmer* emphasizes relatively mundane work: "'Programmer' sounds like 'anomalously high-cost peon who types some mumbo-jumbo into some other mumbo-jumbo.'" By emphasizing the relatively mundane aspects of producing code, the writing metaphor may likely draw attention away from the higher-order aspects of software design.

16. In *Dreaming in Code,* Rosenberg notes that some programmers favor one language over another because of its aesthetic appearance on the screen, and concludes that this is not unreasonable, since you spend more time reading the code you have written than writing it (78–79).

17. John Gruber, "Markdown," *Daring Fireball,* December 17, 2004, http://daringfireball.net/projects/markdown/.

18. Ben Yagoda, "The Rise of 'Logical Punctuation.'" *Slate,* May 12, 2011, http://www.slate.com/articles/life/the_good_word/2011/05/the_rise_of_logical_punctuation.html.

19. James Gleick, *The Information: A History, a Theory, a Flood* (New York: Pantheon Books, 2011), 53.

20. Donald E. Knuth, *Literate Programming* (Stanford, Calif.: Center for the Study of Language and Information, 1992), ix.

21. Rosenberg, *Dreaming in Code,* 299.

22. Knuth, *Literate Programming,* 100.

23. Ibid., ix.

24. Quoted in Loren Glass, *Authors Inc.: Literary Celebrity in the Modern United States, 1880–1980* (New York: New York University Press, 2004), 12.

25. Leonard J. Leff, *Hemingway and His Conspirators: Hollywood, Scribners, and the Making of American Celebrity Culture* (Lanham, Md.: Rowman and Littlefield, 1997), 52.

26. Glass, *Authors Inc.,* 140.

27. Ibid., 1.

28. Ibid.

29. It is worth noting that this model of authorship from the 1920s may not apply perfectly to contemporary writing. In *Star Authors: Literary Celebrity in America* (London: Pluto Press, 2000), Joe Moran has argued that the celebrity culture that surrounded Hemingway and his contemporaries has changed in the later part of the twentieth century. Moran has argued for the rise of the "author-recluse" embodied in writers like Salinger and Pynchon (54), but he also notes that postmodern writers like Paul Auster playfully embrace the public nature of contemporary authorship (79).

30. Richard Florida, *The Rise of the Creative Class: And How It's Transforming Work, Leisure, Community and Everyday Life* (New York: Basic Books, 2002), 23.

31. Quoted in Rosenberg, *Dreaming in Code,* 261.

32. Jenna Wortham, "The iPhone Gold Rush," *New York Times,* April 3, 2009, http://www.nytimes.com/2009/04/05/fashion/05iphone.html.

33. In *The Economy of Literary Form: English Literature and the Industrialization of Publishing, 1800–1850* (Baltimore, Md.: Johns Hopkins University Press, 1996), Lee Erickson notes that authors in the nineteenth century shifted between the writing of essays and fiction based on the economics of the time: "Only when the market for fiction began to offer greater rewards than the market for prose did the publishers and authors turn elsewhere. Dickens ceased to be a parliamentary reporter and began to write stories" (103). Although the shift between the writing of novels and games for mobile devices seems like a much more radical change, we might argue that the expression of creativity in contemporary U.S. culture in part reflects these kinds of economic opportunities.

34. Bradley Dilger and Jeff Rice, "Introduction: Making a Vocabulary for <HTML>," in *From A to <A>: Keywords of Markup,* ed. Bradley Dilger and Jeff Rice (Minneapolis: University of Minnesota Press, 2010), xi.

35. Alan Cooper, Robert Reimann, and Dave Cronin, *About Face 3: The Essentials of Interaction Design* (Indianapolis, Ind.: Wiley, 2007), xxx.

36. Astrid Ensslin, *Canonizing Hypertext: Explorations and Constructions* (New York: Continuum, 2007).

37. Michael Joyce, *Of Two Minds: Hypertext Pedagogy and Poetics* (Ann Arbor: University of Michigan Press, 1995), 40.

38. See Markku Eskelinen, "Towards Computer Game Studies," in *First Person: New Media as Story, Performance, and Game,* ed. Noah Wardrip-Fruin and Pat Harrigan (Cambridge, Mass.: MIT Press, 2004), 36–44.

39. N. Katherine Hayles, *Electronic Literature: New Horizons for the Literary* (Notre Dame, Ind.: University of Notre Dame Press, 2008), ix.

40. In "Deeper into the Machine: Learning to Speak Digital" (*Computers and Composition* 19 [2002]) Hayles contrasts first-generation textual electronic literature to second-generation works that "are fully multimedia" (372) but still translates both kinds of electronic work into writing. She questions "the relation between machine, work, and user to discover what it means to write, read, and inhabit a coded medium" (ibid.).

41. Joyce, *Of Two Minds,* 31.

42. Neal Stephenson, *In the Beginning . . . Was the Command Line* (New York: Perennial, 2003), 38.

43. For the legality of this, see Marybeth Peters's decision for the Register of Copyrights, "Recommendation of the Register of Copyrights in RM-2008–8; Rulemaking on Exemptions from Prohibition on Circumvention of Copyright Protection Systems for Access Control Technologies," June 11, 2010, http://www.copyright.gov/1201/2010/initialed-registers-recommendation-june-11–2010.pdf. See also the Electronic Frontier Foundation's response to the rule, for which they were an advocate, "EFF Wins New Legal Protections for Video Artists, Cell Phone Jailbreakers, and Unlockers," July 26, 2010, https://www.eff.org/press/archives/2010/07/26.

44. The case of DVD encryption is especially problematic because it makes illegal actions that would normally have fallen under fair use provisions in the past. James Boyle explains in *The Public Domain: Enclosing the Commons of the Mind* (New Haven, Conn.: Yale University Press, 2008), "By using a few simple technological measures, they could distribute a work in a particular format and yet, because of their new intellectual property right, they could make illegal an otherwise lawful process of gaining access for the purposes of making fair use" (95). The same sorts of DRM schemes have been extended to computer game disks, which sometimes require connecting to a corporate server to verify the authenticity of the disk.

45. For a transcript of these remarks, see "Apple's CEO Discusses F4Q10 Results-Earning Call Transcript," *Seeking Alpha,* October 18, 2010, http://seekingalpha.com/article/230710-apple-s-ceo-discusses-f4q10-results-earnings-call-transcript.

46. Andy Rubin (Arubin), "the definition of open: 'mkdir android; cd android; repo init -u git://android.git.kernel.org/platform/manifest.git; repo sync; make,'" 11:21 PP, October 18, 2010, Tweet.

*4. E-Books, Libraries, and Feelies*

1. See Amazon's May 19, 2011 press release "Amazon.com Now Selling More Kindle Books than Print Books," May 19, 2011, http://phx.corporate-ir.net/phoenix.zhtml?c=176060&p=irol-newsArticle&ID=1565581&highlight.

2. Sven Birkerts, *The Gutenberg Elegies: The Fate of Reading in an Electronic Age* (New York: Fawcett Columbine, 1994), 6.

3. "Does the Brain Like E-Books?" *New York Times,* October 14, 2009, http://room fordebate.blogs.nytimes.com/2009/10/14/does-the-brain-like-e-books/.

4. In "Why E-Books Look So Ugly" (*Wired,* May 18, 2009, http://www.wired.com /gadgetlab/2009/05/e-book-design/), Priya Ganapati reports on common complaints: "'There's a dearth of typographic expression in e-books today,' says Pablo Defendini, digital producer for Tor.com, the online arm of science fiction and fantasy publisher Tor Books. 'Right now it's just about taking a digital file and pushing it on to a e-book reader without much consideration for layout and flow of text.'"

5. See, for example, Joe Clark's "Web Standards for E-Books," *A List Apart,* March 9, 2010, http://www.alistapart.com/articles/ebookstandards.

6. Anita Singh, "Jonathan Franzen: E-Books are Damaging Society," *Telegraph,* January 29, 2012, http://www.telegraph.co.uk/culture/hay-festival/9047981/Jonathan -Franzen-e-books-are-damaging-society.html.

7. Message posted to the Kindle user forum, July 23, 2009.

8. Henry Petroski, *The Book on the Bookshelf* (New York: Vintage, 1999), 4.

9. Alberto Manguel, *A History of Reading* (New York: Penguin Books, 1996), 199.

10. Alex Allain, "Introduction to C," Cprogramming.com, http://www.cprogram ming.com/tutorial/c/lesson1.html.

11. See, for example, Steve Jobs's very careful response to claims of Apple's monopoly in his 2007 post "Thoughts on Music," February 6, 2007, http://www.apple.com/hotnews /thoughtsonmusic/.

12. This is very much the case with Apple's iPhone operating system (iOS), where users cannot see the file structure directly but can only interact with files through the applications that have generated them. In other words, Apple has worked to bundle the application and its data.

13. Robert Filliou, *Ample Food for Stupid Thought* (New York: Something Else Press, 1965).

14. Janine Barchas, *Graphic Design, Print Culture, and the Eighteenth-Century Novel* (Cambridge: Cambridge University Press, 2003).

15. Jon Stone, *The Monster at the End of this Book,* illus. Michael Smollin (New York: Golden Books, 2004).

16. This focus on design is in addition to broader political concerns about the issue of *access* to books. For a vigorous argument in favor of open access to digital texts, see Gary Hall, *Digitalize This Book! The Politics of New Media, or Why We Need Open Access Now* (Minneapolis: Minnesota University Press, 2008).

17. This is attributed to Alan Kay in the 1982 seminar "Creative Think." See Andy Hertzfeld, *Revolution in the Valley: The Insanely Great Story of How the Mac Was Made* (Sebastopol, Calif.: O'Reilly, 2005), 114–15.

18. *Classic Text Adventure Masterpieces of Infocom,* CD-ROM (Cambridge, Mass.: Infocom, 1996).

19. The attitude of resistance toward the library is perhaps best embodied by the idea of a sandpaper cover for a library item. This was used as part of a book cover in Asger Jorn and Guy Debord's *Mémoires* and as an album cover for the punk band Durutti Column. In both cases, the true avant-garde item destroys the other members of the library.

20. See David Pearson's *Books as History: The Importance of Books beyond Their Texts* (London: British Library, 2008) for a discussion of binding in the eighteenth century. He notes that the idea of a uniform edition, in which the publisher selects a single color and material for binding, is a modern one (23).

21. Joan Shelley Rubin, *The Making of Middlebrow Culture* (Chapel Hill: University of North Carolina Press, 1992), 94.

22. Peter J. Rabinowitz, *Before Reading: Narrative Conventions and the Politics of Interpretation* (Ithaca, N.Y.: Cornell University Press, 1987), 176.

23. Birkerts, *Gutenberg Elegies,* 117.

24. Ibid.

25. Manguel, *History of Reading,* 20.

26. Ibid., 189.

27. John Elsner and Roger Cardinal, "Introduction," in *The Cultures of Collecting,* ed. John Elsner and Roger Cardinal (London: Reaktion, 1994), 1–2.

28. In *Museum Trouble: Edwardian Fiction and the Emergence of Modernism* (Charlottesville: University of Virginia Press, 2011), Ruth Hoberman notes that the issue of ownership and purchasing was central to collecting as it emerged in the modern period: "awkwardly positioned between the aristocracy, who inherit their possessions, and the middle classes, who buy them in department stores, is the collector, who buys from dealers or at auctions" (38).

29. Duncan Martell, "Jobs Says Apple Customers Not into Renting Music," *Reuters,* April 26, 2007, http://www.reuters.com/article/2007/04/26/us-apple-jobs-idUS N2546496120070426.

30. *The Hitchhiker's Guide to the Galaxy,* diskette (Cambridge, Mass.: Infocom, 1984); *Leather Goddesses of Phobos,* diskette (Cambridge, Mass.: Infocom, 1986).

31. Henri-Jean Martin, *The History and Power of Writing,* trans. Lydia G. Cochrane (Chicago: University of Chicago Press, 1994), 507.

32. Pearson, *Books as History,* 21.

33. Ibid., 27.

34. Walter Benjamin, *The Arcades Project,* trans. Howard Eiland and Kevin McLaughlin (Cambridge, Mass.: Harvard University Press, 1999), 207.

35. Ibid., 206.

*5. Invention, Patents, and the Technological System*

1. Steven Johnson, *Interface Culture: How New Technology Transforms the Way We Create and Communicate* (New York: Harper Edge, 1997), 18.

2. Theodor H. Nelson, *Computer Lib/Dream Machines* (Redmond, Wash.: Tempus Books, 1987), 4.

3. Joshua Gunn and Mirko M. Hall, "Stick It in Your Ear: The Psychodynamics of iPod Enjoyment," *Communication and Critical/Cultural Studies* 5, no. 2 (June 2008): 136.

4. Laurence A. Rickels, *The Vampire Lectures* (Minneapolis: University of Minnesota Press, 1999), 62.

5. William Gibson, *Neuromancer* (New York: Ace, 1984), 76–77.

6. Vannevar Bush, "As We May Think," in *From Memex to Hypertext: Vannevar Bush and the Mind's Machine,* ed. James M. Nyce and Paul Kahn (Boston: Academic Press, 1991), 91.

7. Ibid.

8. Jacques Derrida, *Archive Fever: A Freudian Impression,* trans. Eric Prenowitz (Chicago: University of Chicago Press, 1995), 13, 25.

9. Martin Heidegger, *Being and Time,* trans. John Macquarrie and Edward Robinson (New York: Harper and Row, 1962). Heidegger begins his inquiry into the nature of the "Worldhood of the World" (91) by attending to "those entities which we encounter as closest to us" (95). Heidegger adopts the problematic term *thing* and notes that we do not see these objects as independent entities in the world, but rather as extensions of

ourselves with which we engage in specific activities: "in dealings such as this, where something is put to use, our concern subordinates itself to the 'in-order-to' which is constitutive for the equipment we are employing at the time; the less we just stare at the hammer-Thing, and the more we seize hold of it and use it, the more primordial does our relationship to it become, and the more unveiledly is it encountered as that which it is—as equipment" (98).

10. Ibid., 98–99.

11. George Lakoff and Mark Johnson, *Philosophy in the Flesh: The Embodied Mind and Its Challenge to Western Thought* (New York: Basic Books, 1999), 266.

12. Manuel Imaz and David Benyon, *Designing with Blends: Conceptual Foundations of Human–Computer Interaction and Software Engineering* (Cambridge, Mass.: MIT Press, 2007), 24.

13. See Alan F. Blackwell, "The Reification of Metaphor as a Design Tool," *ACM: Transactions on Computer–Human Interaction* 13, no. 4 (2006): 490–530; see also John M. Carroll and John C. Thomas, "Metaphor and the Cognitive Representation of Computing Systems," *IEEE: Transactions on Systems, Man, and Cybernetics* 12, no. 2 (1982): 107–16.

14. See Rita M. Denny and Patricia L. Sunderland, "Researching Cultural Metaphors in Action: Metaphors of Computing Technology in Contemporary U.S. Life," *Journal of Business Research* 58 (2005): 1456–63.

15. Ivan E. Sutherland, "Sketchpad: A Man-Machine Graphical Communication System," *AFIPS Conference Proceedings* 23 (1963): 329.

16. Ibid.

17. Imaz and Benyon, *Designing with Blends,* 7, 6.

18. Heidegger, *Being and Time,* 97n1.

19. Ibid., 97.

20. Byron Hawk and David M. Rieder, "Introduction: On Small Tech and Complex Ecologies," in *Small Tech: The Culture of Digital Tools,* ed. Byron Hawk, David M. Rieder, and Ollie Oviedo (Minneapolis: University of Minnesota Press, 2008), xvii.

21. Hubert L. Dreyfus, *Being in the World: A Commentary on Heidegger's* Being and Time, *Division I* (Cambridge, Mass.: MIT Press, 1991), 62.

22. Neil Postman, *Technopoly: The Surrender of Culture to Technology* (New York: Vintage, [1992] 1993), 23.

23. Vilém Flusser, *Does Writing Have a Future?,* trans. Nancy Ann Roth (Minneapolis: University of Minnesota Press, 2011), 123.

24. U.S. Constitution, art. I, § 8.

25. Bilski v. Kappos, 561 U.S. 593 (2010).

26. Hotel Security Checking Co v. Lorraine Co, 160 F 467 (1908).

27. O'Reilly v. Morse, 56 U.S. 62 (1853).

28. Gottschalk v. Benson, 409 U.S. 63 (1972).

29. Diamond v. Diehr, 450 U.S. 175 (1981).

30. Patent Act of 1790, Ch. 7, 1 Stat. 109-112 (April 10, 1790).

31. Title 35 U.S.C section 111. Models do show up in the code as something that the director "may require" along with specimens (114), but they have clearly been given a subordinate role in the application in 1952.

32. For the example of speculative patents in genetic research, see Ikechi Mgbeoji and Byron Allen, "Patent First, Litigate Later! The Scramble for Speculative and Overly Broad Genetic Patents: Implications for Access to Health Care and Biomedical Research," *Canadian Journal of Law and Technology* 2, no. 2 (2003): 83–98. See also Mark Nowotarski, "Breakthroughs & Abandonment: Patent Abandon Rate Is a Reliable Measure of

Speculative Portfolios" (*IP Watchdog,* September 27, 2010, http://www.ipwatchdog.com/2010/09/27/abandon-rate-measure-speculative-portfolios), which calculates the degree to which individual patents are speculative by their rate of abandonment.

33. O'Reilly v. Morse, 56 U.S. 62 (1853).

34. In *Authors and Owners: The Invention of Copyright* (Cambridge, Mass.: Harvard University Press, 1993), Mark Rose cites a 1774 essay that contrasts the obvious utility of the patentable machine and the more subtle quality of the literary work: "every common capacity can find out the use of a machine; it is a length of time before the value of a literary publication is discovered and acknowledged by the vulgar" (107).

35. Diamond v. Diehr, 450 U.S. 175 (1981) at 195.

36. Bilski v. Kappos, 561 U.S. 593 (2010) at 621.

37. Stevens writes, "the Court posits that the word 'process' must be understood in light of its 'ordinary, contemporary, common meaning.' . . . Although this is a fine approach to statutory interpretation in general, it is a deeply flawed approach to a statute that relies on complex terms of art developed against a particular historical background. Indeed, the approach would render §101 almost comical. A process for training a dog, a series of dance steps, a method of shooting a basketball, maybe even words, stories, or songs if framed as the steps of typing letters or uttering sounds—all would be patent—eligible. I am confident that the term 'process' in §101 is not nearly so capacious."

38. Martin Heidegger, *Basic Writings,* ed. David Farrell Krell (New York: Harper and Row, 1977), 287–88.

39. See, for example, Nelson Goodman's description of art as a "fair sample" in *Ways of Worldmaking* (Indianapolis, Ind.: Hackett, 1978), 133–40.

40. Bruno Latour, *We Have Never Been Modern,* trans. Catherine Porter (Cambridge, Mass.: Harvard University Press, 1993), 23.

41. Ibid., 25.

42. Ibid., 2.

43. Ibid., 7.

44. Michel Foucault, *The Archaeology of Knowledge and the Discourse on Language,* trans. A. M. Sheridan Smith (New York: Pantheon, 1972), 41.

45. John Bender and Michael Marrinan, *The Culture of Diagram* (Stanford, Calif.: Stanford University Press, 2010), 1.

46. Ibid., 7.

47. Ibid.

48. Flusser, *Does Writing,* 28.

49. Apple Computer Inc. v. Microsoft Corp. 35 F.3d 1435 (9th Cir. 1994).

50. Bas Ording, Scott Forstall, Greg Christie, Stephen O. Lemay, and Imran Chaudhri, "Portable Electronic Device with Multi-Touch Input," U.S. Patent 7,812,826, filed December 30, 2005, issued October 12, 2010. Imran Chaudhri et al., "Unlocking a Device by Performing Gestures on an Unlock Image," U.S. Patent 7,657,849, filed June 2, 2009, issued February 2, 2010.

51. Peri Hartman, Jeffrey P. Bezos, Shel Kaphan, and Joel Spiegel, "Method and System for Placing a Purchase Order via a Communications Network," U.S. Patent 5,960,411, filed September 12, 1997, issued September 28, 1999.

52. Michael A. Hiltzik, *Dealers of Lightning: Xerox PARC and the Dawn of the Computer Age* (New York: Harper, 1999), 141.

53. Alan Liu, *The Laws of Cool: Knowledge Work and the Culture of Information* (Chicago: University of Chicago Press, 2004), 215.

54. Michael Hardt and Antonio Negri, *Empire* (Cambridge, Mass.: Harvard University Press, 2000), 290–91.

55. Eugene Thacker, "Foreword: Protocol Is as Protocol Does," in *Protocol: How Control Exists after Decentralization,* by Alexander R Galloway (Cambridge, Mass.: MIT Press, 2004), xiii.

56. Ibid., xiii.

57. Galloway, *Protocol,* 196–97.

58. Latour, *We Have Never Been Modern,* 6.

59. Galloway, *Protocol,* 11.

60. Gilles Deleuze and Félix Guattari, *A Thousand Plateaus: Capitalism and Schizophrenia,* trans. Brian Massumi (Minneapolis: University of Minnesota Press, 1987), 153.

61. Ibid., 149–50.

62. Frederick P. Brooks Jr., *The Mythical Man-Month: Essays on Software Engineering,* anniversary ed. (Boston: Addison Wesley Longman, 1995), 7.

63. James Higgs describes this schizophrenia in his post, "Apple's Aesthetic Dichotomy," *Made by Many,* October 24, 2011, http://madebymany.com/blog/apples-aesthetic-dichotomy.

64. This attitude is on display in Steve Jobs's well-known complaint about the Android operating system as "stolen." Walter Isaacson's biography, *Steve Jobs* (New York: Simon and Schuster, 2011), quotes Jobs as dismissing the possibility of licensing patents to Android: "If you offer me $5 billion, I don't want it. I've got plenty of money. I want you to stop using our ideas in Android, that's what I want" (513). In fact, Apple appears to have weakened its embrace of skeuomorphism in the two years since Jobs's death; likewise, the post-Jobs Apple appears to be at least somewhat less confrontational legally with its rivals. It may be that this particular link between skeuomorphism and patent claims was championed by Jobs's particular view of his company's place within the market.

65. N. Katherine Hayles, *How We Became Posthuman: Virtual Bodies in Cybernetics, Literature, and Informatics* (Chicago: University of Chicago Press, 1999), 17.

66. Ibid., 18.

*6. Audience Today*

1. Espen J. Aarseth, *Cybertext: Perspectives on Ergodic Literature* (Baltimore, Md.: Johns Hopkins University Press, 1997), 62.

2. Lev Manovich, *The Language of New Media* (Cambridge, Mass.: MIT Press, 2001), 36.

3. Richard Powers, *The Gold Bug Variations* (New York: Harper Perennial, 1992), 414.

4. John Cayley, "The Code Is Not the Text (Unless It Is the Text)," *Electronic Book Review,* September 10, 2002, http://www.electronicbookreview.com/thread/electropoetics/net.writing.

5. Rita Raley, "Interferences: [Net.Writing] and the Practice of Codework," *Electronic Book Review,* September 9, 2002, http://www.electronicbookreview.com/thread/electropoetics/net.writing.

6. Talan Memmott, *Lexia to Perplexia,* http://collection.eliterature.org/1/works/memmott__lexia_to_perplexia.html. For a good summary of the goals of codework poetry from Memmott's perspective, see his essay "E_RUPTURE://Codework. Serration in Electronic Literature," http://talanmemmott.com/pdf/e_rupture.pdf.

7. Mez, "The Art of M[ex]ang.elle.ing: Constructing Polysemic & Neology Fic/Fac tions Online," *BeeHive* 3, no. 4 (December 2000), http://beehive.temporalimage.com/content_apps34/mez/0.html.

8. McKenzie Wark, "From Hypertext to Codework," *NJS* 3, no. 1 (2002), http://hjs.ff.cuni.cz/archives/v3/wark.html.

9. Cayley, "The Code Is Not the Text."

10. See, for example, Raley's introduction to the term in "Interferences."

11. Quoted in N. Katherine Hayles, *My Mother Was a Computer: Digital Subjects and Literary Texts* (Chicago: University of Chicago Press, 2005), 48. In *Close to the Machine: Technophilia and Its Discontents* (San Francisco: City Lights, 1997), Ullman comments on the phrase "just do it": "If I just sit here and code, you think, I can make something run. When the humans come back to talk changes, I can just run the program. Show them: Here. Look at this. See? This is not just talk. This runs. Whatever you might say, whatever the consequences, all you have are words and what I have is this, this thing I've built, this operational system. Talk all you want, but this thing here: it *works*" (24).

12. Theodor H. Nelson, *Computer Lib/Dream Machines* (Redmond, Wash.: Tempus Books, 1987), 56.

13. Donald E. Knuth, *Literate Programming* (Stanford, Calif.: Center for the Study of Language and Information, 1992), 9.

14. Hayles, *My Mother,* 116.

15. Ibid., 128.

16. Erich Auerbach, *Mimesis: The Representation of Reality in Western Literature,* trans. Willard Trask (New York: Anchor, 1957), 19.

17. M. H. Abrams, *The Mirror and the Lamp: Romantic Theory and the Critical Tradition* (London: Oxford University Press, 1953), 21–22.

18. Paul de Man is particularly eager to reclaim the concept of rhetoric as a break from formalist models in *Allegories of Reading: Figural Language in Rousseau, Nietzsche, Rilke, and Proust* (New Haven, Conn.: Yale University Press, 1979), see especially 8–9. He also describes the transition away from rhetorical culture with the rise of romanticism in *Blindness and Insight: Essays in the Rhetoric of Contemporary Criticism,* 2nd ed. (Minneapolis: University of Minnesota Press, 1983), 187–88.

19. *The Social Network,* directed by David Fincher (2010; Culver City, Calif.: Sony Pictures, 2011), DVD. *Tron,* directed by Steven Lisberger (1982; Burbank, Calif.: Buena Vista Home Entertainment, 1998), DVD. *The Matrix,* Andy and Larry Wachowski (1999; Burbank, Calif.: Warner Home Video, 2001), DVD. *Tron: Legacy,* directed by Joseph Kosinski (2010; Burbank, Calif.: Buena Vista Home Entertainment, 2011), DVD. *Office Space,* directed by Mike Judge (1999; Beverly Hills, Calif.: Twentieth Century Fox Home Entertainment, 2002), DVD.

20. There seems to be a growing acceptance of the representation of actual programming and typing of commands in films. In the recent *Tron: Legacy* the audience sees the protagonist actually typing the "whois" command to find out who is logged into the computer.

21. Linda Hutcheon, *A Poetics of Postmodernism: History, Theory, Fiction* (New York: Routledge, 1988), 77.

22. See Aarseth, *Cybertext,* 106.

23. Jaishree K. Odin, *Hypertext and the Female Imaginary* (Minneapolis: University of Minnesota Press, 2010), 14.

24. Raoul Eshelman, *Performatism, or the End of Postmodernism* (Aurora, Colo.: Davies Group, 2008), 1.

25. Wark, "From Hypertext to Codework."

26. Rita Raley, "Reveal Codes: Hypertext and Performance," *Postmodern Culture* 12, no. 1 (2001), http://muse.jhu.edu/journals/pmc/v012/12.1raley.html.

27. Michel Foucault, *The History of Sexuality,* vol. 2, *The Use of Pleasure,* trans. Robert Hurley (New York: Vintage, 1990), 5.

28. For example, at the beginning of *Discipline and Punish: The Birth of the Prison,* trans. Alan Sheridan (New York: Vintage, 1977), Foucault describes his interest in "'epistemologico-juridicial' formation" and its productive effects: "make the technology of power the very principle of both the humanization of the penal system and the knowledge of man" (23).

29. At the beginning of *Bodies That Matter: On the Discursive Limits of "Sex"* (New York: Routledge, 1993), Butler writes, "'sex' not only functions as a norm, but is part of a regulatory practice that produces the bodies it governs, that is, whose regulatory force is made clear as a kind of productive power, the power to produce—demarcate, circulate, differentiate—the bodies it controls" (1). In *Gender Trouble: Feminism and the Subversion of Identity* (New York: Routledge, 1990), Butler describes gender as "*a corporeal style,* an 'act,' as it were, which is both intentional and performative, where '*performative*' suggests a dramatic and contingent construction of meaning" (139).

30. Michael Hardt and Antonio Negri, *Multitude: War and Democracy in the Age of Empire* (New York: Penguin, 2004), 200.

31. James E. Porter, "Rhetoric in (as) a Digital Economy," in *Rhetorics and Technologies: New Directions in Writing and Communication,* ed. Stuart A. Selber (Columbia: University of South Carolina Press, 2010), 173.

32. Ibid., 175.

33. Collin Gifford Brooke, *Lingua Fracta: Toward a Rhetoric of New Media* (Cresskill, N.J.: Hampton Press, 2009), 34.

34. Cass R. Sunstein, *Republic 2.0* (Princeton, N.J.: Princeton University Press, 2007), 1.

35. Donald Barthelme, "After Joyce," in *Not-Knowing: The Essays and Interviews of Donald Barthelme,* ed. Kim Herzinger (New York: Random House, 1997), 3–4.

36. Ibid., 4.

37. For the former interpretation of postmodernism, see Robert Venturi, Denise Scott Brown, and Steven Izenour, *Learning from Las Vegas,* rev. ed. (Cambridge, Mass.: MIT Press, 1977). For the latter, see Charles Newman, *The Post-Modern Aura: The Act of Fiction in the Age of Inflation* (Evanston, Ill.: Northwestern University Press, 1985); Mark McGurl, *The Novel Art: Elevations of American Fiction after Henry James* (Princeton, N.J.: Princeton University Press, 2001).

38. Jill Walker Rettberg, *Blogging* (Cambridge: Polity, 2008), 46.

39. Sunstein, *Republic 2.0*, 5.

40. Ibid., 23.

41. Chris Anderson, *The Long Tail: Why the Future of Business is Selling Less of More* (New York: Hyperion, 2006), 1.

42. Theodor W. Adorno, *The Culture Industry: Selected Essays on Mass Culture,* trans. J. M. Bernstein (London: Routledge, 1991), 47–48.

43. Ibid., 40.

44. Sarah Weinman, "Are Authors Who Twitter Any Fitter?" *Poets & Writers,* May/June 2009, http://www.pw.org/content/are_authors_who_twitter_any_fitter.

45. Anne Trubek, "Why Authors Tweet," *New York Times,* January 6, 2012, http://www.nytimes.com/2012/01/08/books/review/why-authors-tweet.html.

46. Henry Jenkins, *Textual Poachers: Television Fans and Participatory Culture* (New York: Routledge, 1992), 23.

47. Ibid., 17.

48. Ibid., 23–24.

49. Henry Jenkins, *Fans, Bloggers, and Gamers: Exploring Participatory Culture* (New York: New York University Press, 2006), 136.

50. Ibid., 141.

51. Ibid., 145.

52. Henry Jenkins, *Convergence Culture: Where Old and New Media Collide* (New York: New York University Press, 2006), 46.

53. Ibid., 26.

54. Jenkins, *Textual Poachers,* 45.

55. Jenkins, *Fans, Bloggers,* 129.

56. Jenkins, *Convergence,* 46.

57. Michel Foucault, *Language, Counter-Memory, Practice: Selected Essays and Interviews,* ed. Donald F. Bouchard, trans. Donald F. Bouchard and Sherry Simon (Ithaca, N.Y.: Cornell University Press, 1977), 124.

58. Jean Burgess and Joshua Green, *YouTube: Online Video and Participatory Culture* (Cambridge: Polity, 2009), 14.

59. Terry Gross, "Novelist Jonathan Franzen," *NPR,* October 15, 2001, http://www.npr.org/templates/story/story.php?storyId=1131456.

60. In a 1956 interview conducted by Jean Stein for the *Paris Review* (Spring 1956, http://www.theparisreview.org/interviews/4954/the-art-of-fiction-no-12-william-faulkner), Faulkner explains the author's obligation: "His obligation is to get the work done the best he can do it; whatever obligation he has left over after that he can spend any way he likes. I myself am too busy to care about the public. I have no time to wonder who is reading me. I don't care about John Doe's opinion on my or anyone else's. Mine is the standard which has to be met."

61. Paul Dawson, *The Return of the Omniscient Narrator: Authorship and Authority in Twenty-First Century Fiction* (Columbus: Ohio State University Press, 2013), 15.

62. Jonathan Franzen, *How to Be Alone: Essays* (New York: Picador, 2002), 5–6.

63. Shayna Garlick, "Harry Potter and the Magic of Reading," *Christian Science Monitor,* May 2, 2007, http://www.csmonitor.com/2007/0502/p13s01-legn.html.

64. Warner Bros. Entertainment Inc. and J. K. Rowling v. RDR Books, 575 F. Supp. 2d 513.

65. RDR Books, "Memorandum of Law in Opposition to Plaintiffs' Motion for a Preliminary Injunction," February 8, 2008, http://cyberlaw.stanford.edu/files/blogs/Final%20Memo%20in%20Opposition%20to%20Rowling%27s%20PI%20Moiton.pdf.

66. J. K. Rowling, *Harry Potter and the Chamber of Secrets* (New York: Scholastic, 1999), 240.

67. *Myst III: Exile,* CD-ROM (San Francisco: Ubi Soft, 2001).

68. Rand Miller and Robyn Miller, *Myst,* CD-ROM (Novato, Calif.: Brøderbund, 1993).

69. Charles R. Acland, ed., *Residual Media* (Minneapolis: University of Minnesota Press, 2007).

## Conclusion

1. See the Conference on College Composition and Communication, "CCCC Position Statement on Teaching, Learning, and Assessing Writing in Digital Environments," February 25, 2004, http://www.ncte.org/cccc/resources/positions/digitalenvironments. This statement focuses mostly on how our understanding of composition must expand to include new processes and textual features: "The focus of writing instruction is expanding: the curriculum of composition is widening to include not one but two literacies: a literacy of print and a literacy of the screen. In addition, work in one medium is used to enhance learning in the other."

2. There are, of course, many exceptions to this very broad generalization. In particular, research by Anthony Paré and others focusing on how student writers move from school to work attempts to analyze "writing in knowledge societies" broadly—to borrow the title of a recent collection. Despite valuable focus on concepts like the habitus and informal mentoring, emphasis in this research tends to focus, nonetheless, on how students adapt to particular genres or learn new techniques rather than on how they tend to conceptualize writing more generally.

3. The Conference on College Composition and Communication, "CCCC Statement on the Multiple Uses of Writing," November 19, 2007, http://www.ncte.org/cccc/resources /positions/multipleuseswriting.

4. Kenneth Goldsmith, *Uncreative Writing: Managing Language in the Digital Age* (New York: Columbia University Press, 2011), 8.

# Index

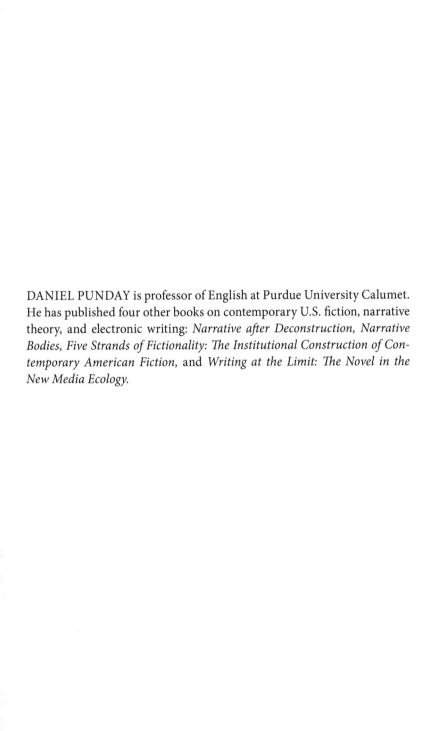

DANIEL PUNDAY is professor of English at Purdue University Calumet. He has published four other books on contemporary U.S. fiction, narrative theory, and electronic writing: *Narrative after Deconstruction, Narrative Bodies, Five Strands of Fictionality: The Institutional Construction of Contemporary American Fiction,* and *Writing at the Limit: The Novel in the New Media Ecology.*